INNOV 2017

The Sixth International Conference on Communications, Computation, Networks and Technologies

October 8 - 12, 2017

Athens, Greece

INNOV 2017 Editors

Alexandros Kaloxylos, University of Peloponnese, Greece

Igor Kotenko, ITMO University and Russian Academy of Sciences (SPIIRAS), Russia

Kiriakos Patriarcheas, Hellenic Open University, Greece

Ioannis Moscholios, University of Peloponnese - Tripolis, Greece

Printed from e-media with permission by:

Curran Associates, Inc.
57 Morehouse Lane
Red Hook, NY 12571

Some format issues inherent in the e-media version may also appear in this print version.

Printed by Curran Associates, Inc. (2017)

International Academy, Research, and Industry Association (IARIA)
412 Derby Way
Wilmington, DE 19810

Phone: (408) 893-6407
Fax: (408) 527-6351

petre@iaria.org

Additional copies of this publication are available from:

Curran Associates, Inc.
57 Morehouse Lane
Red Hook, NY 12571 USA
Phone: 845-758-0400
Fax: 845-758-2633
Email: curran@proceedings.com
Web: www.proceedings.com

Table of Contents

INNOV 2017

Forward

The Sixth International Conference on Communications, Computation, Networks and Technologies (INNOV 2017), held on October 8 - 12, 2017- Athens, Greece, aimed at addressing recent research results and forecasting challenges on selected topics related to communications, computation, networks and technologies.

Considering the importance of innovative topics in today's technology-driven society, there is a paradigm shift in classical-by-now approaches, such as networking, communications, resource sharing, collaboration and telecommunications. Recent achievements demand rethinking available technologies and considering the emerging ones.

The conference had the following tracks:

☐ Communications
☐ Networking
☐ Computing
☐ Web Semantic and Data Processing
☐ Security, Trust, and Privacy

We take here the opportunity to warmly thank all the members of the INNOV 2017 technical program committee, as well as the numerous reviewers. The creation of such a high quality conference program would not have been possible without their involvement. We also kindly thank all the authors that dedicated much of their time and effort to contribute to INNOV 2017. We truly believe that, thanks to all these efforts, the final conference program consisted of top quality contributions.

Also, this event could not have been a reality without the support of many individuals, organizations and sponsors. We also gratefully thank the members of the INNOV 2017 organizing committee for their help in handling the logistics and for their work that made this professional meeting a success.

We hope that INNOV 2017 was a successful international forum for the exchange of ideas and results between academia and industry and to promote further progress in the areas of communication, computation, networks and technologies. We also hope Athens provided a pleasant environment during the conference and everyone saved some time for exploring this beautiful historic city.

INNOV Steering Committee

Yu-Chen Hu, Providence University, Taiwan
Carlos Becker Westphall, University of Santa Catarina, Brazil
Shih-Chang Huang, National Formosa University, Taiwan
Kiriakos Patriarcheas, Hellenic Open University, Greece
Jaime Lloret Mauri, Universitat Politècnica de València, Spain

INNOV Industry/Research Advisory Committee

Igor Kotenko, ITMO University and Russian Academy of Sciences (SPIIRAS), Russia
Sung-soon Park, Anyang University and Gluesys Co. LTD, Republic of Korea
Binod Kumar, JSPM Jayawant Institute of Computer Applications, Pune, India

INNOV 2017

Committee

Copyright Information

TCP Vegas-L An Adaptive End-to-End Congestion Control Algorithm over Satellite Communications

Lianqiang Li, Jie Zhu and Ningyu He
Department of Electronic Engineering, Shanghai Jiao Tong University (SJTU), Shanghai 200240, China
Emails: {sjtu_llq, zhujie, NingyuHe_ruby}@sjtu.edu.cn

***Abstract*—Satellite communications is one of the wireless communication technologies, which is widely spread all over the world. Vegas is a kind of the Transmission Control Protocols (TCPs) over satellite communications. However, there are some shortcomings with this protocol, such as being less aggressive and unfair. These would penalize its performance over satellite communications to a certain extent by taking into account the long round trip time and high packet error rates. In this paper, an adaptive end-to-end congestion control algorithm (Vegas-L) is proposed to overcome these issues. Vegas-L can take full advantage of the historical information of network to divide network conditions into more detailed states, then carry out some adaptive and reasonable adjustments according to the specific network state. Simulation results show that Vegas-L is not only able to improve the aggressiveness to gain high throughput but also has the ability to enhance its fairness over satellite networks.**

Keywords–satellite communications; wireless communications; TCP Vegas; aggressiveness; throughput; fairness

I. Introduction

With the continuous development of satellite communications, their advantages, such as global coverage, bandwidth flexibility and access convenience have been gradually reflected [1]–[3]. However, satellite environments have some intrinsic characteristics including long round trip time (RTT) and high packet error rate (PER) [4], which would degrade the performance of traditional transport layer protocol heavily [5], such as TCP Reno [6]. Some studies have demonstrated that TCP Vegas [7] outperforms TCP Reno with respect to the overall network utilization, throughput and packet loss [8]–[11]. As a result, Consultative Committee for Space Data Systems (CCSDS) has set TCP Vegas as a part of the Space Communications Protocol Standard Transport Protocol (SCPS-TP).

However, there are two main issues with original Vegas over satellite communications. One is that Vegas is too conservative to increase its congestion window size ($Cwnd$) to gain satisfying throughput. The other is unfairness when it competes with Reno. To cope with these shortcomings, several enhanced variants of Vegas have been proposed like Vegas-A [12] and Veno [13]; they increase throughput and fairness by enhancing Vegas's aggressiveness. The strategies employed by them may work in some cases, but they are not general for different PER satellite environments.

In this paper, inspired by the variation of throughput used in Vegas-A, we propose an adaptive end-to-end congestion control algorithm called TCP Vegas-L. Vegas-L will employ more historical information of network to adjust $Cwnd$ and other key variables according to the specific network state. Also, Vegas-L does not add any new parameters and only needs some modifications on the sending ends. Simulation results prove that the proposed Vegas is competitive and even better than Vegas, Vegas-A and Veno over satellite communications under different PER environments.

The rest of this paper is organized as follows. Section II provides a brief description of related works. Section III introduces the proposed Vegas-L. Section IV presents the performance of evaluation under different PER environments over satellite networks. Finally, we summarize the conclusions and present our future research direction in section V.

II. Related Works

There are some variants of Vegas that have been proposed to solve the above issues over satellite communications. We will review Vegas, Vegas-A and Veno. They would be studied in this paper. Among them, Vegas-A is the referenced version of Vegas-L.

A. Vegas

Vegas is a delay based congestion control algorithm. It is not bias against connections with long $RTTs$, which is crucial to satellite communications. There are three key variables $Cwnd$, α and β. The latter two are the thresholds of extra data to be kept in the network. The pivotal mechanism of it is that Vegas uses measured RTT to calculate the difference ($Diff$) between expected throughput ($Expected\_Th$) and actual throughput ($Actual\_Th$) to estimate the congestion level in the early stage. The core algorithm behind it can be expressed as follows:

$$Expected\_Th = Cwnd/Base \tag{1}$$

$$Actual\_Th = Cwnd/RTT \tag{2}$$

$$Diff = (Expected\_Th - Actual\_Th)Base \tag{3}$$

$$Cwnd = \begin{cases} Cwnd + 1, & \text{if } Diff < \alpha \\ Cwnd, & \text{if } \alpha < Diff < \beta \\ Cwnd - 1, & \text{if } Diff > \beta \end{cases} \tag{4}$$

where $Base$ is the minimum RTT of observation. The thresholds α and β employed by Vegas are fixed, with default values to be 1 and 3.

B. Vegas-A

The main idea of Vegas-A is that rather than fix key variables, they could be adjusted dynamically [12]. Vegas-A uses the difference between present round trip throughput ($Th\_(i)$) and the throughput of last round trip ($Th\_(i-1)$) to adjust its congestion control mechanism more flexibly. The core algorithm of Vegas-A is shown in Figure 1.

Input: $Th\_(i)$ and $Th\_(i-1)$
Output: $Cwnd(i+1)$, α and β

```
if α<Diff<β then
    if Th_(i)>Th_(i-1) then
        Cwnd(i+1)=Cwnd(i)+1, α=α+1, β=β+1
    else
        No update of Cwnd(i+1), α and β
    end if
else if Diff<α then
    if α>1 then
        if Th_(i)>Th_(i-1) then
            Cwnd(i+1)=Cwnd(i)+1
        else
            Cwnd(i+1)=Cwnd(i)-1, α=α-1, β=β-1
        end if
    else if α=1 then
        Cwnd(i+1)=Cwnd(i)+1
    end if
else if Diff>β then
    if α>1 then
        Cwnd(i+1)=Cwnd(i)-1, α=α-1, β=β-1
    else
        No update of Cwnd(i+1), α and β
    end if
end if
```

Figure 1. Vegas-A Congestion Control Algorithm

Where $Cwnd(i)$ is the congestion window size under the current round trip, $Cwnd(i+1)$ is the congestion window size of the next round trip.

C. Veno

Veno is a combination of Vegas and Reno. It uses original Vegas's estimation algorithm to carry out early detection of network congestion. But unlike Vegas, the estimation algorithm is only used for adjusting the increase/decrease coefficient of the Reno congestion control algorithm [14].

Compared with original Vegas, there are two enhancements adopted by Veno. On one hand, the sender will probe network resources very conservatively when the estimation algorithm indicates a congestion state. On the other hand, Veno will have the ability to determine whether the loss of data is due to network congestion or channel errors to a certain extent. The second enhancement is very important for satellite communications as Veno would not ascribe all the losses to congestion under a high PER environment.

III. TCP VEGAS-L

As we were studying the above algorithms, we realized that none of them has enough network status information. In other words, the utilization of historical information of the three algorithms is not sufficient. Taking into account their deficiencies, Vegas-L brings the network probing capability into its congestion avoidance phase by employing the recent network status and the far time network status simultaneously.

First, let us declare a number of variables. In Vegas-L, we use $Th\_(i-2)$ to denote the throughput of two $RTTs$ before. The difference between $Th\_(i)$ and $Th\_(i-1)$ is $Diff\_Now$ while the difference between $Th\_(i-1)$ and $Th\_(i-2)$ is $Diff\_Before$. They are shown as follows:

$$Diff\_Now = Th\_(i) - Th\_(i-1) \tag{5}$$

$$Diff\_Before = Th\_(i-1) - Th\_(i-2) \tag{6}$$

Vegas-L employes the variables to classify network circumstances into 6 cases and carries out some adaptive adjustments. The adjustments are shown in Figure 2.

Input: $Diff\_Now$ and $Diff\_Before$
Output: $Cwnd(i+1)$, α and β

```
if Diff_Now>0 then
    if Diff_Before>0 then
        if Diff_Now>Diff_Before then
            Case 1
        else
            Case 2
        end if
    else
        Case 3
    end if
else
    if Diff_Before>0 then
        Case 4
    else
        if Diff_Now>Diff_Before then
            Case 5
        else
            Case 6
        end if
    end if
end if
```

Figure 2. Vegas-L Congestion Control Algorithm

Case 1: The network has just experienced the growth of throughput for two consecutive $RTTs$. Furthermore, the value of increased in the second RTT is bigger than that in the first one. We can judge that the network is experiencing a rapid growth phase and the remaining bandwidth is sufficient, so we adjust the growth rate of $Cwnd$, α and β as twice as the condition of $Th\_(i) > Th\_(i-1)$ in Vegas-A.

Case 2: Even if the network has just experienced the growth of throughput for two consecutive $RTTs$, the value of increased throughput in the second RTT is smaller than that in the first one. We could infer that the network is experiencing a slow growth phase and the remaining bandwidth is not abundant, so we just follow the strategy of Vegas-A as $Th\_(i) > Th\_(i-1)$.

Case 3: In this case, the throughput has just come from the reduction phase to the growth phase. There is a slight improvement in the network condition, but the remaining bandwidth would not be too much. So we set the growth rate of $Cwnd$, α and β more moderately. As a result, they are half of Vegas-A's strategy as $Th\_(i) > Th\_(i-1)$.

Case 4: In this case, the throughput has just come from the growth phase to the reduction phase. There is a slight deterioration in the network condition, but the degree of congestion level would not be very serious. So we set the reduction rate of $Cwnd$, α and β to be half of Vegas-A's strategy as $Th\_(i) < Th\_(i-1)$.

Case 5: In spite of network has just experienced the reduction of throughput for two consecutive $RTTs$, the throughput reduced in the second RTT is smaller than that in the first one. It indicates that network begins to relieve its congestion level. We just keep the strategy of Vegas-A as $Th\_(i) < Th\_(i-1)$.

Case 6: The network has just experienced the reduction of throughput for two consecutive $RTTs$. Moreover, the throughput reduced in the second RTT is bigger than that in the first one. We can assume that the network is experiencing a very congested phase. As a result, the reduction rate of $Cwnd$, α and β are set to be as twice as Vegas-A's strategy when $Th\_(i) < Th\_(i-1)$.

These more particular network states and adaptive adjustments will enable Vegas-L to gain better performance over satellite communications.

IV. Performance Evaluation

We use Network Simulator 2 (ns2.35) [15] to validate the effectiveness of Vegas-L. The simulation settings and simulation results are shown as follows.

A. Simulation Settings

The employed satellite network topology is expressed in Figure 3. The first ground launching node is placed in Beijing (39.4°N,116.4°E), corresponding receiver is in New York (40.7°N,74°W). The first data flow is attached with original Vegas, Vegas-A, Veno and Vegas-L respectively. The second ground launching node is collocated at Shanghai (31.2°N,121.5°E) and receiver is collocated at Washington (28.9°N,77°E). The second data flow is attached with the enhanced Reno, NewReno [16].

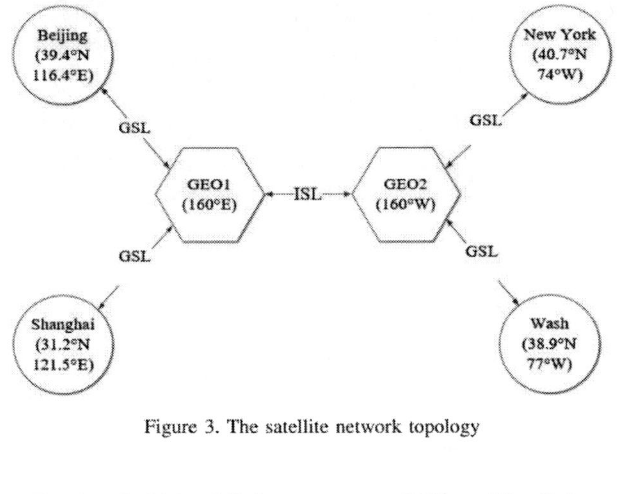

Figure 3. The satellite network topology

The bandwidth of links are set as $5Mbps$. The link type is LL/Sat while the queue management type of node buffer is DropTail. TCP packet size is 1024 bytes. Simulation lasts for 1000 seconds to get steady results. We evaluate the performance by considering two circumstances. In the first one, PER is low, just 10^{-6}, and the PER is as high as 10^{-3} in the second one.

B. Simulation Results

The dynamics of $Cwnd$ is the basic metric for evaluating a congestion control algorithm. It could reflect real-time network state during the simulation. The evolution of $Cwnds$ of Vegas, Vegas-A, Veno and Vegas-L under different PER environments over the satellite network is shown in Figure 4.

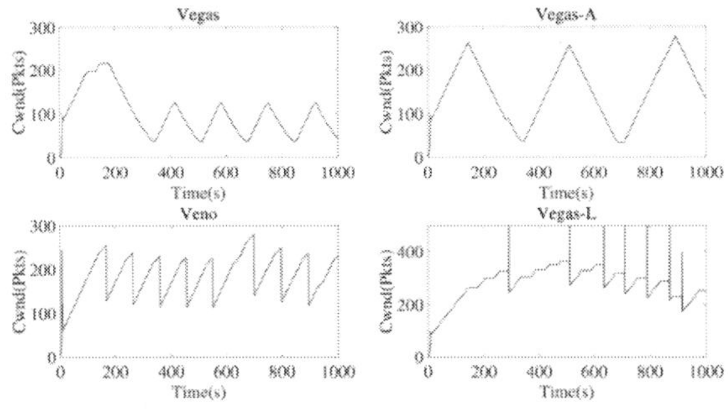

(a) The dynamics of Cwnd under low PER environment

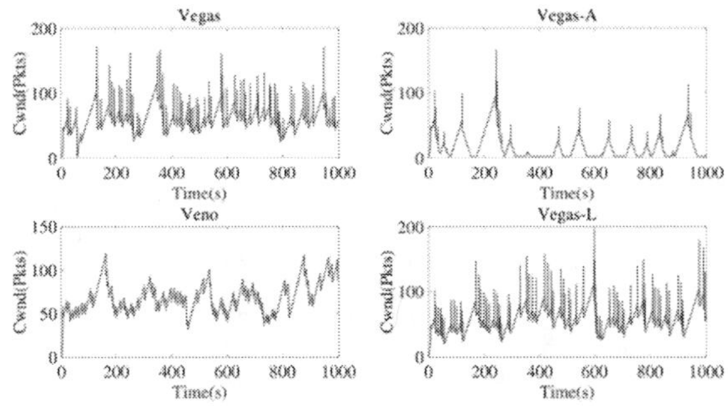

(b) The dynamics of Cwnd under high PER environment

Figure 4. The dynamics of Cwnds under different PERs environments

By observing Figure 4(a), we can see that the performance of $Cwnd$ of Vegas-L under the low PER environment is the best one. More concretely, the $Cwnds$ of these algorithms are similar to each other in the first 150 seconds. Then there are some fluctuations in original Vegas, Vegas-A and Veno. On the contrary, Vegas-L begins to enter a steady growth phase. There is little fluctuation in its $Cwnd$. Furthermore, the steady value of Vegas-L is 350 packets, which is not only 200% larger than that in original Vegas but also larger than those in Vegas-A and Veno. Next, we can also see from Figure 4(b) that the performance of all four algorithms has declined under the high PER environment. There are more dense fluctuations. The values of $Cwnd$ are much smaller than those in low PER environment. However, from the whole point of view, the $Cwnd$ value of Vegas-L is still similar to Vegas and Veno. Their performance is tied for the best one, which is better than Vegas-A.

The performance of $Cwnd$ is related to strategies used by the protocols. As far as Vegas and Vegas-A are concerned, their congestion control algorithms are relatively conservative. As a result, their $Cwnds$ change gradually in low PER environment. Veno is the combination of Vegas and Reno. It also has the intrinsic of loss-based algorithms to gain network resources aggressively. Vegas-L is not as sensitive and dull as Vegas, it could be more active to adjust its $Cwnd$ according to specific network state. Consequently, Veno and Vegas-L will have some sharp fluctuations in $Cwnds$ when the PER is low. The performance of $Cwnd$ which degrades with the increases of PER over satellite network is unavoidable. But Vegas-L is always gaining the best performance either under low PER environment or under high PER environment. The good performance of Vegas-L is due to that Vegas-L not only always monitors the satellite network status but also improves its $Cwnd$ and other key variables adaptively. Vegas-L inherits the stability from Vegas. As contrast, the performance of Vegas-A is the worst one in the high PER environment. Although Vegas-A also inherits the stability from Vegas, the congestion control algorithm employed by Vegas-A is too fragile to ensure a good performance in a high PER environment over satellite communications.

Network throughput is another basic metric to show the effectiveness of a congestion control algorithm. The final average throughput of the four algorithms under different PER environments over the satellite network is shown in Figure 5.

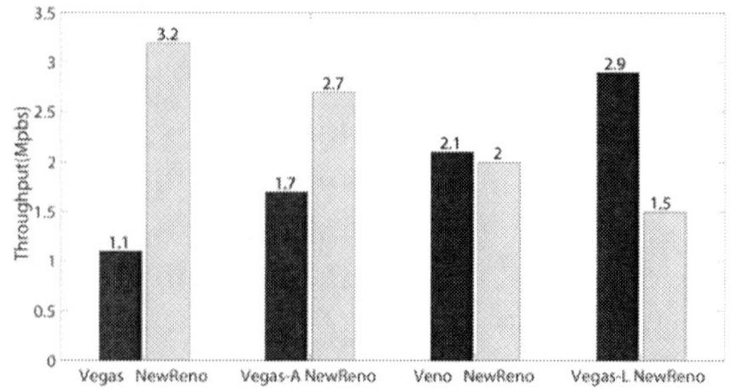

(a) The average throughput under low PER environment

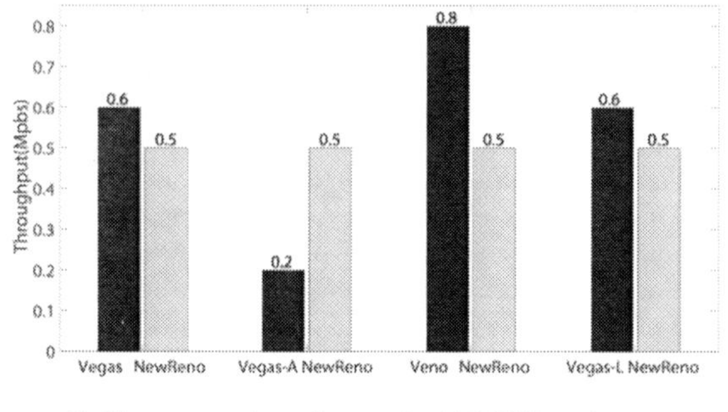

(b) The average throughput under high PER environment

Figure 5. The average throughput under different PER environments

As illustrated in Figure 5(a), the throughput of Vegas is $1.1Mbps$ under low PER environment over the satellite network. The throughput is improved in Vegas-A and Veno, but the highest one is Vegas-L with $2.9Mbps$. We could also find that the throughput of NewReno varies widely under low PER environment. It reaches $3.2Mbps$ when competes with original Vegas while only gains $1.5Mbps$ when competes with Vegas-L. As shown in Figure 5(b), all of these algorithms' performance becomes poor with the increases of PER. Among them, Vegas-A decreases rapidly, its throughput is the smallest one. Conversely, Veno is the largest one, followed by original Vegas and Vegas-L. The throughput of NewReno is always $0.5Mbps$ when it competes with variants of Vegas under high PER environment.

The performance of throughput is corresponding to the values of their $Cwnds$. Vegas-L has more historical information, detailed network states and dynamical strategies. It would not revise its $Cwnd$ recklessly. In consequence, Vegas-L has a better $Cwnd$, which leads to better throughput under different $PERs$ over the satellite network. These phenomena also demonstrate that Vegas-L has much better aggressiveness.

The fairness index is closely related to throughput. In this paper, we use Jain's fairness index [17], which is defined as Eq.7:

$$f(x_1, x_2, \ldots, x_n) = (\sum_{i=1}^{n} x_i)^2 / (n \sum_{i=1}^{n} x_i^2) \qquad (7)$$

where n represents the number of data flows and x_i is the throughput of the ith data flow. The results are shown in Figure 6.

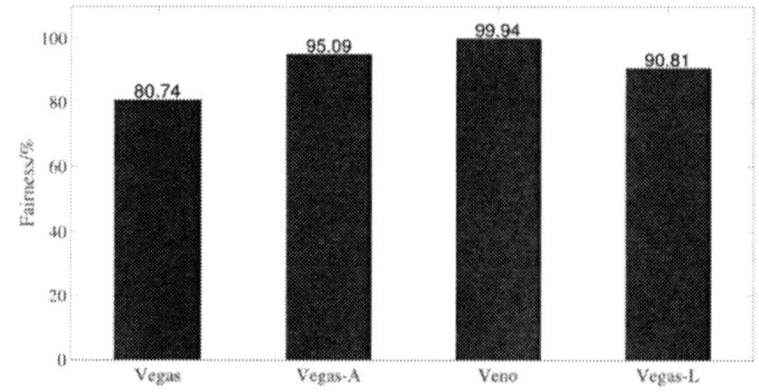

(a) The fairness under low PER environment

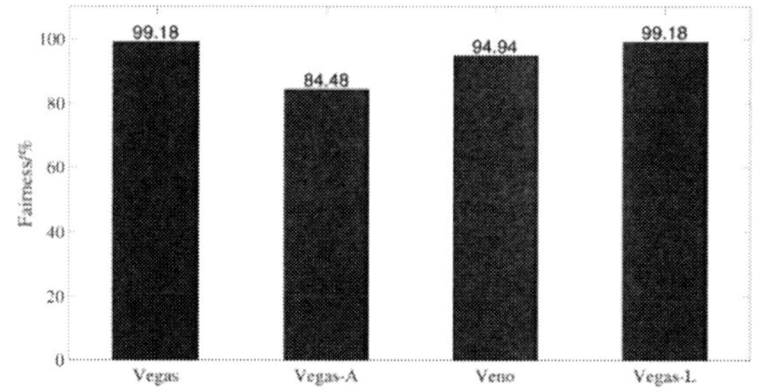

(b) The fairness under high PER environment

Figure 6. The fairness under different PER environments

It is clear from Figure 6(a) that the fairness index of original Vegas is just 80.74%, which is the smallest one. The fairness performance is enhanced in Vegas-A, Veno and Vegas-L. Particularly, the fairness index of Veno is as high as 99.94%. As shown in Figure 6(b), the fairness performance of original Vegas and Vegas-L are tied for the best one under high PER environment over the satellite network, followed by Veno. Compared with them, Vegas-A owns the worst performance.

We should point out that the throughput of Vegas-L is larger than the throughput of corresponding NewReno under low PER circumstance. Vegas-L not only has the ability to share bandwidth equally with NewReno but also can occupy a leading role, which results in the ordinary fairness performance. Similarly, Veno has the ability to distinguish whether packet loss is due to network congestion or channel errors.

V. Conclusions

In this paper, we have proposed an adaptive end-to-end congestion control algorithm called TCP Vegas-L for satellite communications. It can take full advantage of more historical information to adjust its congestion control strategies dynamically. The modifications introduced by Vegas-L are related to specific network state. After a comprehensive comparison of original Vegas, Vegas-A, Veno and Vegas-L, we can draw some conclusions as follows:

1) Vegas-L could gain outstanding performance in terms of $Cwnd$, throughput and fairness under low PER environment over satellite communications.
2) Vegas-L is able to gain satisfying performance with respect to $Cwnd$, throughput and fairness under high PER environment over satellite communications.
3) Vegas-L is competitive and even better than Vegas, Vegas-A and Veno over satellite communications under different PER environments.

However, there is still some room to improve the performance of Vegas-L. On the one hand, adjusting the aggressiveness and fairness of Vegas according to particular state of network is a novel method, but how to optimize its strategies is still worth studying. On the other hand, we could see that the performance of Vegas-L under high PER satellite environment is not the best one; how to modify Vegas-L to make it more suitable for high PER satellite environments would be another challenge.

Acknowledgement

This work is supported by Shanghai Aerospace Science and Technology Innovation Foundation of China (grant No. SAST2015039) and the National Natural Science Foundation of China (grant Nos.11433002 and 61371147).

References

[1] L. Li, H. You, J. Zhu, and Y. Yang, "A novel design on multi-layer satellite constellation," Journal of Shanghai Normal University, vol. 45, no. 2, 2016, pp. 248–252.

[2] L. Li, J. Zhu, Y. Yang, and Z. Hu, "Evaluation of tcp congestion control algorithms on satellite ip networks," Journal of Aerospace Shanghai, vol. 33, no. 6, 2016, pp. 109–114.

[3] Q. Zhao, H. Zhou, and H. Deng, "An enhanced vegas congestion control algorithm based on beidou navigation system," IEICE Communications Express, vol. 1, no. 7, 2012, pp. 275–281.

[4] L. Yang, D. Wei, C. Pan, and K. Wang, "Congestion control algorithm based on dual model control over satellite network," in Wireless Communications & Signal Processing (WCSP), 2015 International Conference on. IEEE, 2015, pp. 1–6.

[5] H. Obata, K. Tamehiro, and K. Ishida, "Experimental evaluation of tcp-star for satellite internet over winds," in 2011 Tenth International Symposium on Autonomous Decentralized Systems. IEEE, 2011, pp. 605–610.

[6] V. Jacobson, "Modified tcp congestion avoidance algorithm," end2end-interest mailing list, 1990.

[7] L. S. Brakmo, S. W. O'Malley, and L. L. Peterson, "Tcp vegas: New techniques for congestion detection and avoidance," vol. 24, no. 4, 1994, pp. 24–35.

[8] S. A. Nor, A. N. Maulana, F. A. A. Nifa, M. N. M. Nawi, and A. Hussain, "Performance of tcp variants over lte network," in AIP Conference Proceedings, vol. 1761, no. 1. AIP Publishing, 2016, pp. 020–021.

[9] E. Abolfazli and V. Shah-Mansouri, "Dynamic adjustment of queue levels in tcp vegas-based networks," Electronics Letters, vol. 52, no. 5, 2016, pp. 361–363.

[10] J. Qu, "An enhanced tcp vegas algorithm based on route surveillance and bandwidth estimation over geo satellite networks," in 2010 International Conference on Measuring Technology and Mechatronics Automation, vol. 1. IEEE, 2010, pp. 464–467.

[11] M. Nirmala and R. V. Pujeri, "Evaluation of tcp congestion control algorithms on different satellite constellations," in Advanced Computing and Communication Systems (ICACCS), 2013 International Conference on. IEEE, 2013, pp. 1–7.

[12] K. Srijith, L. Jacob, and A. L. Ananda, "Tcp vegas-a: Improving the performance of tcp vegas," Computer communications, vol. 28, no. 4, 2005, pp. 429–440.

[13] C. P. Fu and S. C. Liew, "Tcp veno: Tcp enhancement for transmission over wireless access networks," IEEE Journal on selected areas in communications, vol. 21, no. 2, 2003, pp. 216–228.

[14] A. Afanasyev, N. Tilley, P. Reiher, and L. Kleinrock, "Host-to-host congestion control for tcp," IEEE Communications surveys & tutorials, vol. 12, no. 3, 2010, pp. 304–342.

[15] "The network simulator 2.35," http://www.http://www.isi.edu/nsnam/.

[16] S. Floyd, T. Henderson, and A. Gurtov, "The newreno modification to tcp's fast recovery algorithm," 2004.

[17] R. Jain, A. Durresi, and G. Babic, "Throughput fairness index: An explanation," Tech. rep., Department of CIS, The Ohio State University, Tech. Rep., 1999.

A Study on the Improvement of National R&D History Data Management

Eungyeong Kim, Chulsu Lim
National Science & Technology Information Service Center
Korea Institute of Science and Technology Information
Daejeon, Republic of Korea
e-mail: {eungyeong, cslim}@kisti.re.kr

***Abstract*—In order to share and open national R&D information to researchers, providing user-participation service is required. With the integrated service of the National Science & Technology Information Service (NTIS), it is available to check information on R&D projects including human resources and outcomes. However, researchers are not able to see research history (research outcome) due to the possibility of the leak of personal data. Thus, this study distributed and implemented API for issuing and verifying research number (RN), which would eventually contribute to constructing national one-stop project application service and unify DB of researchers. Using the RM, it is feasible for NTIS to provide one-stop service of checking and applying for national R&D projects. Therefore, to manage the process of announcing and applying for R&D projects, this paper conducted research on examining ways to improve management of information on research history.**

Keywords-Linkage of Research History Data; Project Management System; National R&D; Project Application and Submission.

I. INTRODUCTION

The NTIS is a national R&D portal system designed to support the efficiency of R&D throughout R&D life-cycle, from R&D planning to the utilization of research outcome [1]. It has gradually evolved from 2006 (from NTIS1.0 to NTIS4.0) under the influence of external environment, changes in governmental organization, and entities of research management. By integrating with 17 national departments and agencies and constructing DB, NTIS set a goal of sharing and proliferating information on national R&D including projects, human resources, outcomes, and facilities.

As a part of 'Government 3.0 for science and technology', the purpose of this study is to construct national one-stop project application service and unify DB of researchers. Thus, we conducted research on distributing and implementing API for issuing and verifying RN. We focused on RN, as it allows researchers to use one-stop service of checking and applying for national R&D projects [2]. While [2] suggested how to provide service of integrating research history data to representative research management institutes (RRMIs), this paper expanded the subjects of the service by including research management institutes (RMIs) where there were no research management systems.

Information on participants, equipment & facilities, research outcome and collaborative research are available in the NTIS website through linkage with 17 government departments and agencies. This study was able to check research history data in the NTIS, but the one (research outcome) linked with other researchers was not. In NTIS, a researcher can search for his or her own research history (research outcome), but cannot search for others'. Therefore, user-participating services need to be developed for the opening and sharing of national R&D information.

II. THE CURRENT STATE OF NATIONAL R&D INFORMATION MANAGEMENT

Similar to NTIS, Japan and Europe also manage national R&D information. Japan's national R&D data system is called 'Japan Science and Technology (JST)'. The projects are approved by the government or implemented by the JST internally. The national R&D data system in the EU is called Community Research and Development Information Service (CORDIS). CORDIS provides R&D and technology innovation-related data [3].

TABLE I. NATIONAL R&D DATA SYSTEMS AND DATA ITEMS

National R&D Data Systems	Data Items
NTIS	Projects, participants, research results, equipment & facilities, research outcome, science & technology statistics, etc.
JST	Science & technology report, researcher career management service, Bio information service, patent & research outcome data, etc.
CORDIS	R&D expense support, research outcome, projects, programs, R&D agencies, researchers, latest trends, etc.

Table 1 above summarizes what data items NTIS, JST, and CORIDS manage and provide.

III. IMPROVEMENT IN THE MANAGEMENT OF RESEARCH HISTORY DATA

At present, RMIs transfer information to the NTIS through information integration once an agreement for projects/programs is signed. Then, project serial numbers are given to each project or program, linking to the transferred information. Accordingly, on the NTIS website, one can search for the information on national R&D, such as participants, equipment & facilities, outcomes, or collaborative research.

In case of retrieval of information on research history of a researcher, due to the concern of leaking personal information, a researcher is allowed to access to only his or her own R&D history, implying that he or she has no authority to access to others'. However, in order to share and publicly open national R&D information, the user-participation service is required.

Thus, this paper developed alternative solution to improve the management of information on research history by promoting NTIS to integrate with both RRMIs and RMIs so that the process of announcing, applying, and conducting national R&D projects can be managed.

A. Integrating with RRMIs with SSO

To integrate research history data, this study constructed a single channel to let the procedures of announcing, applying and modifying the R&D projects to be performed in one-stop process. For the single channel, however, a heterogeneous login solution exists, which causes the problem of multi-login when integrating NTIS with the RRMIs. Hence, single sign on (SSO) was interlocked between the NTIS and the institutes. As the resident registration number cannot be used for personal identification, by using the RN, a token is issued and verified in the SSO server.

As the result, SSO interlocking was designed to be flowed in both ways between RRMIs' research management system and NTIS. In the NTIS, furthermore, DB of announcement and application of R&D was interlocked with the RRMIs, and the systems were linked to allow researchers to be able to apply for, edit and submit a project through the single channel. It indicates that RRMIs administer and manage the procedures of applying and modifying R&D projects, whereas NTIS presents the current status of application and provides the channel ('Go To') to modify.

B. Developing Process to Integrate with RMIs

In South Korea, there are RMIs where research management systems are not used as RRMIs do. Thus, this paper constructed another single channel for RMIs to integrate research history data. Unlike the RRMIs, due to the absence of the research management systems, researchers have to send mails to RMIs when applying for R&D projects.

Thus, as shown in Figure 1, this study developed the process of applying and receiving the projects on online by using NTIS.

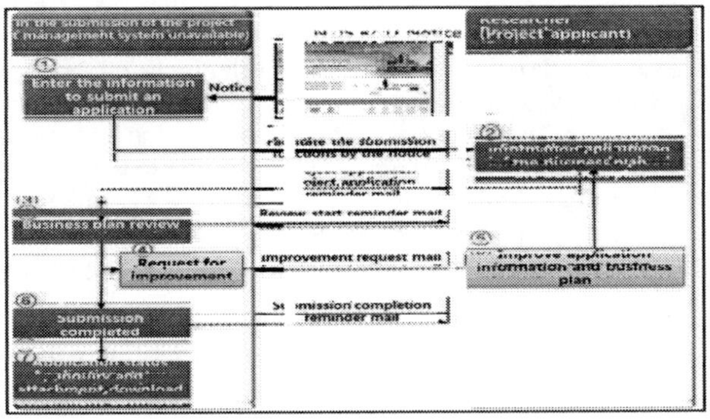

Figure 1. NTIS Project Application-Submission Process.

The program (reception) manager selects the program announcement from the NTIS R&D announcements and inputs management information that is needed for the reception. Then, researchers upload their business plan to apply for the projects.

IV. CONCLUSION AND FUTURE WORKS

This study examined on integration of research history data for the purpose of managing and monitoring the data. As a result, the management of ongoing projects, applied projects, researchers and participating agencies has become more convenient. Figure 2 below shows the result of this research, demonstrating the state of a researcher's participation and application project. In the table of the figure, there are names of projects, the amount of government fund, research period, and participation rate.

In sum, this paper developed one-stop project service using RN to improve the management and utilization of R&D information. The result indicates that researchers will able to check and manage such projects in 'My Project' from the NTIS.

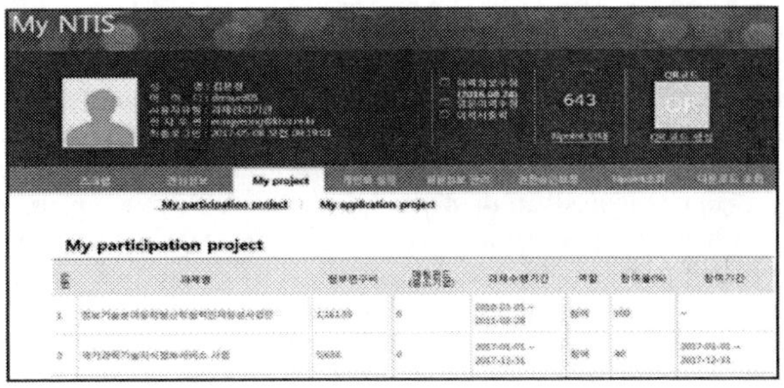

Figure 2. Management of My Project

However, further research is needed for NTIS to provide user-participation service to researchers. In details, to manage research history data, RN needs to perform duties of identifying individuals and managing the information linked to them. Also, more studies are needed to strengthen the security of personal information.

ACKNOWLEDGMENT

This research was supported by Construction of National Science and Technology Information Service (NTIS) funded by the Korea Institute of Science and Technology Information (KISTI).

REFERENCES

[1] National Science & Technology Information Service (NTIS), www.ntis.go.kr [retrieved: July, 2017]

[2] E. Kim, C. Lim, and H. Jeong, "Integration of National R&D Information Management Systems to Enhance Research Productivity", International Conference on Convergence Technology, Vol. 6, pp. 492-493, 2016.

[3] K. Choi, M. Park, and Y. Kim, "A Study on Construction of Integrated National R&D", Journal of the Society of Korea Industrial and Systems Engineering, Vol. 32, No. 4, pp.25-37, 2009.

A Solution for Bufferbloat Problem in Upload TCP Communication over IEEE 802.11n WLAN Only by Modifying Access Point

Masataka Nomoto, Celimuge Wu, Satoshi Ohzahata, and Toshihiko Kato
University of Electro-Communications
Tokyo, Japan
e-mail: noch@net.is.uec.ac.jp, clmg@is.uec.ac.jp, ohzahata@is.uec.ac.jp, kato@is.uec.ac.jp

***Abstract*—IEEE 802.11n Wireless Local Area Networks (WLANs) suffer from Bufferbloat problem such that the round-trip delay increases in upload Transmission Control Protocol (TCP) communications when the Media Access Control (MAC) level data rate is low such as 6.5 Mbps. This problem degrades user level quality of service for communications sharing the WLAN transmission queue. In order to resolve it, several methods are proposed including a method based on active queue management, our previous method reducing the MAC retransmission limit at low MAC level data rates, and a method stopping sending TCP level data when the queue contains more than a specific number of packets. However, those methods need to be implemented in data sending stations. In this paper, we propose a new method resolving Bufferbloat problem by providing an effect similar to our previous method at a data receiving access point. This decreases the congestion window size in the sending side TCP and can reduce the delay. This paper also shows the results of the performance evaluation by implementing the proposed method in an access point. According to the results, the proposed method decreases the Round-Trip Time (RTT) for low MAC data rates and does not reduce the TCP throughput. It does not give any influences on the TCP throughput for the stations supporting the conventional methods for Bufferbroat problem.**

Keywords- Wireless LAN; IEEE 802.11n; TCP; Dymamic Rate Switching; Bufferbloat Problem; Block Acknowledgment.

I. INTRODUCTION

WLANs conforming to the IEEE 802.11n standard [1] have adopted new physical and MAC technologies. They include Multiple-Input and Multiple-Output (MIMO), the channel bonding, the frame aggregation, and the Block ACKnowledgment (Block ACK).

On the other hand, similarly with the conventional IEEE WLAN standards, IEEE 802.11n supports multiple data rates and the dynamic rate switching to use the optimal data rate between a STAtion (STA) and an Access Point (AP). When an STA is located close to an AP and the radio condition is good, the high data rate such as 300 Mbps can be used. But, when an STA moves to the location far from an AP and the receiving radio signal strength becomes weak, the data rate gets lower, for example down to 6.5 Mbps.

When an STA communicates by TCP while it is using a low data rate, the packet losses do not increase, but the RTT increases largely, up to several seconds [2]. This long delay is considered as a sort of Bufferbloat problem, which is discussed widely in the networking community [3]-[5].

In order to solve this problem, there are some proposals [6]-[8]. All of them intend to decrease TCP traffic load when packets in a WLAN transmission queue pile up and the transfer delay increases. They are classified into two categories. One is a scheme that generates packet losses intentionally against increased transfer delay, which in turn decreases TCP congestion window (cwnd). CoDel [6], which is an active queue management based method, uses a packet-sojourn time in a transmission queue as a control parameter, and drops a packet in the situation when packets stay too long in the queue. In our previous paper [2], we inferred that one of the reasons for the large queuing delay is the powerful data retransmission function in 802.11n MAC level, which uses the frame aggregation and the Block ACK. So, we proposed a method that intentionally weakens the capability of retransmission realized by Block ACK frames, only when the data rate is low in TCP communications [7]. It increases the possibility of TCP packet losses at low data rate. The second category is a scheme that TCP stops sending data segments when many packets are stored in a MAC level transmission queue. An example is TCP small queues [8], which is implemented in the Linux operating system with 3.6 and later versions. For resolving Bufferbloat problem in upload TCP communications, all of those methods require to be implemented in every STA. The Linux operating system implements CoDel and/or TCP small queues, but as far as we know, the Windows and MAC operating systems do not implement either of them.

In this paper, we propose a new method which resolves Bufferbloat problem by providing an effect at a receiving side access point, which is similar to reducing the MAC level retransmission limit in STAs when the data rate is low. This decreases cwnd in the sending side and can reduce the delay. This paper also shows the results of the performance evaluation by implementing the proposed method in a Personal Computer (PC) based AP. According to the results, the proposed method decreases RTT for low MAC data rates and does not reduce the TCP throughput. It does not give any influences on the TCP throughput for STAs supporting CoDel or TCP small queues.

The rest of this paper is organized as follows. Section II explains the frame aggregation and Block ACK procedures and the related work. Section III describes the proposed method, and Section IV gives the results of performance evaluation. In the end, Section V concludes this paper.

II. PROCEDURE OF 802.11N AND RELATED WORK

This section describes the high throughput data transfer function of 802.11n and the related work on Bufferbloat problem.

A. *Frame aggregation and Block ACK in 802.11n WLAN*

IEEE 802.11n allows multiple data frames (called MAC Protocol Data Units: MPDUs) to be aggregated and sent together in order to increase the efficiency of data sending (see Figure 1). The whole transmitted frame is called Aggregation MPDU (A-MPDU), and is a collection of A-MPDU subframes, each of which includes an MPDU delimiter, and MPDU body, and a padding. An MPDU delimiter contains the MPDU length, a Cyclic Redundancy Check (CRC) to detect bit errors within the delimiter itself. A padding consists of 0 through 3 bytes, which makes the length of an A-MPDU subframe a multiple of 4 bytes.

The IEEE 802.11n standard adopts an acknowledgment scheme called High Throughput (HT)-immediate Block ACK. When a receiver receives an A-MPDU, it replies a Block ACK frame which contains a Block ACK Bitmap parameter indicating whether it correctly receives a MPDU with a specific sequence number. The Bitmap indicates receipt or non-receipt of 64 MPDUs. The data sender retransmits non-received MPDUs according to the Bitmap. When a Block ACK frame itself is lost, the whole A-MPDU is retransmitted by timeout.

These procedures are implemented by the WLAN device drivers and WLAN hardware at the data sender and receiver. The details are shown in Figure 2. At the data sender side, the device driver selects MPDUs to be aggregated in an A-MPDU. They include some retransmitted MPDUs determined by the Block ACK Bitmap. The device driver also determines the retry-out of MPDUs independently if the retransmission count of the MPDU reaches the retransmission limit. On the other hand, the WLAN hardware at the sender side realizes the actual formatting and sending out of A-MPDUs, timeout retransmission of A-MPDUs, and reporting of Block ACK Bitmap to the device driver.

At the data receiver side, the WLAN hardware handles the reporting of received MPDUs to the device driver and the sending of Block ACKs. The hardware also notifies the device driver of the information on MPDUs with CRC error. On the other hand, the device driver handles the sequencing of MPDUs and the retry-out decisions. The retry-out decision at the data receiver side is realized by the timeout basis, not by counting the MPDU retransmissions.

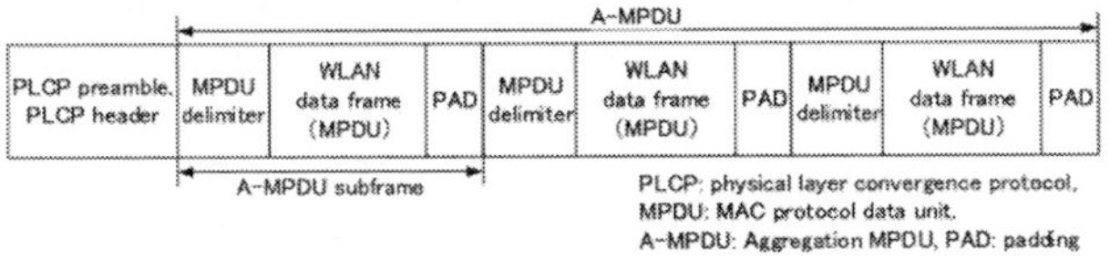

Figure 1. Format of A-MPDU.

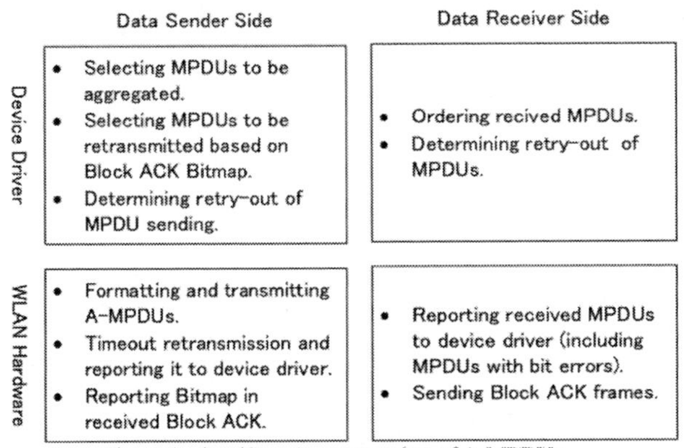

Figure 2. Send/Receive processing of A-MPDUs.

B. *Related work*

(1) CoDel

As described above, CoDel uses a packet-sojourn time in the queue. Specifically, when any packet stays in the queue longer than a specific duration, called *target* in CoDel, during a predefined interval, called *interval* in CoDel, the last packet in the queue is dropped. As for the value of *target*, 5 msec is used in [6]. The *interval* takes 100 msec at the beginning of the procedure, and if a packet is dropped, the value is decreased in inverse proportion to the square root of the number of drops since the dropping state started.

(2) Decreasing retransmission limit at low data rate

The second method is our previous proposal, which is based on the MAC level retransmission limit adjustment. It aims at causing an MPDU loss intentionally by setting the retransmission limit to some value between 2 and 8 when the data rate is smaller than 100 Mbps, and use 10, which is the default value, when the data rate is larger than 100 Mbps [7].

(3) TCP small queues

In an ordinary TCP communication, data that an application sent are stored in the send socket buffer and transferred under the limitation of advertised window and cwnd. In contrast, TCP small queues is a method that transfers TCP data segments by taking account of the status of transmission queues within the operating system scheduler and the WLAN device driver [8]. When the total size of TCP data segments stored in those transmission queues becomes a specific threshold (128 Kbytes in the default setting), new data generated by applications are not handled in TCP and keep staying in the send socket buffer. After the TCP data size stored in the transmission queue becomes smaller than the threshold, TCP module resumes the processing of data stored in the send socket buffer. As a result, TCP small queues can suppress the queuing delay without invoking intentional packet losses even if a low data rate is used.

As described above, all of those methods resolve Bufferbloat problem over 802.11n WLAN, but they need to be implemented in individual STAs. Although the recent versions of Linux implement CoDel and TCP small queues, it is expected that some of the major operating systems, such as Windows and Mac OS, support neither of them.

III. PROPOSAL

The primary goal of our proposal is to resolve Bufferbloat problem in upload TCP communications over 802.11n WLANs only by modifying an AP, which is an MPDU receiver. We adopt a method similar with our previous proposal, which increases MPDU losses by decreasing the MAC level retransmission limit when the data rate is low. The retransmission of lost MPDUs is controlled only by data senders; by STAs not APs in the upload data transfer. The proposed method emulates the limited number of retransmissions only at an AP working as an MPDU receiver, for MPDUs including TCP segments transferred in a low data rate. This will increase the loss possibility of MPDUs and invoke the cwnd shrinking. This section describes detailed design of the proposed method.

A. Design principles

In order to design the proposed method, we have adopted the following principles. The first one is that we design the proposed method under the restriction to implement it inside the WLAN device driver. As described in the previous section, the retransmission of MPDUs and the sending of Block ACK are implemented in the WLAN hardware. So, the device driver at data receiver side cannot control the MPDU retransmission behavior that a data sender goes up to the retransmission limit. So, we adopt an approach that, when MAC level data rate is low, the receiver side device driver behaves as if retry-out occurred in response to a smaller retransmission count, and goes further to handling the following MPDUs. The retransmission count used as the retry-out limit is called a *retry-out index* in this paper.

The second principle is that we utilize the information reported from the WLAN hardware to the device driver as much as possible. As described above, the WLAN hardware reports the sequence number of an MPDU which suffers from transmission error (with CRC error). The proposed method uses this information as far as it maintains consistency with other information.

Figure 3 shows the idea of our proposal. STA and Access Point is connected through WLAN, and Access Point has an access to Ethernet. Figure 3 (a) shows the idea of our previous proposal [7]. The retransmission limit is set to 1 in STA. Frame 3 is transferred with CRC error twice, and so it is handled as a retry-out event. As a result, Access Point relays Frame 4 to Ethernet without sending Frame 3. Figure 3 (b) shows the idea of the method proposed in this paper. While STA has a large retransmission limit, Access Point supposes that it is 1. So, at the timing of the second erroneous reception (the first retransmission) of Frame 3, it is handled as if the retry-out happens (pseudo retry-out), and the next frame (Frame 4) is relayed to Ethernet. Even if Frame 3 is received correctly later, it is ignored.

B. Detailed design

The followings give the details on how to implement the proposed method.

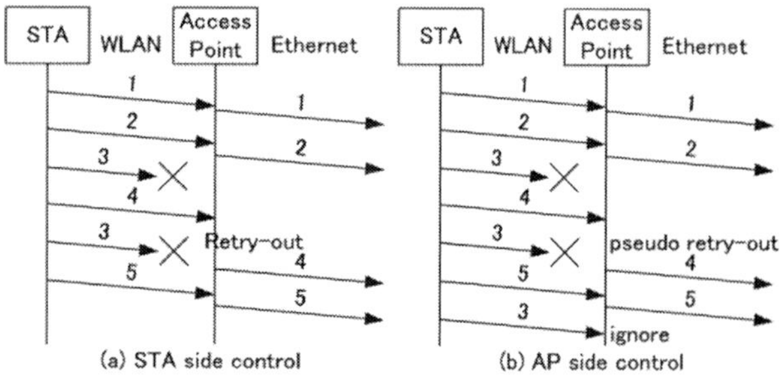

Figure 3. Idea of our proposal.

TABLE I. RETRY-OUT INDEX.

Smoothed data rate (Mbps)	~25	25~50	50~100	100~
Retry-out index	2	5	8	out of scope

(1) Retry-out index

The value of retry-out index is selected as shown in Table I. The value are the same as the retransmission limits used in our previous proposal [7]. The smoothed data rate used for the retry-out index selection is calculated according to the exponential moving average with coefficient 0.25. That is, the *smoothed data rate* in Table I is calculated by the following equation at each of MPDU reception.

$$\begin{aligned} &smoothed\ data\ rate \leftarrow \\ &0.75 \times smoothed\ data\ rate\ (previous) \\ &+ 0.25 \times data\ rate\ used\ by\ received\ MPDU \end{aligned}$$

(2) Estimation of retransmission count

An AP, an MPDU receiver, estimates the retransmission count per MPDU basis. The estimation is done based on the signaling of MPDUs with CRC error from the WLAN hardware. That is, when an MPDU with CRC error is reported, the proposed method increases (or set to 1) the estimated count of receiving this specific MPDU supposing that the signaled number of MPDU is correct. The retransmission count is the estimated receiving count minis one. It should be noted that the retransmission count covers both the Block ACK based MPDU retransmission and the timeout based A-MPDU retransmission.

(3) Handling as lost frames when reaching retry-out index

When an MPDU is received with CRC error and it contains a TCP segment, the estimated retransmission count is compared with the retry-out index. If the count reaches the retry-out index, the MPDU is marked as a lost frame. If there are any buffered MPDUs waiting for being reported to the upper layer whose sequence numbers follow the number of the MPDU marked as lost, they will be reported to the upper layer. Even though an MPDU is marked as lost, an STA continues the retransmission until its retransmission limit, and so an AP may receive such an MPDU.

(4) Non-error MPDU handling

When an AP receives an MPDU without any errors, it takes one of the followings. If the MPDU is marked as lost, it is ignored. (Note that a Block ACK is sent by the WLAN hardware.) Otherwise, if the MPDU is an in-sequence one, it is reported to the upper layer. Otherwise, it is buffered within the WLAN device driver for waiting in-sequence MPDUs.

C. Example of behavior at AP

Figure 4 shows an example of behavior at AP supporting the proposed method. The first row in the table indicates received A-MPDUs; A-MPDU(1) through A-MPDU(7). The second row indicates the sequence number assigned to individual MPDUs; 1 to 10. The slash mark over the number means that the corresponding MPDU is received with CRC error. For example, A-MPDU(1) includes five MPDUs, and among them, MPDUs with sequence number 2 and 4 are received with CRC error.

	A-MPDU(1)					A-MPDU(2)			A-MPDU(3)				A-MPDU(4)				(5)	(6)		(7)
	1	~~2~~	3	~~4~~	5	~~6~~	7	8	~~2~~	~~4~~	~~9~~	~~10~~	2	~~4~~	9	~~10~~	6	~~4~~	10	4
1	✔																			
2		0							1				✔							
3			Keep										✔							
4				0						1				2/Lost				3		Ignore
5					Keep									✔						
6						0											✔			
7							Keep										✔			
8								Keep									✔			
9											0				Keep		✔			
10												0				1			✔	

✔: Reporting received MPDU to upper layer
Keep: Buffering received MPDU within device driver
Lost: Handles MPDU as it is lost
Ignore: Ignoring received MPDU
Numbers: indicate retransmission counts

Figure 4. Example behavior of proposed method. .

Each cell in the table shows how the MPDU given in the second row is handled. The sequence number is indicated in the first column in the table. Non-blank cells mean the followings:

- Mark ✔ means the user data contained in the received MPDU is reported to the upper layer.
- "Keep" means that the received MPDU is buffered within the device driver.
- "Ignore" means that the user data in the received MPDU is ignored.
- "Lost" means that the received MPDU is marked as a lost frame.
- The number in a cell corresponds to the estimated retransmission count.

In this example, we suppose the retry-out index is two. In the beginning, A-MPDU(1) contains five MPDUs, among which MPDU-2 and 4 has CRC error. So, MPDU-1 is reported to the upper layer and MPDU-3 and 5 are buffered. For MPDU-2 and 4, the estimated retransmission count is set to 0.

Similarly, for A-MPDU(2), the estimated retransmission count of MPDU-6 is set to 0, and MPDU-7 and 8 are buffered.

A-MPDU(3) is an example of the case where a whole A-MPDU is corrupted. In this case, the information on MPDU sequence numbers is also reported to the device driver, which we have confirmed actually. As a result, the values of estimated retransmission count for MPDU-2, 4, 9 and 10 are incremented to 1 or set to 0, respectively.

A-MPDU(4) is a timeout based retransmission of A-MPDU(3), in which MPDU-2 and 9 are correctly received and MPDU-4 and 10 are corrupted. The receipt of MPDU-2 makes user data within MPDU-2 and 3 reported to the upper layer. MPDU-9 is buffered, and the estimated retransmission count for MPDU-4 and 10 is incremented. Since the count for MPDU-4 reaches 2 (retry-out index), MPDU-4 is handled as a lost frame at this time. Since buffered MPDU-5 follows the MPDU marked as lost (MPDU-4), its user data is reported to the upper layer.

Then, A-MPDU(5) containing only MPDU-6 is received. Since this is an in-sequence MPDU and MPDU-7 through 9 are buffered within the device driver, user data contained in all of those MPDUs are reported to the upper layer.

Next, A-MPDU(6) containing MPDU-4 and 10 is received, and MPDU-4 is again corrupted. Since MPDU-4 is marked as lost, its retransmission count is just incremented and user data in MPDU-10 is passed to the upper layer.

In the end, A-MPDU(7) containing MPDU-4 correctly is received. For MPDU-4, the WLAN hardware sends a Block ACK, but the device driver just ignores it.

In this way, an AP, an MPDU receiver, sets the retry-out index to the smaller value than the retransmission limit at an STA, an MPDU sender, and handles an MPDU as a lost frame earlier than an STA.

IV. Performance Evaluation

This section describes the results of experiments measuring the TCP throughput and the RTT of Ping (Internet Control Message Protocol (ICMP) Echo request/response) in the situation where Bufferbloat problem occurs. More specifically, the following points are examined.

- Whether the proposed method suppresses the increase of RTT or not. As for STA, we use PCs which run the Linux operating system, Windows and Mac OS.
- Whether MPDU losses introduced by the proposed method reduce the TCP throughput or not.
- Whether the proposed method gives any influence or not to the TCP throughput of STAs implementing CoDel or TCP small queues.

A. Experimental settings

Figure 5 shows the network configuration of our experiment. An STA and an AP use 5GHz band WLAN conforming to IEEE 802.11n. The AP and a server are connected via Gigabit Ethernet link through a bridge, which provides just bridging in this experiment.

The experiment is performed in a two-storied Japanese style house built of wood. The server, the AP and the bridge are located in the 2nd floor. The STA is located at various locations in the 1st and 2nd floors, and the stairs between them. The distance between the STA and the AP is about 1.2 meter at the nearest position and about 10 meter at the far most position. At one position, the STA is fixed and performs TCP and Ping communications for 60 seconds.

The AP is implemented using a Linux PC. For STA, we prepared a Linux PC, a Windows PC and a Mac PC. The specification of the AP and the STA is given in Table II. As for the Linux PC, we prepared three versions; a PC without any methods preventing Bufferbloat problem, a PC with TCP

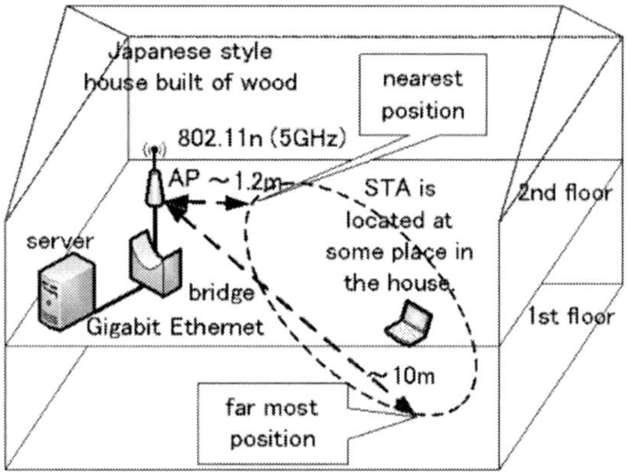

Figure 5. Experiment configuration.

TABLE II. SPECIFICATION OF AP AND PC.

	AP	Linux PC	Windows PC	Mac
model	Lenovo ThinkPad X61		Mac Book Pro	
kernel	Linux 3.2.38	Linux 3.13.0	Window 10	Mac OS 10.11
WLAN MAC	IEEE 802.11n (5GHz)			
TCP congestion control	—	CUBIC TCP [9]	Default method of OS	
AP software	Hostapd 0.7.3	—	—	—
NIC	NEC Aterm WL300NE-AG		Broadcom	
Driver	ath9k [10]		Default software of OS	

small queues, and a PC with CoDel. As for the PC with TCP small queues, we used a Linux PC with version 3.13 as it is. As for the PC without any methods, we used a Linux PC with version 3.13 by setting the queue limit to 10,000 packets, which is large enough to suppress the function of TCP small queues. As for the PC with CoDel, we used a Linux PC with large TCP small queues' limit by adding the function of CoDel.

B. Results of performance evaluation

In the experiment, we executed a 60 sec TCP data transfer from STA to AP, and a 60 sec Ping communication invoked by STA, simultaneously. TCP data transfer is done by use of iperf [11]. In the Ping communication, STA sends a Ping request (ICMP Echo request packet) once a second. For one measurement run, we measured the average of TCP throughput, Ping RTT, and transmission queue length in WLAN driver. As for the last item, we measured only for a Linux PC.

As for the parameter which characterizes the position of the STA, we used the average data rate for all A-MPDUs transmitted during a 60 sec communication. We mapped the measured values with the average data rate. This is a similar approach with our previous paper [7].

Figure 6 shows the result of average Ping RTT versus average data rate. One plot in the graph corresponds an average during one measurement run. "none", "tsq" and "codel" indicate the results of Linux PC without any methods, Linux PC with TCP small queues, and Linux PC with Codel, respectively. "windows" and "mac" indicate the results of Windows PC and Mac PC, respectively.

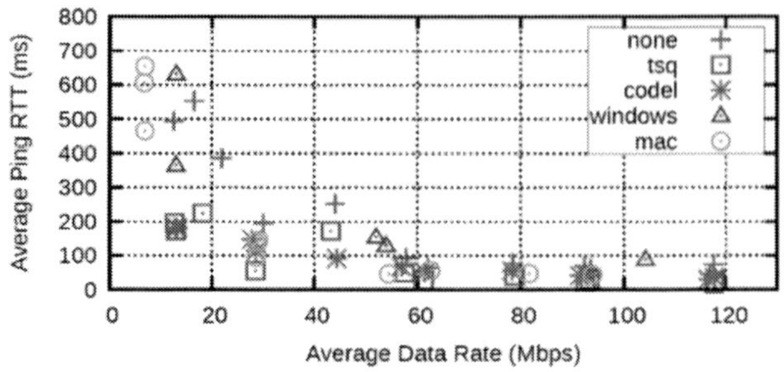

(a) Without proposed method in AP.

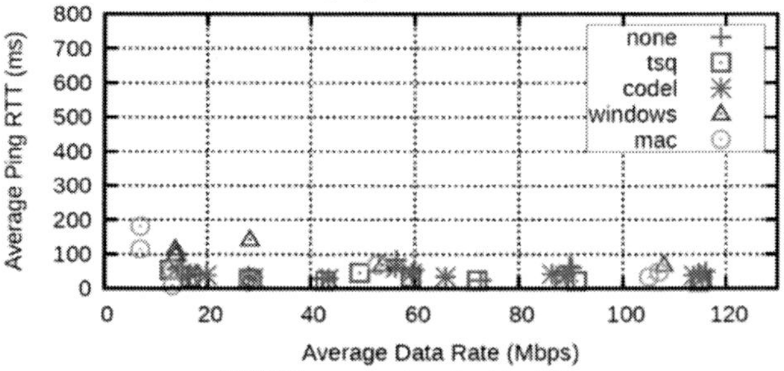

(b) With proposed method in AP.

Figure 6. Average Ping RTT vs. average data rate.

Figure 6 (a) shows that, in the case the proposed method is not introduced in the AP, the Ping RTT of Linux PC without any methods, Windows PC, and Mac PC becomes large when the average data rate is lower than 20 Mbps. The worst case is around 700 msec. In Linux PC with TCP small queues or CoDel, the Ping RTT is around 200 msec when the average data rate is lower than 20 Mbps.

These results mean that Windows 10 and Mac OS X do not support any mechanisms to prevent Bufferbloat problem, and that TCP small queues and CoDel can suppress the increase of delay.

Figure 6 (b) shows that, when the proposed method is implemented in the AP, all of Linux PCs, Windows PC and Mac PC do not suffer from large delay even if the average data rate is lower than 20 Mbps. Especially, the reduction of Ping RTT is clear for Linux PC without any methods, Windows PC and Mac PC, which do not care about Bufferbloat problem. This result means that the proposed method is effective for preventing the increase of delay caused by Bufferbloat problem.

Figure 7 shows the result of average WLAN transmission queue length versus average data rate, in Linux PCs. In the case the proposed method is not introduced, around 600 packets are stored in transmission queue for any data rate in a Linux PC without any methods (Figure 7 (a)). This length is considered as cwnd in TCP communication [2]. On the other hand, in a Linux PC introducing TCP small queues or CoDel, the average queue length is reduced to around 100 packets, and as a result, the delay is reduced.

Figure 7 (b) shows that, when the proposed method is introduced, the average queue length in STA is suppressed to less than 50 packets when the average data rate is lower than 50 Mbps. As a result, the delay is also suppressed. When the average data rate is higher than 50 Mbps, the average queue length increases in a PC without any methods, but it is not a problem because the Ping RTT itself is small as shown in Figures 6 (a) and 6 (b).

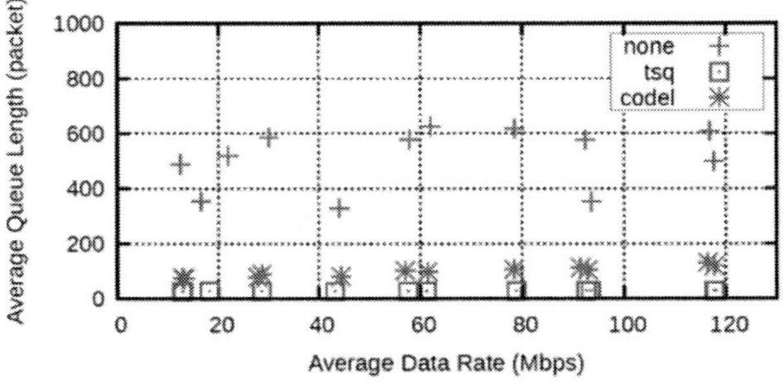

(a) Without proposed method in AP.

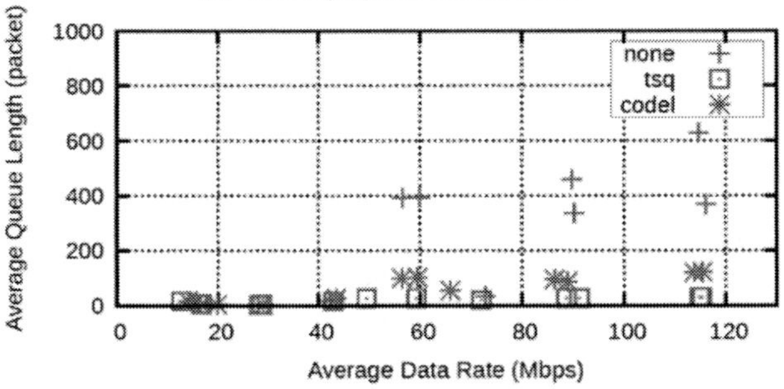

(b) With proposed method in AP.

Figure 7. Average transmission queue length vs. average data rate.

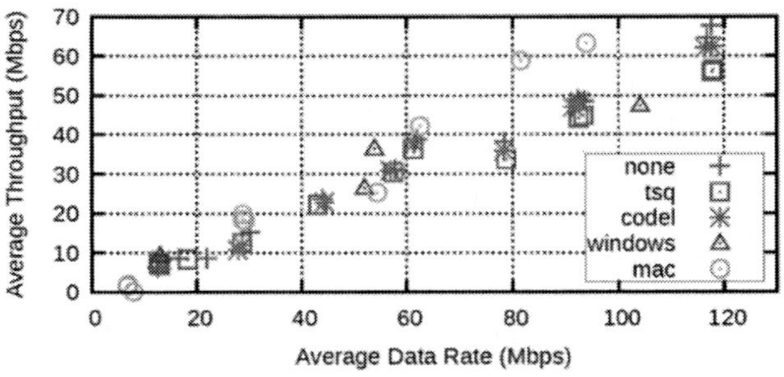

(a) Without proposed method in AP.

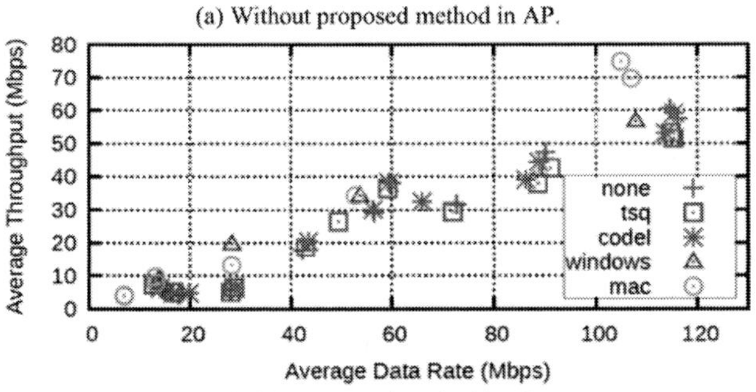

(b) With proposed method in AP.

Figure 8. Average TCP throughput vs. average data rate.

Figure 8 shows the result of average TCP throughput versus average data rate. As shown in Figure 8 (a), the TCP throughput is not affected by Bufferbloat problem. Besides, Figure 8 (b) shows that the result of TCP throughput is similar for both cases with and without the proposed method installed in the AP. This means that the proposed method does not influence the TCP throughput of STAs implementing TCP small queues or CoDel.

V. CONCLUSIONS

This paper has proposed a new method that is installed only at an IEEE 802.11n AP and can reduce the delay in upload TCP communications. The proposed method realizes similar effect with decreasing the retransmission limit at low MAC level data rate. The proposed method can prevent Bufferbloat problem in upload TCP communication without modifying sender side STAs at all. This paper also presented the detailed performance evaluation. The results clarified that the proposed method surely reduces the Ping RTT from STA when TCP bulk data transfer co-exists, that it does not reduce the TCP throughput, and that it does not give any influence to that of STAs implementing TCP small queues or CoDel, which are well-known methods for resolving Bufferbloat problem.

REFERENCES

[1] IEEE Standard for Information technology,"Local and metropolitan area networks Part 11: Wireless LAN Medium Access Control (MAC) and Physical Layer (PHY) Specifications," 2012.

[2] M. Nomoto, T. Kato, C. Wu, and S. Ohzahata, "Resolving Bufferbloat Problem in 802.11n WLAN by Weakening MAC Loss Recovery for TCP Stream," Proc.12th IASTED PDCN, pp. 293-300, Feb. 2014.

[3] J. Gettys and K. Nichols, "Bufferbloat: Dark Buffers in the Internet," ACM Queue, Virtualization, vol. 9, no.11, pp. 1-15, Nov. 2011.

[4] M. Allman, "Comments on Bufferbloat," ACM SIGCOMM Computer Communication Review, vol.43, no.1, pp. 31-37, Jan. 2013.

[5] A. Showail, K., Jamshaid, and B. Shihada, "An Empirical Evaluation of Bufferbloat in IEEE 802.11n Wireless Networks," Proc. IEEE WCNC '14, pp. 3088-3093, Apr. 2014.

[6] K. Nichols and V. Jacobson, "Controlling Queue Delay," ACM Queue, Networks, vol.10, no.5, pp. 1-15, May 2012.

[7] M. Nomoto, C. Wu, S. Ohzahata, and T. Kato, "Resolving Bufferbloat in TCP communication over IEEE 802.11n WLAN by Reducing MAC Retransmission Limit at Low Data Rate," in Proc. ICN 2017, pp. 69-74, Apr. 2017.

[8] E. Dumazet, "[PATCH v3 net-next] tcp: TCP Small Queues," Jul. 2012, http://article.gmame.org, [retrieved: Aug. 2017].

[9] I. Rhee and L. Xu, "CUBIC: a new TCP-friendly high-speed TCP variant," SIGOPS Operating Systems Review, vol.42, no. 5, pp. 64-74, July 2008.

[10] ath9k Linux Wireless, http://wireless.kernel.org/en/users/Drivers/ath9k, [retrieved: Aug. 2017].

[11] iperf, https://github.com/esnet/iperf, [retrieved: Aug. 2017].

A Study on Support of Project Planning Competency for Small & Mid-sized Enterprises Using National Science & Technology Data

Sunghee Lee, Wonkyun Joo, Myungseok Yang, Eunji Yu, Kiseok Choi
NTIS Center
Korea Institute of Science and Technology Information
Daejeon, Republic of Korea
e-mail : {sunghee.lee, joo, msyang, eunjiyu08, choi}@kisti.re.kr

Abstract— **There have been a lot of policies to support small and mid-sized enterprises (SMSEs), which have recently emerged as leading figures in technology innovation. The National Science and Technology Information Service (NTIS), which has provided national R&D data also launched a business support service in late 2015 and has helped the SMSEs build project planning capability since then. This study attempted to review the NTIS' business support service system and examine its improvement and development plan.**

Keywords- National R&D; R&D information; SMSEs; small and mid-sized enterprises; business support service; NTIS.

I. INTRODUCTION

Among the profit-making businesses in the Republic of Korea, the percentage of small and mid-sized enterprises (SMSEs) is as large as 99.9%, having a considerable effect on national economy [1]. Even though they have emerged as key players for technology innovation, they are still short of funds, technology, knowledge and manpower, compared to big businesses [2][3]. In particular, approximately 70% of them are incapable of implementing R&Ds due to difficulty in securing R&D staff and turnover of current R&D personnel [4]. Considering these obstacles, the National Science & Technology Information Service (NTIS) has provided special services for the SMSEs to help them build project planning capability, which is needed to create new programs.

The NTIS is a national R&D data knowledge portal which provides information on government-funded R&D programs, such as national R&D programs and projects, personnel, research outcome and R&D equipment and facilities [5]. In connection with 17 government offices and bureaus, it collects standard national R&D data under 422 different categories and has opened 295 items to the public through the related services such as integrated search. The government-led portal has nearly 150,000 members. Among them, government bureaus and project management institutes account for 6% while businesses and colleges & government-funded research institutes are 34% and 44.6% respectively. In average, it records 2.11 million page views per month.

The NTIS developed a dedicated webpage for business users in late 2015 and has provided support since then to encourage them to actively use national R&D data for diverse purposes such as project proposal and data analysis.

This study investigates the NTIS' business support service in Section II and proposes a development and improvement direction to support SMSEs' R&D activities in Section III.

II. CURRENT SERVICES

In terms of SMSEs' needs derived through a demand survey, the followings were found: research trend and technical trend data on key technology, experts for collaboration and new national R&D projects. In addition, there was a necessity for linkage with experts who can back up analytical ability. Therefore, NTIS's business support service consists of two parts: providing customized information and supporting expert analysis based on users' demand.

A. Customized Information service

SMSEs are in high demand for research trends, collaboration partner and national R&D project information to apply for government R&D funds. For this need, NTIS provides such information through customized information service. As shown in Figure 1, a business user enters keywords and requirements of interest, and the NTIS manager extracts the projects in which the user-entered keywords are matched with the keywords on the national R&D program and project database. Then, they are provided with linkage information to allow users to check the projects in detail. In addition, the system supports the search of expert information which requires collaboration by providing major research outcome along with the information of chief researchers who implemented the projects (e.g., name, institute name, number of the related projects implemented, total project budget).

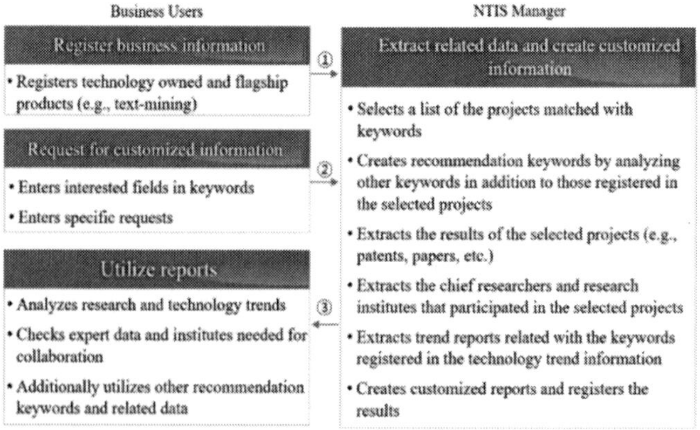

Figure 1. Customized Information Service

B. *Expert Analysis service*

If SMSEs need analysis information and experts' opinions on the interested fields, NTIS provides such information through expert analysis service. As shown in Figure 2, SMSEs enter keywords and requests and ask for expert analysis. In connection with experts on the Global Network of Korean Scientists and Engineers (KOSEN), the NTIS provides text summary and expert opinions to the users who want text analysis and related data and experts' opinions to those who need national R&D results. The NTIS pays all the costs needed for the expert support service so that businesses are able to use it free of charge.

The business support service may be of some help to SMSEs which have found it hard to invest their manpower and time in data acquisition and analysis. In particular, data search time was significantly reduced, allowing users to find the information they want in a quick and easy fashion.

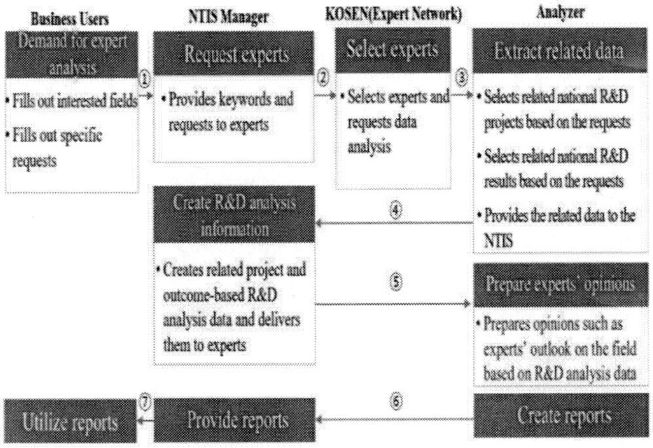

Figure 2. Expert Analysis Service

C. *Service Status*

Business support has been in service since Dec. 2015, and Figure 3 shows the business support service page currently being offered. 162 cases of customized information and 18 cases of expert analysis information are provided.

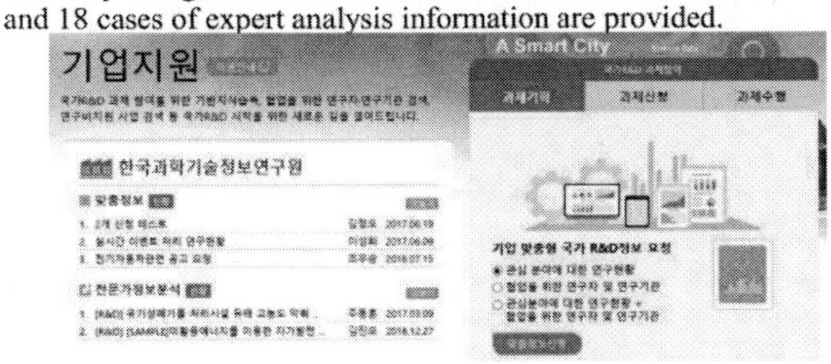

Figure 3. Business Support Service Web Page in NTIS

III. IMPROVEMENT AND DEVELOPMENT DIRECTION

The customized information service which is currently available is a one-time service, which provides analysis results to business users. Under this service, a report file is provided within three days from the date of request. For active business support, a smart push service which creates customized information regularly based on profile data and makes it available readily is needed. For this, there should be a system which can register profile information needed for analyzing data, such as keywords and interested products, and automatically extract and analyze related information.

With rapid technology development, R&D cooperation has become more important. Under these circumstances, it is required to establish a core competency-based collaboration system to implement national R&D programs. Even if SMSEs need to know who has the knowledge they want ('know-who') and where it is ('know-where'), they have found it hard to approach 'know-who' and 'know-where' with a poor personnel network [6]. In Europe, collaboration partner services are provided via CORDIS. It supports an expert-centric collaboration system by connecting projects with institutes and/or businesses.

The NTIS which provides national R&D data in an integrated manner can also offer SMSEs that are competent in academia-industry-research collaboration-based R&D projects an opportunity to participate by providing a collaboration partner service for the purpose of establishing a transparent and effective collaboration system.

IV. CONCLUSION

This study investigated the NTIS' business support service which helps the SMSEs that have no room for spending time and manpower in data acquisition and analysis build project planning capability. To upgrade the current business support service to an active and effective one, i) business profile information-based smart push service and ii) academia-industry-research collaboration-based R&D collaboration system support service are needed. The NTIS plans to keep moving forward to eliminate the obstacles of the SMSEs by analyzing their needs.

ACKNOWLEDGMENT

This research was supported by Maximize the Value of National Science and Technology by Strengthen Sharing/Collaboration of National R&D Information funded by the Korea Institute of Science and Technology Information (KISTI).

REFERENCES

[1] 2014 SMSE's Status Indicators, Small Medium Business Administration (SMBA).

[2] D. Ahn, "Some Theses for the Promotion of Technological Innovation of Small and Medium Firms-based on the survey materials about the innovation hindrances", Koreanstudies Information Service System, Vol.22, pp.25-50, 2004.

[3] Y. Lee, J. Shin, J. Shin and J. Yoo, "A Study on Direction of Support on Domestic Small & Mid-sized Enterprises under Open Innovation Environment" , Korean Institute of Industrial Engineers, pp.46-50, 2010

[4] C. Lee, M. Park, P. Kim and H. Shim, "A Study of the Improvement of Partner System Efficiency to Strengthen Government-funded Research Institutes' Support on Small and Mid-sized Enterprises", Korea Technology Innovation Society, pp.47-58, 2014

[5] http://www.ntis.go.kr[retrieved: 5, 2017]

[6] Y. Lee, "The Open Innovation Value and Policy Implications of Small and Mid-sized Enterprises' ICT R&D", Information & Communications Policy, Vol.25, No.22, pp.22~46, 2013

Implementation of An Access Control Technology for Internet of Things Environments

Daewon Kim and Jeongnyeo Kim
Information Security Research Division
Electronics and Telecommunications Research Institute
Daejeon, Korea
emails: {dwkim77, jnkim}@etri.re.kr

Abstract—**In this paper, we introduce an implementation for the access control on Internet of Things (IoT) environments. For the implementation, we designed the components and processes required for the access control technology. To show the feasibility, we implemented the technology based on an oneM2M architecture and experimented the processing steps.**

Keywords-Interner of Things; security; access control; role based access control; oneM2M.

I. INTRODUCTION

For security, Internet of Things (IoT) platforms need some access control technologies to control the information access authorities of the joined devices. Normally, under the activation of an access control technology, each device can access only its own resources and the owner or manager device can access the resources of other devices.

Among various IoT platforms, oneM2M-based platforms have been actively researched and implemented. OneM2M [1] is the global standard for machine-to-machine (M2M) communications and the IoT. Eight regional standards associations and over 200 companies are participating in the oneM2M standards. The important point is that oneM2M provides many useful specifications for constructing the oneM2M-based IoT platforms to researchers and developers.

For controlling the resource access, oneM2M defines and describes various components such as resources, attributes, and parameters [2]. However, the information is not sufficient to be practically implemented because it provides the general descriptions and procedures for the access control mechanism. In this paper, we present the implementation for an access control on an oneM2M platform. Among various access control researches, our implementation is based on Role Based Access Control (RBAC) [3][6].

For the access control, some studies have been processed. Representatively, there are Capability-based Access Control (CapBAC) [4][5] and RBAC [3][6]. They basically use token structures and certificates. An important problem of such researches is, even for sending small main contents to other IoT devices, that they may include the security information of bigger size than main contents.

The contribution of our paper is to introduce an implementation technique for the access control in IoT environments and to show the feasibility controlling the accesses only with a lightweight permission information which is known as a token identifier.

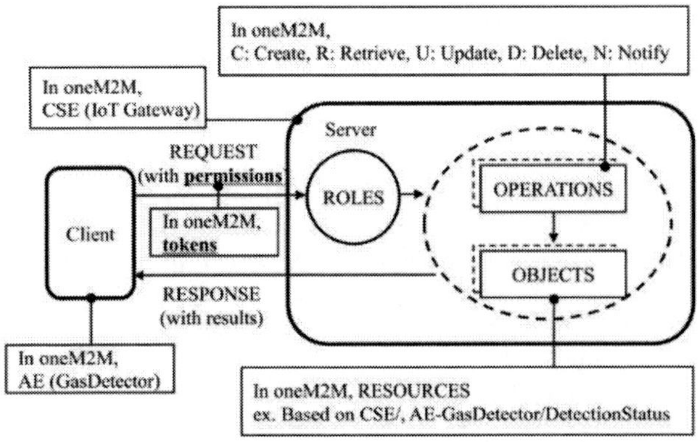

Figure 1. The simplied relationship of RBAC and oneM2M.

The rest of the paper is organized as follows. In Section 2, we introduce the background information related to the RBAC and oneM2M. In Section 3, we present the operation processes for our implementation. In Section 4, we show the experiment results for the feasibility and finally we conclude the paper in Section 5.

II. BACKGROUNDS

Figure 1 shows the simplified relationship of RBAC [3] and oneM2M. The core of RBAC is that permissions are assigned to roles rather than to devices. The role is a job function for some associated semantics regarding the authorities of devices. The semantics mean the operations for objects.

In the oneM2M architecture, common service entity (CSE) and application entity (AE) have the relationship of a server and a client. Mainly, AE sends service requests to CSE and CSE responds the processed results to AE. The resources, which are the objects in RBAC, can be addressed as the paths of the data storage including some values. For controlling the resources, the oneM2M entities can use 5 operations, such as create, retrieve, update, delete, and notify. The permissions of RBAC can be represented as the tokens in the oneM2M architecture.

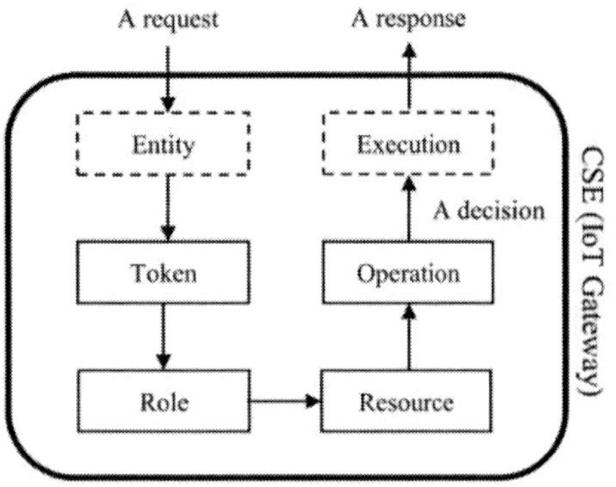

Figure 2. The processes for our access control technology.

III. THE OPERATION PROCESSES FOR IMPLEMENTING OUR ACCESS CONTROL TECHNOLOGY

Figure 2 shows the processes of our implementation to control the resource accesses. If one of the processes fails, the IoT Gateway sends an error response to the request originator. The solid line rectangles are the core processes for the access control. Each core process is composed of an identifier (ID) table and the job function.

A request is received to the IoT Gateway. The request normally includes a source ID, a destination ID, a target resource, an operation for the resource, and a token. First, in the Entity processing, the source ID is verified whether it is already registered into the Entity ID table. In the Token processing, the request token is verified whether it is already registered into the Token ID table. From the Token ID table, a role ID related to the token is extracted. From the Role ID table by the Role processing, a resource ID and the permitted operations are extracted. In the Resource processing, a resource related to the resource ID is extracted. Finally, if the target resource and operation in the request message are same with the resource and operation extracted from the tables in the IoT Gateway, the resource access of request is executed successfully.

IV. EXPERIMENTS

In this section, for verifying the feasibility, we show the detailed operations of our implementation about a scenario.

A. A Simple Operation Scenario based on An oneM2M Architecture

For an experiment, as an oneM2M-based practical scenario, in Figure 1, we assume that the IoT Gateway has the value 'no' in the resource CSE/AE-GasDetector/DetectionStatus. When gas leak is detected by the GasDetector, it sends an update request to the IoT Gateway for changing the resource value from 'no' to 'yes'.

B. Request and Response Messages for The Scenario

Figure 3 shows the request and response messages for the above scenario. The pseudo XML type messages are based on the oneM2M primitive parameters. Table I shows the brief descriptions for the XML tags.

```
[REQUEST: GasDetector to IoT Gateway]

<op>3</op>
<to>/AE-GasDetector/</to>
<fr>65934</fr>
<rqi>16807</rqi>
<tkid>1085377743</tkid>
<pc>
    <DetectionStatus>yes</DetectionStatus>
</pc>

[RESPONSE: IoT Gateway to GasDetector]

<rsc>2000</rsc>
<rqi>16807</rqi>
```

Figure 3. The request and response messages for the scenario.

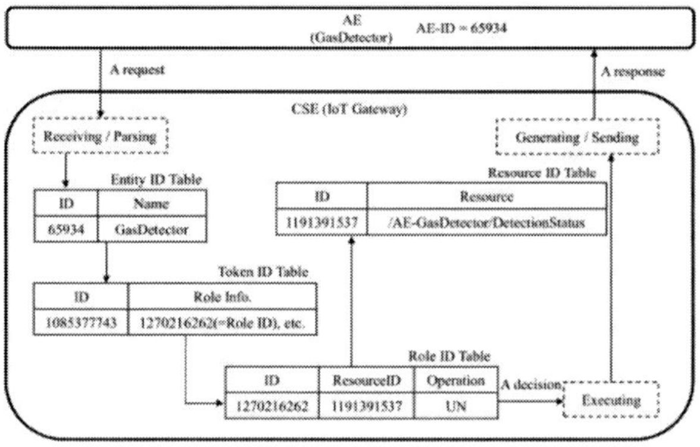

Figure 4. The detailed operations for the scenario.

TABLE I. THE BRIEF DESCRIPTIONS OF FIGURE 3

Short Name	Full Name	Description
op	OPeration	UPDATE(3)
to	TO	destination or target resource
fr	FRom	source
rqi	ReQuest Id	request identifier
tkid	ToKen ID	token identifier
pc	Primitive Content	serialized representation for accessing the target resource
rsc	Response Status Code	OK(2000)

Through the request message of Figure 3, the GasDetector requests to update the value 'no' of target resource '/AE-GasDetector/DetectionStatus' to 'yes'.

C. The Detailed Operations for The Scenario

Figure 4 shows the detailed operations about the request and response messages of Figure 3. We assume that the GasDetector ID and a token ID have been already allocated. The IoT Gateway receives a request message from the

GasDetector the source ID 65934 in the tag <fr> is verified whether it is already registered into the Entity ID table. The request token 1085377743 in the tag <tkid> is verified whether it is already registered into the Token ID table. A role ID 1270216262 related to the token 1085377743 is extracted from the Token ID table. A resource ID 1191391537 and the permitted UN operations, which are update and notify, are extracted from the Role ID table. The IoT Gateway executes the request and sends an OK response to the GasDetector because the update and notify operations are permitted about the target resource '/AE-GasDetection/DetectionStatus'.

V. CONCLUSIONS

In this paper, we introduced an RBAC-based implementation for controlling the IoT resource accesses. Through the experiments for an operation scenario, we showed the implementation feasibility and the operation clarity. As the future works, our implementation will be extended for some management issues, such as role creation, role assigning, and the device to device direct communication.

ACKNOWLEDGMENT

This work was supported by Institute for Information & communications Technology Promotion (IITP) grant funded by the Korea government (MSIT) (No.2015-0-00508, Development of Operating System Security Core Technology for the Smart Lightweight IoT Devices).

REFERENCES

[1] "oneM2M Functional Architecture," oneM2M-TS-0001, vol. 2.10.0, Aug. 2016.

[2] "oneM2M Security," oneM2M-TR-0008, vol. 2.0.0, Aug. 2016.

[3] "American National Standard for Information Technology-Role Based Access Control", American National Standard Institute, Inc., ANSI INCITS 359-2004, 2004.

[4] R. Hummen, H. Shafagh, S. Raza, T. Voig, and K. Wehrle, "Delegationbased authentication and authorization for the IP-based Internet of Things," in SECON. IEEE, 2014.

[5] S. Cirani, M. Picone, P. Gonizzi, L. Veltri, and G. Ferrari, "IoT-OAS: An OAuth-based authorization service architecture for secure services in IoT scenarios," Journal of Sensors, 2015.

[6] D. F. Ferraiolo, R. Sandhu, S. Gavrila, D. R. Kuhn, and R. Chandramouli, "Proposed nist standard for role-based access control," TISSEC, 2001.

Formal Verification of Key Establishment for Dual Connectivity in Small Cell LTE Networks

Vassilios G. Vassilakis*, Ioannis D. Moscholios†, Michael D. Logothetis‡, Michael N. Koukias‡
* Dept. of Computer Science, University of York, York, United Kingdom
† Dept. of Informatics & Telecommunications, University of Peloponnese, Tripolis, Greece
‡ Dept. of Electrical & Computer Engineering, University of Patras, Patras, Greece
e-mail: vv573@york.ac.uk, idm@uop.gr, {mlogo,mkoukias}@upatras.gr

***Abstract*—Dual connectivity (DC) has been included in the Release 12 of the long-term evolution (LTE) standard. In this paper, we perform a formal security verification of the key establishment protocol for DC in small cell LTE networks. In particular, the security verification is performed using a popular tool called Scyther. The considered security properties include secrecy and reachability. We also simulate a key leakage and show that some security claims in this case can be falsified.**

Keywords–Dual connectivity; long-term evolution (LTE); key establishment; Scyther tool.

I. INTRODUCTION

The exponential growth in mobile data traffic in the last years necessitates the development of novel applications and equipment to satisfy customer needs [1]. Standards bodies, such as the 3rd generation partnership project (3GPP), are working towards defining and enhancing the specifications for mobile communications. The current mobile broadband technology developed by 3GPP is known as long-term evolution (LTE) and was initially specified in 3GPP's Release 8 document series.

Since Release 12 [2], LTE provides enhanced support for small cells, such as dual connectivity (DC) and carrier aggregation. The main motivation for these enhancements is to support dense small cell deployments by reducing the mobility signaling and improving user data rates by using macro and small cells together. In this context, heterogeneous networks (HetNets) [3] are considered as a promising approach to enhance network capacity. In a HetNet, small cells typically provide improved capacity in hot spots, whereas macro cells are responsible for reliable wide-area coverage and fast moving user equipments (UEs). A macro base station in the LTE terminology is known as the evolved Node B (eNB).

According to the DC framework, the control plane, which transmits system information and handles user connectivity, is spit from the user plane, which transmits user data [4]. This split provides greater flexibility in terms of network management and administration, since the small cells can be used to operate in the user plane only, while the macro cells operate in both the control plane and the user plane by providing additional quality-of-service (QoS) support [5]. The DC feature of LTE, essentially, allows a UE to be connected to two cells simultaneously.

In this paper, we perform a formal security verification of the key establishment protocol for DC in small cell LTE networks [6]. In particular, the security verification is performed using a popular tool called Scyther [7]. The considered security properties include secrecy, agreement, and key freshness. Our considered model for the key establishment is in line with [8].

The rest of the paper is structured as follows. In Section II, we describe our considered model for DC in small cell LTE networks and introduce the necessary notation. In Section III, we describe the considered key establishment protocol for DC. In Section IV, we briefly introduce the Scyther's input language. In Section V, we describe our Scyther implementation of the key establishment protocol. In Section VI, we present our security verification results for the protocol. Finally, in Section VII, we conclude and discuss possible future directions. Also, in Table I, we present the list of abbreviations used in this paper.

II. DUAL CONNECTIVITY IN LTE NETWORKS

In this section we describe our considered model for DC in small cell LTE networks.

A. *Preliminaries*

Consider a UE and two eNBs involved in DC. The first eNB is called a Master eNB (MeNB) and is responsible for maintaining the control of the radio resource management. The second eNB, called Secondary eNB (SeNB), is controlled by the MeNB and provides additional radio resources to the UE. In a realistic scenario the MeNB is typically a macro eNB, while the SeNB could be a small cell eNB.

All the radio control traffic between the UE and the MeNB is transported over the established signaling radio bearer (SRB). All the data traffic between the UE and the eNBs (both MeNB and SeNB) is transported over the established data radio bearers (DRBs) with each eNB. Each DRB has a unique identifier (ID). The ID of the i-th DRB between the UE and the MeNB is denoted by DRB_i^{mu}. Similarly, the ID of the j-th DRB between the UE and the SeNB is denoted by DRB_j^{su}.

From UE's perspective, one SRB is established with the MeNB and multiple DRBs can be established with the MeNB and the SeNB.

B. *Trust Model*

The considered trust model is as follows [8]:

- A secure channel between the MeNB and the SeNB.
- A secure channel between the MeNB and the UE.
- The channel between the UE and the SeNB is insecure. This introduces a particular challenge for the selection of an appropriate key establishment mechanism.
- The MeNB, the SeNB, and the UE cannot be compromised.

TABLE I. LIST OF ABBREVIATIONS

3GPP	3rd Generation Partnership Project
AES	Advanced Encryption Standard
DC	Dual Connectivity
DL	Downlink
DRB	Data Radio Bearer
eNB	evolved Node B
HetNet	Heterogeneous Network
KDF	Key Derivation Function
ID	Identifier
LTE	Long Term Evolution
MeNB	Master eNB
QoS	Quality of Service
SCC	Small Cell Counter
SeNB	Secondary eNB
SRB	Signaling Radio Bearer
UE	User Equipment
UL	Uplink
UP	User Plane

In particular, the aforementioned secure channels provide *encryption*, *integrity*, and protection against *replay attacks*.

C. Security Parameters

The security parameters of the considered model are as follows [8]:

- $Algs$: A list IDs of encryption algorithms supported by the UE and shared with the MeNB.
- SCC: The small cell counter (SCC) that is used to keep track of the established DRBs.
- $KDF()$: A key derivation function (KDF).
- K_{MeNB}: The secret key shared between the UE and the MeNB. This is used to derive other keys.
- K_{SeNB}: The secret key shared between the UE and the SeNB. The UE can derive this key using formula (1), discussed below. The SeNB receives this key from the MeNB, which in turn derives this key using formula (1).
- $K_{UPenc,j}$: The secret key shared between the UE and the SeNB for DRB_j^{su}. This key is used to encrypt the user plane (UP) traffic. That is, the data traffic between the UE and the SeNB for the j-th DRB. The UE and the SeNB can derive this key using formula (2).

D. Adversary Model

For the adversary, we adopt the widely used Dolev-Yao model [9]. According to this model, the adversary is able to intercept all messages. They are also able to forward, drop, or replay old messages. However, the adversary is not able to decrypt messages, unless they are in possession of the required keys.

III. KEY ESTABLISHMENT PROTOCOL

A. First Data Radio Bearer (DRB)

Below we describe the key establishment process for the first DRB between the UE and SeNB. At the end of the process, the UE and the SeNB are in the possession of the shared key $K_{UPenc,1}$, which will be used to encrypt the traffic in the first DRB.

- Step 1: The MeNB generates the key K_{SeNB} based on (1).
- Step 2: The MeNB sends to the SeNB a message containing: K_{SeNB}, $Algs$, and DRB_1^{su}.
- Step 3: The SeNB establishes the first DRB with the UE.
- Step 4: The SeNB selects some encryption algorithm ID $a \in Algs$ and derives the key $K_{UPenc,1}$ via (2), where $j = 1$.
- Step 5: The SeNB sends the selected algorithm ID, a, to the MeNB.
- Step 6: The MeNB sends to the UE a message containing: SCC, DRB_1^{su}, and a.
- Step 7: The UE derives the key $K_{UPenc,1}$ via (2), where $j = 1$.

$$K_{SeNB} = KDF(K_{MeNB,SCC}) \tag{1}$$

where SCC is the small cell counter (SCC) that is used to keep track of the used DRBs.

$$K_{UPenc,j} = KDF(K_{SeNB}, DRB_j^{su}, a) \tag{2}$$

B. Subsequent Data Radio Bearers (DRBs)

Having described the key establishment process for the first DRB, below we describe the key establishment for subsequent DRBs between the UE and SeNB. At the end of the process, the UE and the SeNB are in the possession of the shared key $K_{UPenc,j}$ ($j > 1$). At this stage the SeNB is already in possession of the key K_{SeNB} and has selected some encryption algorithm a.

- Step 1: The MeNB sends to the SeNB the ID of the j-th DRB, DRB_j^{su}, where $j > 1$.
- Step 2: The SeNB establishes the j-th DRB with the UE.
- Step 3: The SeNB derives the key $K_{UPenc,j}$ via (2).
- Step 4: The MeNB sends to the UE the ID of the j-th DRB, DRB_j^{su}.
- Step 5: The UE derives the key $K_{UPenc,j}$ via (2).

IV. SCYTHER'S LANGUAGE

Scyther is a widely used formal verification tool and has been designed for the automatic verification of security protocols. In this section, we briefly describe the Scyther' input language. Additional language features are also introduced and explained later, in Section V, which describes the protocol implementation. Scyther's language is loosely based on C/Java-like syntax [7]. At the most basic level, Scyther manipulates the *terms*. Terms could be *atomic* or *complex*. An atomic term could be any identifier, for example a string of alphanumeric characters that represents user data. Atomic terms can be combined into more complex terms by operators, such as pairing or encryption. This could refer, for example, to encrypted user data. Encryption of a term m with a key k is denoted in Scyther as $\{m\}k$.

The main purpose of the language is to describe protocols which are defined by a set of roles. A role could represent, for example, a network node, such as eNB or UE. Roles, in turn are defined by a sequence of events, such as sending/receiving terms (e.g., signaling messages or user data) and security claims. In particular, message sending and receiving can be specified by the pair $send\_i(S,R,m)$ and $recv\_i(S,R,m)$, where i denotes the i-th message, S is the sender, R is the receiver, and m is the message. Claims are used to specify security requirements, such as message secrecy and node aliveness. For example, $claim(X, Alive)$ means that role X claims to be alive, and $claim(Y, Secret, m)$ means that role Y claims that the message m must be unknown to an adversary.

Scyther has a predefined symmetric key infrastructure: $k(X,Y)$ denotes the long-term symmetric key shared between the roles X and Y. Also, Scyther has a predefined adversary model, which is based on the Delev-Yao model, mentioned in Section II. This greatly simplifies the implementation task, since there is no need to implement the adversary model from scratch.

V. Protocol Implementation using Scyther

In this section, we describe the Scyther implementation of the key establishment protocol of Section III. In the interest of space, we only present the implementation for the first DRB. The key establishment for subsequent DRBs is implemented in a similar way.

A. Initial Definitions

In Figure 1, we present the initial type definitions and term declarations. As we observe, the KDF has been defined as a hash function (line 2). In Scyther, this is done by using the keyword *hashfunction*. Next, in lines 3-6 we define four types: ALG, SCC, DRB, and DATA. A user-defined type can be specified in Scyther using the keyword *usertype*. The names of the these types are self-explanatory. For example, the ALG type will be used to represent various encryption algorithms.

Having specified the user-defined types, in lines 8-10 we declare various terms that will be used by the protocol. The keyword *const* specifies terms whose value remains constant throughout the whole protocol verification process. For example, the constants $a1$ and $a2$ have been declared of ALG type and will refer to different encryption algorithms supported by the UE, such as the SNOW-3G and the advanced encryption standard (AES).

B. The MeNB Role

In Figure 2, we begin specifying the protocol and start with the MeNB role. A protocol definition (line 12) specifies the protocol name and takes as a parameter a sequence of roles, which are then defined in the protocol's body. The MeNB role definition is shown in lines 14-24, starting with the role's name in line 14. In line 15, we assign the value of the shared key K_{MeNB} to the term *kmenb*. Recall that the key K_{MeNB} is shared between the MeNB and the UE. Hence, it is predefined in Scyther as $k(MeNB, UE)$. The keyword *macro* is used to define abbreviations for particular terms. In line 16, we define a new term $n1$ of type *Nonce*. Nonce is a predefined type and is used to define terms that must be used only once. The keyword *fresh* is used to declare a *freshly generated* term of arbitrary/random value. This means that different instances of the same role will generate different values. In line 17, the term $ksenb$, which refers to the key K_{SeNB}, is assigned its value according to (1). Note that the value assignment in line 17 is also based on $n1$. This is to ensure that different MeNB instances will generate different keys K_{SeNB}. Line 18

```
1  # Type Definitions
2 hashfunction KDF; # key derivation function
3 usertype ALG; # encryption algorithm
4 usertype SCC; # small cell counter
5 usertype DRB; # data radio bearer
6 usertype DATA; # user data
7  # Term Definitions
8 const a1, a2: ALG;
9 const scc: SCC;
10 const drb1, drb2: DRB;
```

Figure 1. Initial Definitions.

```
11 # Protocol Specification: Key Establishment for Dual Connectivity
12 protocol DC-LTE(MeNB,SeNB,UE){
13  # MeNB role specification
14  role MeNB {
15  macro kmenb=k(MeNB,UE); #shared key between MeNB and UE
16  fresh n1: Nonce;
17  macro ksenb=KDF(kmenb,scc,n1);
18  send_1(MeNB,SeNB,{ksenb,(a1,a2),drb1}k(MeNB,SeNB));
19  claim(MeNB,Secret,ksenb);
20  var a: ALG;
21  recv_2(SeNB,MeNB,{a}k(MeNB,UE));
22  send_3(MeNB,UE,{scc,a,drb1}mkenb);
23  claim(MeNB,Reachable);
24  }
```

Figure 2. The MeNB Role Implementation in Scyther.

declares the first *send* event. The MeNB sends to the SeNB an encrypted message that contains the key K_{SeNB}, a list of encryption algorithms supported by the UE, and the ID of the DRB. The corresponding *recv* event appears in line 28 of Figure 3, which defines the SeNB role and will be explained in Subsection V-C. Returning back to Figure 2, line 19 declares the first *claim* event. The MeNB claims that the key K_{SeNB} must be unknown to an adversary. In line 20, using the keyword *var*, we declare the term a as a variable of type *Nonce*. Variables are used to store received terms. In this case, the variable a will be used to store the encryption algorithm ID received from $recv_2$ in line 21. The corresponding $send_2$ event is defined in line 31 of Figure 3. Having received from the SeNB the selected algorithm ID, the MeNB forwards it to the UE together with other required parameters, such as the SCC and the ID of the DRB (line 22). These parameters will be used by the UE to determine the key $K_{UPenc,j}$, based on (2), with $j = 1$, which corresponds to the first DRB. Finally, line 23 declares the *claim* event using the keyword *Reachable*. This is used to check whether this claim can be reached at all. It returns true if and only if there exists a trace in which this claim occurs.

C. The SeNB Role

The specification of the SeNB role is provided in Figure 3. Having provided a detailed explanation for the specification of the MeNB role in Subsection V-B, most of the code in Figure 3 should now be self-explanatory. Hence, below we explain only some selected parts of the code. In line 32 we define a term $dataDL$ of DATA type. This term represents the downlink (DL) data that will be sent to the UE. As shown in line 34, $dataDL$ is encrypted using the key $K_{UPenc,j}$, with $j = 1$. Similarly, the term $dataUL$ will be used to store the received

```
25    # SeNB role specification
26  role SeNB {
27    var n1: Nonce;
28    recv_1(MeNB,SeNB,{ksenb,(a1,a2),drb1}k(MeNB,SeNB));
29    claim(SeNB,Secret,ksenb);
30    macro kupenc1=KDF(ksenb,drb1,a1);
31    send_2(SeNB,MeNB,{a1}k(MeNB,SeNB));
32    fresh dataDL: DATA;
33    fresh n2: Nonce;
34    send_4(SeNB,UE,{dataDL,n1}kupenc1);
35    claim(SeNB,Secret,dataDL);
36    var dataUL: DATA;
37    var n3: Nonce;
38    recv_5(UE,SeNB,{dataUL,n3)kupenc1);
39    claim(SeNB,Secret,dataUL);
40    claim(SeNB,Reachable);
41  }
```

Figure 3. The SeNB Role Implementation in Scyther.

```
42    # UE role specification
43  role UE {
44    var a: ALG;
45    var n1, n2: Nonce;
46    recv_3(MeNB,UE,{scc,a,drb1}k(MeNB,UE));
47    var dataDL: DATA;
48    recv_4(SeNB,UE,{dataDL,n1}kupenc1);
49    claim(UE,Secret,kupenc1);
50    claim(UE,Secret,dataDL);
51    fresh n3: Nonce;
52    fresh dataUL: DATA;
53    send_5(UE,SeNB,{dataUL,n3}kupenc1);
54    claim(UE,Secret,dataUL);
55    claim(UE,Reachable);
56  }# end of UE tole specification
57 } #end of protocol specification
```

Figure 4. The UE Role Implementation in Scyther.

uplink (UL) data from the UE (line 38). In lines 35 and 39, the SeNB claims that these DL and UL data will remain secret (i.e., unknown to the adversary).

D. The UE Role

The specification of the UE role is provided in Figure 4 and should be self-explanatory.

VI. Security Verification

In this section, we present the security verification results for the key establishment protocol. The verification is based on the Scyther implementation of Section V. In particular, the purpose of the verification is to verify whether the claims defined in various role specifications are true. In the Result Window, shown in Figure 6, Scyther outputs a single line for each claim. The first column shows the protocol in which the claim occurs, the second column shows the role, etc.

We observe that for each claim the verification process returns its status (i.e., whether the claim has been verified), some claim-specific comments, and the identified trace patterns (if applicable). For all the secrecy claims (lines 19, 29, 35, 39, 49, 50, and 54) we observe that the status is *OK* and *Verified*, i.e., no attacks have been found where an adversary gains knowledge of the confidential information. If a claim is false, the corresponding status message will be *Fail*.

```
30    ...
31    macro kupenc1=KDF(ksenb,drb1,a1);
32    send_!(SeNB,SeNB,kupenc1);
33    ...
```

Figure 5. Leaking the key $K_{UPenc,1}$ to the adversary.

For all the reachability claims (lines 23, 40, and 55) we observe that the status is also *Verified* and the Comments column says *At least 1 trace pattern*. Furthermore, by clicking the *1 trace pattern* button in the Patterns column, it is possible to see a trace identified Scyther.

In the following sections we simulate a key leakage and perform the Scyther verification process. Assume that the key $K_{UPenc,1}$ is leaked to the adversary by the SeNB. This can be simulated in Scyther using a *send* event with an exclamation mark, as follows: $send\_!(X, X, m)$, where X is the role from which the leak occurs and m is the leaked message. Hence, the required code modification of Figure 2 includes adding a new *send* event, as shown in line 32 of Figure 5.

The new verification results are shown in Figure 7. We observe that the status of five claim events changed from *OK* to *Fail*. In particular, the failed claims are: one for the actually leaked key and the other four for the compromised DL/UL data, as a result of key leakage. For each failed claim the Comments column says *At least 1 attack*. By pressing the corresponding button in the Patterns column, we can view one of the possible attack graphs for $dataDL$, which is shown in Figure 8.

In Figure 8, we see one instantiation, Bob, of the SeNB role (denoted as Run #1) and one instantiation, Charlie, of the MeNB role (denoted as Run #2). There is also Alice in the UE role, but Alice is not involved in the particular attack. The boxes represent creation of a run (i.e., an instance of a protocol role), communication events of a run, and claim events. The arrows represent ordering constraints. According to lines 32 and 33 of Figure 3, Bob generates two fresh terms: $dataDL$ and $n2$. Bob's run number is appended to his terms, in order to distinguish them from any homonymous terms of other runs. Hence, these terms appear in the graph as $dataDL\#1$ and $n2\#1$. Bob also generates a variable $n1$ (line 27), which will receive its value from $n1\#2$, generated by Charlie. After receiving ($recv\_1$) the first message from Charlie, Bob generates the key $K_{UPenc,1}$ (not shown in the graph) and leaks ($send\_!$) the key to the adversary, which is represented by an orange oval. When later Bob sends the message $dataDL$ to Alice ($send\_4$), the adversary intercepts this message and decrypts it. Hence, the secrecy claim has been falsified (black rectangular box in Figure 8).

VII. Conclusion and Future Work

In this paper, we perform a formal security verification of the key establishment protocol for dual connectivity in small cell LTE networks. In particular, the key establishment protocol has been implemented and verified using the Scyther tool. The protocol verification includes security properties, such as secrecy and reachability. Although all the security claims have been verified, further protocol analysis is required to identify potential attacks. In our future work, we intend to perform additional security analysis using other popular formal verification tools, such as Tamarin [10] and ProVerif [11].

Scyther results : verify

Claim				Status		Comments	Patterns
DC_LTE	MeNB	DC_LTE,MeNB1	Secret KDF(k(MeNB,UE),scc,n1)	Ok	Verified	No attacks.	
		DC_LTE,MeNB2	Reachable	Ok	Verified	At least 1 trace pattern.	1 trace pattern
	SeNB	DC_LTE,SeNB1	Secret KDF(k(MeNB,UE),scc,n1)	Ok	Verified	No attacks.	
		DC_LTE,SeNB2	Secret dataDL	Ok	Verified	No attacks.	
		DC_LTE,SeNB3	Secret dataUL	Ok	Verified	No attacks.	
		DC_LTE,SeNB4	Reachable	Ok	Verified	At least 1 trace pattern.	1 trace pattern
	UE	DC_LTE,UE1	Secret KDF(KDF(k(MeNB,UE),scc,n1),drb1,a1)	Ok	Verified	No attacks.	
		DC_LTE,UE2	Secret dataDL	Ok	Verified	No attacks.	
		DC_LTE,UE3	Secret dataUL	Ok	Verified	No attacks.	
		DC_LTE,UE4	Reachable	Ok	Verified	At least 1 trace pattern.	1 trace pattern

Done.

Figure 6. Security verification results using Scyther: Key establishment protocol.

Scyther results : verify

Claim				Status		Comments	Patterns
DC_LTE	MeNB	DC_LTE,MeNB1	Secret KDF(k(MeNB,UE),scc,n1)	Ok	Verified	No attacks.	
		DC_LTE,MeNB2	Reachable	Ok	Verified	At least 1 trace pattern.	1 trace pattern
	SeNB	DC_LTE,SeNB1	Secret KDF(k(MeNB,UE),scc,n1)	Ok	Verified	No attacks.	
		DC_LTE,SeNB2	Secret dataDL	Fail	Falsified	At least 1 attack.	1 attack
		DC_LTE,SeNB3	Secret dataUL	Fail	Falsified	At least 1 attack.	1 attack
		DC_LTE,SeNB4	Reachable	Ok	Verified	At least 1 trace pattern.	1 trace pattern
	UE	DC_LTE,UE1	Secret KDF(KDF(k(MeNB,UE),scc,n1),drb1,a1)	Fail	Falsified	At least 1 attack.	1 attack
		DC_LTE,UE2	Secret dataDL	Fail	Falsified	At least 1 attack.	1 attack
		DC_LTE,UE3	Secret dataUL	Fail	Falsified	At least 1 attack.	1 attack
		DC_LTE,UE4	Reachable	Ok	Verified	At least 1 trace pattern.	1 trace pattern

Done.

Figure 7. Security verification results using Scyther: Simulating key leakage.

REFERENCES

[1] Cisco, Cisco Visual Networking Index: Global Mobile Data Traffic Forecast Update, 2016-2021 White Paper, Feb. 2017.

[2] D. Astely, E. Dahlman, G. Fodor, S. Parkvall, and J. Sachs, "LTE release 12 and beyond," IEEE Commun. Mag., vol. 51, no. 7, July 2013, pp. 154-160.

[3] J. G. Andrews, "Seven ways that HetNets are a cellular paradigm shift," IEEE Commun. Mag., vol. 51, no. 3, March 2013, pp. 136-144.

[4] A. Zakrzewska, D. López-Pérez, S. Kucera, and H. Claussen, "Dual connectivity in LTE HetNets with split control-and user-plane," Proc. IEEE Globecom Workshops, Atlanta, USA, Dec. 2013, pp. 391-396.

[5] V. G. Vassilakis, I. D. Moscholios, A. Bontozoglou, and M. D. Logothetis, "Mobility-aware QoS assurance in software-defined radio access networks: An analytical study," Proc. 1st IEEE Conference on Network Softwarization (NetSoft), London, UK, April 2015, pp. 1-6.

[6] S. C. Jha, K. Sivanesan, R. Vannithamby, and A. T. Koc, "Dual connectivity in LTE small cell networks," Proc. IEEE Globecom Workshops (GC Wkshps), Austin, USA, Dec. 2014, pp. 1205-1210.

[7] C. J. F. Cremers, "The scyther tool: Verification, falsification, and analysis of security protocols," Proc. International Conference on Computer Aided Verification, Princeton (CAV), USA, July 2008, pp. 414-418.

[8] N. B. Henda, K. Norrman, and K. Pfeffer, "Formal verification of the security for dual connectivity in LTE," Proc. 3rd FME Workshop on Formal Methods in Software Engineering, Florence, Italy, May 2015, pp. 13-19.

[9] D. Dolev and A. Yao, "On the security of public key protocols," IEEE Transactions on Information Theory, vol. 29, no. 2, March 1983, pp. 198-208.

[10] S. Meier, B. Schmidt, C. Cremers, and D. Basin, "The TAMARIN prover for the symbolic analysis of security protocols," Proc. 25th International Conference on Computer Aided Verification (CAV), Saint Petersburg, Russia, July 2013, pp. 696-701.

[11] B. Blanchet, "An efficient cryptographic protocol verifier based on prolog rules," Proc. 14th Computer Security Foundations Workshop (CSFW), Cape Breton, Canada, June 2001, pp. 82-96.

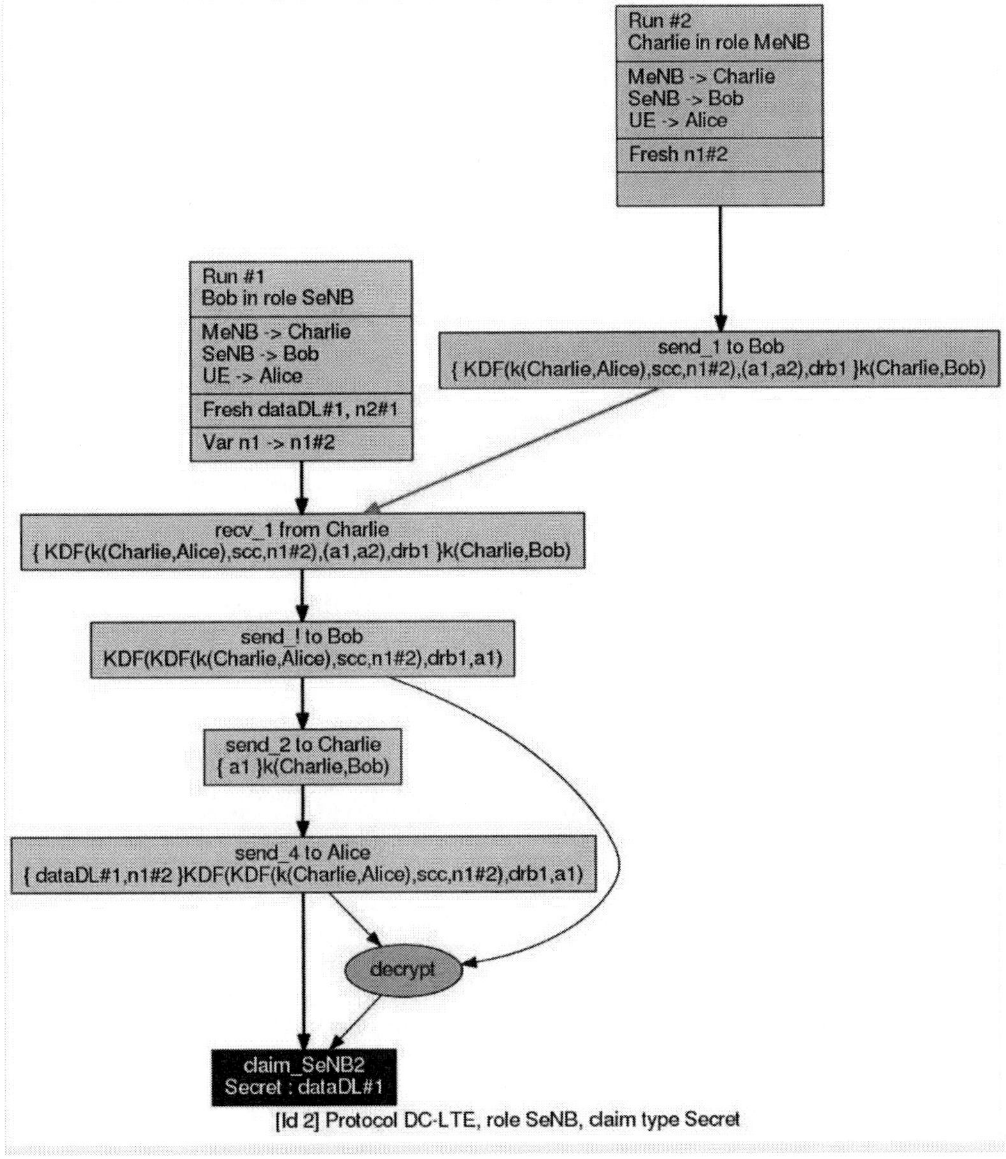

Figure 8. Security verification results using Scyther: Attacking the secrecy of downlink data.

Monitoring the State of Elements of Multi-service Communication Networks on the Basis of Fuzzy Logical Inference

Igor Kotenko[1,2], Igor Saenko[1,2]
[1] St. Petersburg Institute for Informatics and Automation of the Russian Academy of Sciences (SPIIRAS)
[2] ITMO University
Saint-Petersburg, Russia
e-mail: {ivkote, ibsaen}@comsec.spb.ru

Sergey Ageev
Research Center
St. Petersburg Academy of Telecommunications
Saint-Petersburg, Russia
e-mail: serg123_61@mail.ru

***Abstract*—The paper considers an approach for monitoring the state of elements of multi-service communication networks, based on application of fuzzy logical inference. The proposed approach can be implemented to design the systems for operative support of decision making in multi-service communication networks. The results of numerical simulation of the proposed method are analyzed, which showed that the method has high efficiency.**

Keywords- network monitoring; multi-service communication networks; fuzzy logical inference.

I. INTRODUCTION

Multi-service network (MSN) belongs to the class of big complex heterogeneous hierarchical geographically distributed systems. For such systems, the functional characteristics defining the reliability are some of the main characteristics [1]. With the growing size of networks, complexity of equipment and the extension of their functionality, the responsibilities of network administrators for the correctness and validity of decisions made for network effective management significantly increased. Network administrators, which determine the quality and reliability of MSN, as a rule, have sufficiently small time resource to make analysis of the current situation and develop management solutions to minimize the number of errors when making decisions on elimination of arising faults or failures in the network equipment. In addition, they have to make decisions in conditions of incomplete information about the technical state of the network elements. All this leads to discrepancy between physical and functional possibilities of the operator, and to the increasing complexity of the tasks that need to be solved to maintain the network in workable state. In this regard, the development and implementation of an intelligent operational decision-making system (ODMS) for monitoring and diagnostics of technical state of MSN elements is an actual scientific problem.

As an example, Table 1 shows the main managed parameters, which determine the quality of MSN services. Table I shows the diversity of the basic MSN parameters to be managed, their different physical nature, as well as different scales of their measurement. All this determines the complexity of solving the problem of monitoring the state of network elements (NEs) using traditional methods.

TABLE I. PARAMETERS OF MSN SERVICES

#	MSN Element	Parameter
1	Multiplexor, demultiplexor	Efficiency, Electric parameters, Interface
2	Communication lines	Bandwidth, Impedance, Attenuation, Noise Level, Resistance
3	Router	Performance, DBMS, OS, Applied Software, Electrical parameters, Interface, Protocols
4	Commutator	Bandwidth, Electrical parameters, Buffers, Interface, OS
5	Server	Functions, DBMS, OS, Applied Software, Performance, Electrical parameters
6	Gate	Performance, Capacity, Electrical parameters, Protocols, Interface

In this paper, we propose a new approach for the monitoring of the NE state in MSN, based on application of the fuzzy logical inference. The necessity of usage of fuzzy data processing methods in the proposed approach is caused by the following factors: (1) uncertainty of the reasons that can result in failures of nodes and communication channels; (2) incomplete information about the NE state and MSN as a whole, which is subject to processing; (3) delay for transmission of the NE state data to the processing nodes. Theoretical contributions and novelties of the paper are as follows: (1) the mechanism of fuzzy logical inference on NE states with hierarchical structure is proposed; (2) an approach based on the use of intelligent agents for decision making is suggested; (3) an algorithm for fuzzy models training that does not require significant computing resources is offered.

Further structure of the paper is as follows. Section 2 specifies the problem of the operational monitoring of the NE state in MSN. Section 3 discusses the results of relevant works. Section 4 considers the method for assessment of NE states in MSN. Section 5 shows and analyzes the results of experimental evaluation of the proposed approach. Section 6 contains the main conclusions and directions for further research.

II. PROBLEM STATEMENT

The process of functioning of NEs of MSN can be represented as a sequence of time intervals of workable states and outages, including failures and recovery (Figure 1). The duration of these intervals is determined by various factors. The following notations are used in Figure 1: t_i – NE's workability interval; τ_i – NE's outage interval.

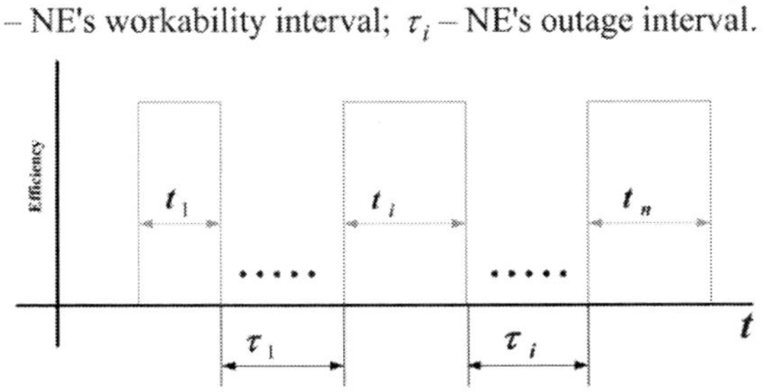

Figure 1. Intervals of workability and outages.

In the first approximation, the intervals can be considered mutually independent random variables, having certain distribution with the average times. The mean time between failures (MTBF) T_0 is calculated as

$$T_0 = \frac{\sum_{i=1}^{n} t_i}{n}. \quad (1)$$

Mean recovery time T_1 is calculated as follows:

$$T_1 = \frac{\sum_{i=1}^{n} \tau_i}{n}. \quad (2)$$

Reliability of NE of MSN is defined as the probability of existing of NE in a workable state in the conditions of failures. It is equal to the mathematical expectation of time during which the NE is in workable state. This definition is equivalent to the concept of the coefficient of availability K_a. In this case, the following expression is true:

$$K_a = \frac{T_0}{T_0 + T_1}, \quad (3)$$

or (for communication line):

$$K_a = \frac{\mu}{\mu + \lambda}, \quad (4)$$

where $\lambda = 1 / T_0$ is the rate of equipment failures; $\mu = 1 / T_1$ is the rate of equipment recovery. The probability of NE failure is determined as follows:

$$K_0 = 1 - K_1. \quad (5)$$

Analysis of expressions (3) and (4) shows that increasing of K_1 value corresponds to reduction of the recovery time of the controlled object T_1, which, in its turn, can be represented as follows and should be minimized:

$$T_1 = t_{\text{det}} + t_{\text{ev}} + t_{\text{des}} + t_{\text{ex}} \rightarrow \min, \quad (6)$$

where t_{det} is the time of detection of deviation from normative functioning mode; t_{ev} is the time of estimation of the new situation relatively to the state of the controlled NE; t_{des} is the time of elaboration and making decision; t_{ex} is the time of decision realization.

Thus, the task of the decision-making support (DMS) system is in production of such decision, in which the condition (6) is met. The time of decision realization is determined by the technical characteristics of the operations support subsystem (OSS). This time does not depend on DMS characteristics.

III. RELATED WORK

Currently, the NE state monitoring is based on the concept of "agent – manager", which is described in details in [2]-[6]. According to this concept, the *agent* pre-accumulates information about the current NE state, and then sends it to the *manager*. The manager, in its turn, provides it in a convenient form to the network administrator. This approach implements the paradigm of "detection – informing". The MSN is controlled by the network administrator. Known and practically implemented approaches to the NE state monitoring are based on the statistical methods [7].

In some papers to reduce the a priori uncertainty and decrease the reaction time to change the NE state, it is proposed to use intelligent techniques [8]-[12]. On their basis it is possible to realize the paradigm of "from the state detection to decision". In a number of papers, it is proposed to use neural networks for network state monitoring [13][14]. Kasabov et al. [15] suggest a dynamic evolutionary fuzzy logic system that implements adaptive training in a near real time. However, it should be noted that, given the diversity of estimated parameters, in the known papers on the NE state monitoring insufficient attention is paid to the DMS elements that are implementing the methods for making optimal and rational decisions. At the same time, the experience of using the mechanisms of fuzzy inference for making decisions to identify anomalous behavior and manage the security risks in the MSN, given in [16][17], allows to assert about appropriateness of its use for the NE state monitoring.

IV. ASSESSMENT OF THE NETWORK ELEMENT STATE

Let us assume that after the block of fuzzification of the Mamdani fuzzy inference machine the input variables, characterizing the NE state in MSN, take the form of linguistic input variables and are defined as follows:

$$\langle x, T, U, G, M \rangle, \quad (7)$$

where x is variable's name; T is term-set, each element of which is determined by the fuzzy set on universal set U; G is syntactic rules, generating the membership functions of terms' names; M is semantic rules, determining the membership rules on fuzzy terms, generated by the syntactic rules from G.

Fuzzy logical inference for generation of estimations of situations of the NE state in MSN based on the Mamdani fuzzy inference has the following form [9][10]:

$$(x_1 = a_{1j}\theta_j ... \theta_j x_n = a_{nj}) \times w_j \Rightarrow y_j = d_j, j = 1,..., m, \quad (8)$$

where a_{ij} is a fuzzy term, by which the variable x_i in j-th rule of the knowledge base is estimated; d_j is conclusion of j-th rule; m is number of rules in the knowledge base; w_j are weight coefficients for each j-th rule of the knowledge base ($w_j \leq 1$); θ_j is logical operation, connecting premises in j-th rule of the knowledge base.

In the expression (8), all values of input and output variables are represented by fuzzy sets. We introduce the following membership functions:

– $\mu_j(x_j)$ – membership function for input x_i, corresponding to fuzzy term a_{ij}, i.e.:

$$a_{ij} = \int \mu(x_i)/x_i, \quad (9)$$

– $\mu(y_i)$ – membership function for output y_i, corresponding to fuzzy term d_{ij}, i.e.:

$$d_{ij} = \int \mu(y_i)/y_i, \quad (10)$$

Then the degree of execution of j-th rule for current input vector $X^* = (x_1^*, x_2^*, ..., x_n^*)$ is determined as

$$\mu_j(X^*) = (\mu_j(x_1^*) \ ... \chi_j \ \mu_j(x_n^*)) \times w_j, \ j = \overline{1, m}, \quad (11)$$

where operator χ_j is determined as

$$\chi_j = \begin{cases} t\text{ - norm when } \chi_j =< \text{AND} >, \\ s\text{ - norm when } \chi_j =< \text{OR} >. \end{cases} \quad (12)$$

Then the result of fuzzy inference may be represented as

$$y^* = \{\frac{\mu_1(x^*)}{d_1}, \frac{\mu_2(x^*)}{d_2}, ..., \frac{\mu_m(x^*)}{d_m}\}. \quad (13)$$

The carrier of the fuzzy set, determined by the expression (13) is the set of fuzzy terms $\{d_1, d_2, ..., d_m\}$. For transition to the fuzzy set, determined on the carrier y, the operations of implications like

$$d_j^* = \int \min \frac{(\mu_j(X^*), \mu(y_j))}{y}, \ j = \overline{1, m}, \quad (14)$$

as well as the operations of aggregation like

$$y^* = \int \max \frac{(\mu_j(X^*), \mu(y_j))}{y}, \ j = \overline{1, m}, \quad (15)$$

are done.

As the result of the defuzzification of the fuzzy set Y (which can be done, for example, using the method of determining the gravity center), the exact value of output y is turned out. Summarizing the above results, to assess the current state of the NE it is proposed to implement in DMS the mechanism of fuzzy inference with two-level hierarchical structure that is represented in Figure 2. In the given structure, the number of levels is conditional and can be modified when solving a specific task. Each hierarchical level comprises the machines of fuzzy inference. The particularity of this structure is the lack of intermediate operations of defuzzification and fuzzification. These operations are fulfilled on the DMS input and output. For each group of controlled functional parameters, defining the NE state, the features vectors $\{X_i\}$ arrive on the inputs of the fuzzy logical inference machines of the first level of the hierarchy.

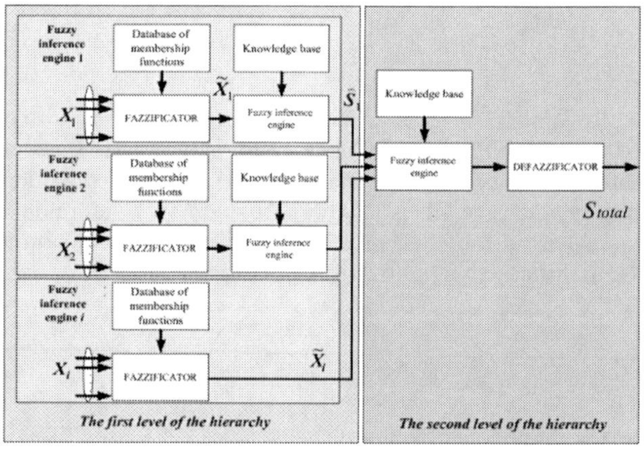

Figure 2. The structure of the mechanism of fuzzy logical inference.

At the output of the hierarchical layer a set of fuzzy assessments of the situation $\{S_i\}$ of the NE state for each functional group of parameters is formed. These estimates are aggregated on the second level of the hierarchy.

Figure 3 shows a variant of the hierarchical structure of the process of the NE state assessment based on cluster analysis. This structure can be used for a large number of input variables, characterizing the NE technical state, and implements a hierarchy of methods of fuzzy cluster analysis with subsequent classification of the obtained results.

The structure of the classifier corresponds to the considered structure of the fuzzy logical inference system.

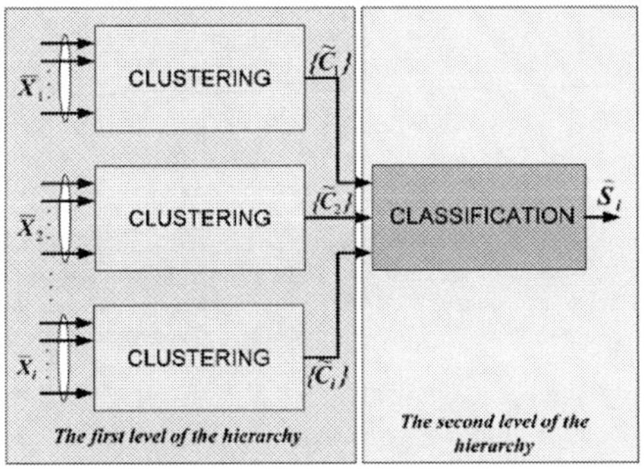

Figure 3. The structure of the NE assessment process.

It is advisable to choose as the main clustering techniques: (1) the method of fuzzy k–means if the number of clusters is known a priori; (2) subtractive clustering methods, if a priori the number of clusters is unknown.

A fuzzy situation of the NE state is formed as follows:

$$S^i_{NE} = F_1\left(\{S^i_{fg}\},\{X^i_{fg}\}, R^i_{fg}\right), \tag{16}$$

where S^i_{NE} is a fuzzy situation of NE state; F_1 is aggregation operator; $\{S^i_{fg}\}$ is a set of fuzzy situations of states of controlled functional NE groups; $\{X^i_{fg}\}$ is a set of fuzzy parameters of states of controlled functional NE groups; R^i_{fg} is a set of functional and technological NE resources.

Then the solution on NE control will be as follows:

$$R^i_{sl,NE} = F^i_{sl,NE}\left(S^i_{NE}, \{X^i_{fg}\}, R^i_{fg}\right) \tag{17}$$

where $R^i_{sl,NE}$ is a solution for NE control; $F^i_{sl,NE}$ is an operator of decision making on NE control.

On the basis of the proposed approach, the generalized algorithm for monitoring of technical state of typical NE can be represented as shown in Figure 4. In this figure, $\{X_i\}$ is a set of input features of the functional groups' state; $\{S_i\}$, $i = \overline{1, N}$, is a set of fuzzy situations, characterizing the state of each functional NE group. These include, for example, the NE performance, electromechanical characteristics (containing the value of the active and wave resistances of interfaces), the current operating temperature of the processor module, the number of software faults per time unit, etc.

There are two variants of decision-making:

1. The decision is made by the intelligent agent (IA) exactly at NE itself, and the higher control level, such as network administrator, is only notified about the decision made. This is possible if such rights are delegated to by the higher level.

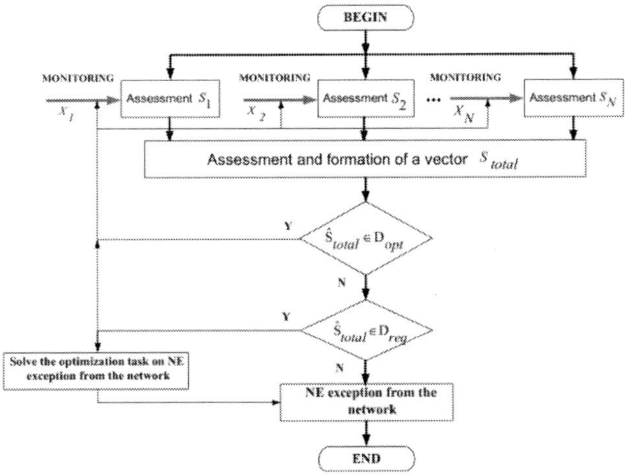

Figure 4. Generalized algorithm of NE monitoring.

2. The solution, as in the first case, made by IA itself, but is acknowledged and can be corrected by a higher control level taking into account its preferences.

It should be noted that the proposed DMS inherits the features of multi-agent systems. These include the following properties:

1. Adaptation. The agents adapt to the network architecture and adequately respond to changes in the network equipment configuration.

2. Rationality of resource allocation. IAs are evenly distributed across all the NEs in the MSN that allows to rationally (optimally) allocate computing resources.

3. Fault tolerance. At failure of one IA a part of its functions can be taken by other IAs.

4. Ensuring a high degree of information security. The security subsystem does not have the dedicated control center (decision-making center), as the agents are evenly distributed throughout the system, therefore it is more difficult to attack the MSN than a network with a centralized security server. Distributed over the network information and distributed protection require the attacker to attack many sites at the same time.

5. The possibility of centralized control. Introducing changes into agents' work can be performed centrally and by agent interaction protocols be transferred to any point.

V. Experimental Results

For numerical simulation, an NE "router" was chosen as an example. The structure of the intelligent agent for NE "router" state assessment is outlined in Figure 5. In the numerical experiment, the NE state was estimated according to the following functional parameters:

1. Electrical parameters: power; active resistance of interfaces; attenuation of communication lines to which the interfaces are connected.

2. Performance: processor unit performance; switching module performance; state of memory buffers.

3. State of software: state of the database management system; software state; number of failures of the software and the operating system.

We denote the estimates for each such group of parameters as S_1, S_2, and S_3, respectively. Numerical simulation was carried out in MATLAB R 2014b.

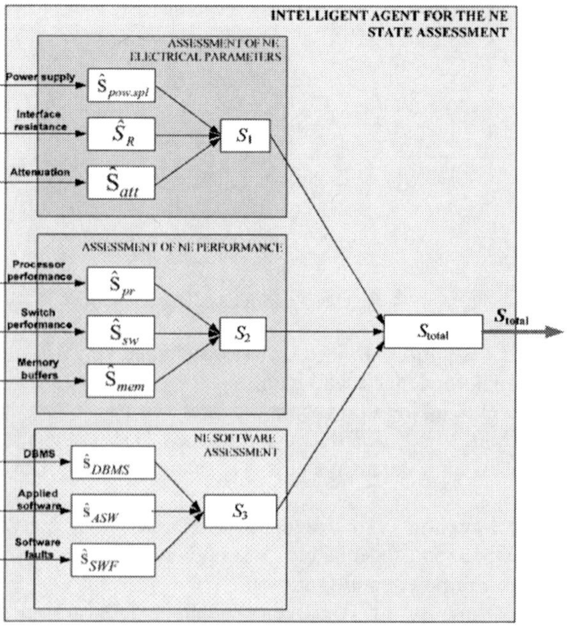

Figure 5. The structure of the intelligent agent.

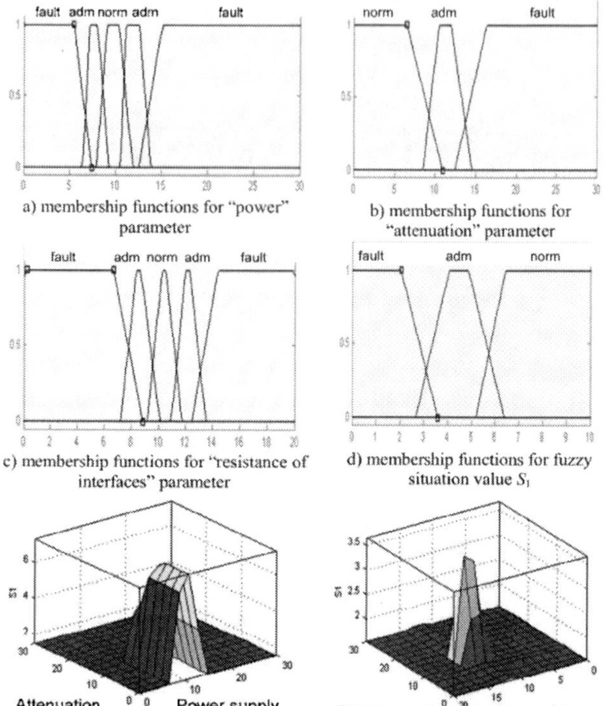

a) membership functions for "power" parameter

b) membership functions for "attenuation" parameter

c) membership functions for "resistance of interfaces" parameter

d) membership functions for fuzzy situation value S_1

e) membership function for "power – attenuation"

f) membership function for "power – resistance of interfaces"

Figure 6. Evaluation of fuzzy situation using the NE electrical parameters.

Figure 6 represents the characteristics of the fuzzy inference system for evaluation of the fuzzy situation using the NE electrical parameters. Figure 6-a shows the membership functions for the "power" parameter. When forming this function, it was assumed that a supply voltage equal to 10 V 5% is considered normal. Deviations of +10% and -15% are considered as the maximum permissible. Values exceeding these values are considered as failures. Similarly, the membership functions for "attenuation" parameter, shown in Figure 6-b, are constructed. It was believed that the signal attenuation corresponds to the norm, if it does not exceed 5-6 dB. Attenuation equal to 8-11 dB is considered acceptable. If the attenuation exceeds 12 dB, then a failure is fixed, since the router will not perform its functions. The approach to building the membership functions for "resistance of interfaces" parameter (Figure 6-c) is similar to the approach discussed above. The membership functions for the fuzzy situation value S_1 are shown in Figure 6-d. These functions perform the aggregation of the membership functions of the individual parameters belonging to group 1, and characterize three states – "normal", "acceptable" and "failure". Figure 6-e and Figure 6-f show sections of the multidimensional function S_1 for possible pairs of separate parameters: "power-attenuation" and "power-resistance of interfaces", respectively.

Figure 7 depicts the characteristics of the fuzzy inference system to evaluate the fuzzy situation using the NE software, and Figure 8 shows the characteristics of the fuzzy inference system to evaluate the fuzzy situation.

The construction of membership functions for these functional groups is similar to the first functional group. Without loss of generality, in this computational experiment all the membership functions are represented by trapezoidal functions. This is due to the simplicity of their practical implementation. The conducted studies confirm their acceptable approximation properties [16][17]. Numerical modeling of the functioning of the intelligent agent was carried out by the Monte Carlo method with a given probability and methods of generating random processes with given statistical characteristics. These events and random processes simulated the numerical, functional, logical and linguistic data of the sensors arriving at the input of the intelligent agent for each monitored functional group of the router. The results of computational evaluation for common fuzzy situation S_{total} concerning the NE state are represented in table II. The rows of the table correspond to possible combinations of estimates of fuzzy situations for individual groups of functional elements.

One of the problems, solved by development and implementation of this class DMS, is the task of preliminary training.

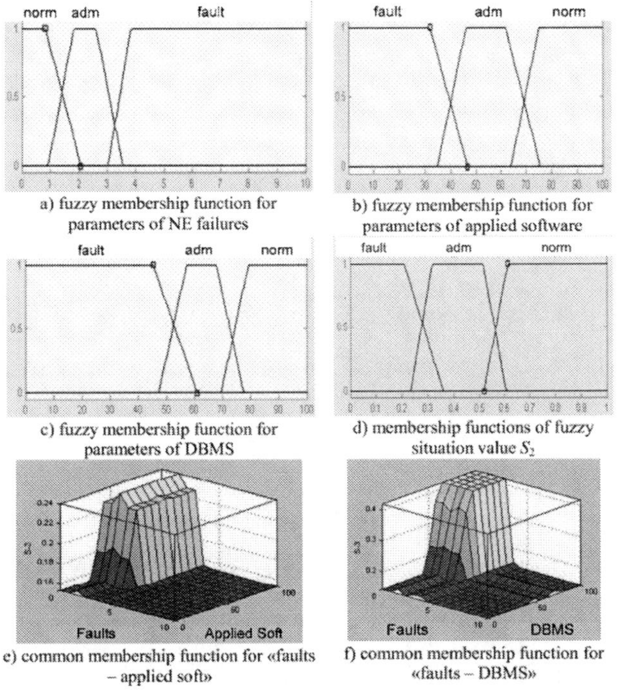

Figure 7. Evaluation of the fuzzy situation using the NE software.

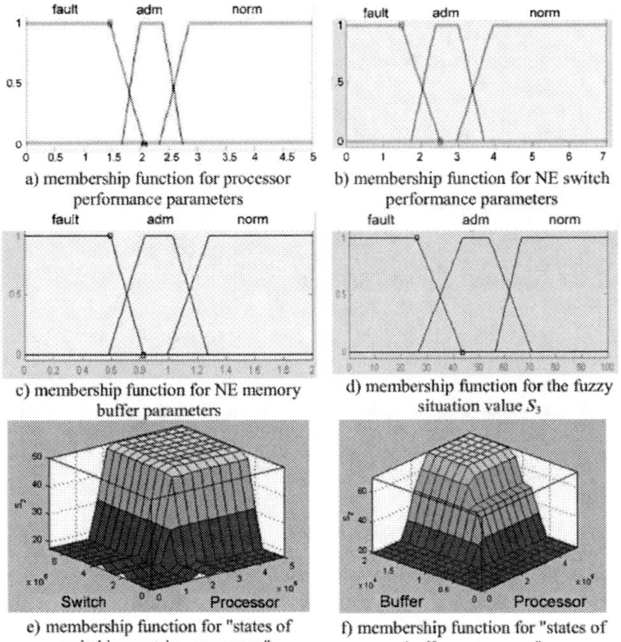

Figure 8. Evaluation of the fuzzy situation using the NE performance.

In [16][17], they tested the training algorithm of fuzzy model using a set of test input data. The proposed modification of the algorithm is presented in Figure 9. In the first step of the algorithm, a set of test training data samples is generated for each monitored functional group.

TABLE II. RESULTS OF EVALUATION OF NE STATE FUZZY SITUATIONS

##	S_1	S_2	S_3	S_{total}
1	norm	norm	norm	norm
2	admissible	admissible	admissible	admissible
3	admissible	norm	norm	admissible
4	fault	admissible	norm	fault
5	norm	fault	admissible	fault
6	admissible	admissible	fault	fault
7	norm	norm	fault	fault

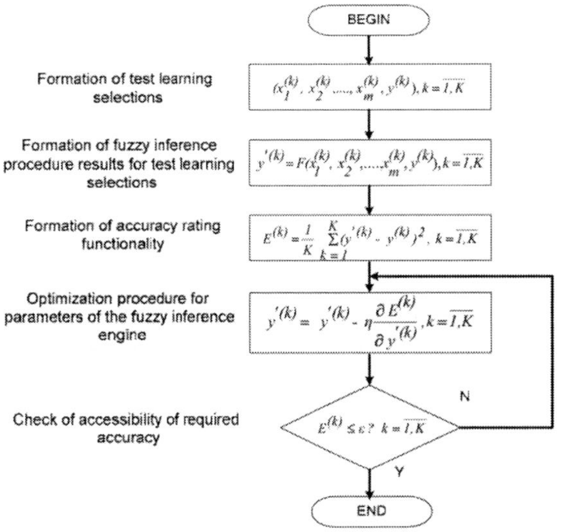

Figure 9. Training algorithm of fuzzy model.

In the second step, the results of fuzzy inference procedures are formed on the basis of training samples of the source data. In this case, the input training samples can be either numerical or linguistic variables. In the third step, the functional of the degree of accuracy is formed. In the overwhelming majority of cases, this functional belongs to the class of quadratic functionals. In the fourth step, an iterative gradient procedure is performed, which allows to optimize the membership functions for the corresponding parameters of the fuzzy inference mechanism. In the final fifth stage, the accuracy of the fuzzy inference system is checked. If this accuracy is acceptable, then the algorithm is completed. If not, it returns to step 4.

The main characteristics and properties of the training algorithm of fuzzy model are as follows: the amount of training samples is much less than the amount of data to compute the sufficient statistics used in statistical methods to ensure the same given accuracy; easy implementation of the algorithm; implementation of this algorithm does not require significant computing resources; the convergence of this algorithm is provided in approximately 5-17 iterations; despite the fact that this algorithm belongs to the class of algorithms of preliminary training, it can be applied also for training of fuzzy inference systems and their operation. The data, obtained in the numerical experiments, indicate high efficiency of the proposed methods of the NE state assessment based on the model of the intelligent agent and the mechanism of logical inference. The *duration of the final NE status assessment* in all cases was in the range from 100 to 150 msec. The *duration of the final NE status assessment* in all cases was in the range from 100 to 150 msec. The calculations were performed on a personal computer of a typical configuration (Intel Xeon 4x2 GHz CPU Cores, 2 GByte). In traditional statistical approaches (considered in [2]-[7]) this duration is related with calculation of correlation dependences. Its value lies between 5 to 30 seconds depending on the composition of the initial data used. Comparison of the obtained duration estimate with the estimate performed according to the traditional approaches shows a gain of 50 to 180 times. Proceeding from expressions (3) and (6), the decrease of the duration of the final NE status assessment leads to decrease the NE recovery time and increase the coefficient of availability respectively from 0.9-0.95 to 0.95-0.99. Thus, the method proposed allows to increase the MSN reliability significantly. *The accuracy of the final NE status assessment* for numerical parameters was not less than 0.95. For symbolic parameters, in all cases, the accuracy was 1.0. For comparison, with the statistical approach, the accuracy for numerical parameters lies in the range from 0.9 to 0.97, and for symbolic values the statistical estimate generally loses its meaning. Thus, this conclusion is justified by the following factors: the high completeness of the representation of heterogeneous primary information about the NE state, which is then analyzed and aggregated; the possibility of learning and self-learning of intelligent agents; the possibility of organizing parallel computational procedures for evaluating the state of NE, which provides the possibility of its operation in real time; high accuracy of NE state estimation; the ability to quickly track various failures and short-term violations in the operation of NE hardware and software; the absence of the need to collect and process various statistical data on the functioning of the NEs. In addition, the use of intelligent agents in conjunction with the developed methods and algorithms ensures to implement the principle of self-organization when providing and restoring the specified state of MSN as a whole.

VI. CONCLUSION

On the basis of the analysis of the methods for ensuring the MSN reliability, the task of the operational monitoring of the NE state was formulated. Using the proposed mechanism for fuzzy hierarchical inference the algorithm for operational monitoring of the NE state was developed. Analysis of the results of the experimental evaluation of the developed algorithm in comparison with the statistical approach has shown its higher speed and accuracy for NE state estimation, as well as the possibility of predicting its further state. All this allows us to speak about the high efficiency of the proposed approach for monitoring of the NE state in MSN. The future research is associated with the use of fuzzy inference for making decisions on MSN control.

ACKNOWLEDGMENT

This research is being supported by the grants of the Russian Foundation of Basic Research (15-07-07451, 16-37-00338, 16-29-09482), partial support of budgetary subjects 0073-2015-0004 and 0073-2015-0007, and Grant 074-U01.

REFERENCES

[1] "ITU-T: General principles and general reference model for Next Generation Networks. Recommendation Y.2011", Geneva, 2004.

[2] "RFC 1450. Management Information Base for version 2 of the Simple Network Management Protocol (SNMP v2)", IETF, April, 1993.

[3] W. Stallings, "SNMP, SNMP v2, SNMP v3 and RMON 1 and 2", Third edition, Reading, MA, Addison-Wesley, 1998.

[4] D. Harrington, R. Presuhn, and B. Wijnen, "An Architecture for Describing SNMP Management Fremeworks", IETF, April, 1999.

[5] "RFC 1450. Management Information Base for version 2 of the Simple Network Management Protocol (SNMP v2)", IETF, April, 1993.

[6] Uy. Black, "Network management standards: SNMP, CMIP, TMN, MIBs and Objects libraries", McGraw-Hill Inc, 1995.

[7] A.L. Goel, "Software Reliability Models: Assumptions, Limitations, and Applicability", IEEE Transactions on Software Engineering, vol. SE-11, is.12, pp.1411-1423, 1985.

[8] R. Zhang-Shen and N. McKeown, "Guaranteeing quality of service to peering traffic", Proc. 27th IEEE International Conference on Computer Communications, IEEE Press, Apr. 2008, pp. 1472-1480, doi: 10.1109/INFOCOM.2008.206.

[9] E. Mamdani and H. Efstathion, "Higher-order logics for handling uncertainty in expert systems", Int. J. Man-Mach. Studies, no.3, pp.243-259, 1985.

[10] E. Mamdani and S. Assilian, "An Experiment in Linguiste Syntheses with Fuzzy Logic Controller", Int. J. Man-Machine Studies, vol. 7, no. 1, pp. 1-13, 1975.

[11] J. Zhang and Y. Leung, "Impruved possibilistic c-means clustering algorithms", IEEE Transactions on Fuzzy Systems, vol. 12, pp. 209-217, 2004.

[12] R. Yager and D. Filev, "Essentials of Fuzzy Modeling and Control", USA: John Wiley&Sons, 1984.

[13] A. Azruddin, R. Gobithasan, B. Rahmat, S. Azman, and R. Sureswaran, "A hybrid rule based fuzzy-neural expert system for passive network monitoring", Proc. of the Arab Conference on Information Technology, pp. 746-752, 2002.

[14] L. Souza and G. Barreto, "Nonlinear system identification using local arx models based on the self-organizing map. Learning and Nonlinear Models", Revista da Sociedade Brasileira de Redes Neurais, vol. 4, no. 2, pp. 112-123, 2006.

[15] N. Kasabov and Q. Song, "DENFIS: Dynamic Evolving Neuro-Fuzzy Inference System and Its Application for Time-Series Prediction", IEEE Transactions on Fuzzy Systems, vol.10, no.2, pp. 144-154, 2002.

[16] I. Saenko, S. Ageev, and I. Kotenko, "Detection of traffic anomalies in multi-service networks based on a fuzzy logical inference", Intelligent Distributed Computing X. Studies in Computational Intelligence, vol. 678. 2016, Springer, doi: 10.1007/978-3-319-48829-5, pp. 79-88, 2016.

[17] I. Kotenko, I. Saenko, and S. Ageev, "Countermeasure Security Risks Management in the Internet of Things based on Fuzzy Logic Inference", Proc. of the 14th IEEE International Conference on Trust, Security and Privacy in Computing and Communications (TrustCom-2015), 20-22 August 2015, Helsinki, Finland, pp. 655-659, 2015.

TCP on Large Scale Network Topologies: Performance Analysis and Issues on Real Networks' Topology Design

Konstantinos Paximadis, Vassilis Triantafillou
Anna Galanopoulou, and Pavlos Kalpakioris
Computer & Informatics Engineering Dept., Western Greece University of Applied Sciences, Antirio, 30020, Greece
email: kpaximadis@gmail.com

Abstract – **The Transmission Control Protocol (TCP) is a traffic carrier protocol and the only one that counts for reliability. TCP incorporates a sliding window mechanism which controls the traffic flow from source to destination. The behavior of the window is of critical importance to TCP's performance. TCP operates on an end-to-end basis, based on routes provided by a routing algorithm. Reliability issues dictate the need of alternate routes serving either as backup routes or as load balancing routes. The exact role of alternate routes is defined by the network manager. We point out that large scale topologies are more close to real networks in many aspects, and so they deserve more attention. We study the TCP window's behavior for two major TCP versions and we address design issues, constraints and tradeoffs for large scale, similar to real, network topologies.**

Keywords-Transmission Control Protocol (TCP); Congestion avoidance and control; Sliding Window mechanism; Network Simulator NS2; Network topology.

I. INTRODUCTION

Nowadays, billions of people are connected to each other, usually via internet. There are two common used traffic carriers used for carrying all this traffic. The Transmission Control Protocol (TCP) and the User Datagram Protocol (UDP). TCP main goal is to reliably carry users' traffic from source to destination. As no one can guarantee links' integrity and limit possible losses or packet delays, TCP's reliability feature lies on a mechanism that can check the received data for errors and/or missing packets. TCP checks the received packets, informs the source and, if needed, requests retransmission of specific data packets.

TCP not only merits for reliable data transmission but also tries to control the flow of data in order to avoid congestion, by incorporating a sliding window mechanism. TCP's sliding window mechanism tries to serve as many users with as much traffic as possible. Sometimes the total amount of traffic posed by users may exceed networks' capacity. If this happens, long delays and high packet losses naturally occur, slowing down the network and degrading its performance.

So, there is a trade off between throughput and delay-losses which has to be judged carefully.

Last but not least, TCP counts for fairness, meaning that it treats all users the same, thus ensuring that all users get a fair share of bandwidth.

TCP operates on an end-to-end basis, transmitting on routes provided by a routing algorithm. Generally, a routing algorithm finds the best route from a source node to a destination one. However, in an Internet provider's core network serving millions of clients, reliability issues dictate the need of alternate routes. Alternate routes may be standing by, to be used in case of a failure, or can be simultaneously used with the best ones for load balancing. This is due to the network manager to decide.

Alternate routes have to be defined prior to transmission, because, when serving millions of connections and a link fails, you do not have the luxury (of time) to wait for the routing algorithm to calculate new routes. So, alternate routes must be known before the network starts transmission and must be used accordingly to the manager's decisions. Other issues to be taken care of are how to define alternate routes, how many should they be and how different from the basic route and from other alternate routes should, or can, be.

This work is organized as follows: Section II deals with the congestion avoidance basics used in TCP networks. Sections III presents some of the existing TCP versions. Section IV describes the network topology. Section V comments and discusses issues on topology design. Section VI presents the simulation results. Finally in Section VII, we present the conclusion and thoughts for future work.

II. CONGESTION AVOIDANCE BASICS

If users enter a network in an uncontrolled manner, the amount of traffic to be carried may exceed the total network capacity. In this case, the effective throughput (thus the number of packets that manage to reach their destinations with success) decreases and may approach zero. The phenomenon during which throughput declines towards zero is called congestion collapse [7].

The main goal of congestion avoidance and congestion control algorithms is to prevent a network from congestion collapse. The main mechanism evolved towards this goal is the sliding window mechanism.

As defined in [7], the congestion window is a TCP sender's estimate of the number of data packets which the network can manage to transmit towards destination, without causing congestion. In this case, we must note that flow control aims to prevent the destination's buffer from overflow and uses the so-called receiver window. Since usually the end (receiving) systems can process the delivered packets faster than the network can transmit them, it is assumed that the congestion window (and not the receiver window) is the main network load limiting factor. So, one easily can understand that the behavior of the congestion window is of critical importance to TCP's performance.

III. TCP VERSIONS

TCP as an end-to-end protocol relies on information gathered at the two network ends. So the communication subnet is viewed like a black box [7]. As mentioned earlier TCP tries to avoid congestion in order to avoid congestion collapse. Another TCP main objective is to maintain fairness that is to equally divide the available network capacity among the bandwidth competing users.

A table giving the main features of the various TCP variants can be found in [7], where we also can found an evolutionary graph of various TCP versions.

TCP versions can be categorized [7] as Reactive ones, which base their decisions on detection of losses, and Proactive ones, which base their decisions on delay measurements.

A. TCP Tahoe

Proposed by V. Jacobson in [1], TCP Tahoe is based on the original TCP specification RFC 793 [8]. It consists of two mechanisms the Slow Start and the Congestion Avoidance.

The window's increase policy is triggered by the in-time reception of an ACK (acknowledgment) which probably means that the network is coping well with the current traffic, and so, naturally, traffic can be increased.

This congestion avoidance algorithm was found quite effective [1] [7]. Its only drawback is its relatively slow discovery and use of the network's capacity due to the conservative nature of the additive increase policy. Also, the combination of Slow Start and Congestion Avoidance mechanisms result in good behaviour regarding fairness [7].

B. TCP Reno

TCP Tahoe sets the congestion window equal to one upon a packet loss, why? Because it "smells" congestion and feels that the session must limit the amount of data that poses into the network. However, this policy is rather strict and can sometimes lead to major throughput degradation, punishing the users for the lost packet they experienced.

So Jacobson et al. [8] renew the Slow Start and Congestion Avoidance mechanisms to count for different congestion states of the network.

A major congestion network state is defined as the state where the network can hardly deliver any packets. In this case a decrease mechanism should be strict in an effort to quickly deal with this unwanted state.

A minor congestion network state is defined as the state where the network can and does deliver some packets. This case is triggered by a supposed loss packet, based on duplicate ACKs evidence.

In this case we prefer a less strict decrease mechanism.

This less strict mechanism is used in TCP Reno and is called Fast Recovery [7] [9].

Incorporating Slow Start, Congestion Avoidance, Fast recovery and Fast retransmit TCP Reno shows a significantly better performance and achieves higher throughputs. TCP slow start approach is also discussed in [2].

C. TCP Vegas

TCP Vegas was presented by Brakmo and Peterson in [6].

As noted in [6], TCP Vegas aims to measure and accurately control a "right" amount of extra traffic in the network. Extra traffic would not otherwise have been accepted in the network.

TCP Vegas uses a proactive mechanism in order to replace the reactive Congestion Avoidance algorithm.

As shown in [7], TCP Vegas has the advantage of achieving rate stabilization in a steady state. Rate stabilization together with the absence of unwanted oscillations of the window size, can lead to higher values of throughput.

Other TCP versions are TCP Africa [3] which is a delay-sensitive congestion avoidance approach incorporated in networks of high bandwidth delay product (BDP) and Compound TCP (CTCP) [10] which a synergy of delay-based and loss-based approach.

IV. LARGE SCALE NETWORK TOPOLOGY: WHY AND WHERE?

TCP variants have been extensively simulated. However, in many studies [3] [4] [6] [7] [10] [13], the topologies tested are somewhat small (and sometimes trivial). In [4], a four-node backbone network topology with numerous nodes attached to the four nodes is used. In [11], a larger topology is tested but with a relatively small network core, and in [13], a fat-tree network topology is used with the question of how it can be applied in data center networks.

As mentioned in [3] several modern applications such as supercomputer grids and large biological simulations often have the need to transfer data between different continents. So, naturally, data need to travel through several nodes, and, apparently, large topologies.

Also, large telecommunication and internet regional providers operate on their private networks which are usually expanded all over the country. Other large institutions with Wide Area Private Networks (such as banks) also operate over a large area.

For all the above reasons we decided to simulate TCP versions over a large scale network topology, which was first introduced in [5] and also used in other studies [12]. By large we mean a network that is close to a regional network provider's backbone network, for example, a provider operating in a medium sized country (i.e. in Europe, not China!) who can use these 19 nodes to locate a router (or a Layer-3 switch) in each of the major country's cities.

Large scale networks provide a realistic simulation environment as they are close to real ones. They have real world's characteristics and if suitably modified can match exactly real networks of providers and/or banks. Figure 1 shows the topology of the network used and Figure 2 shows the 32 sessions simulated.

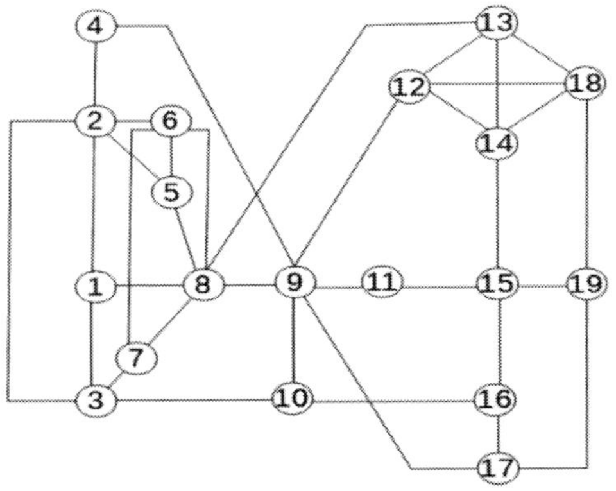

Fig. 1: The large scale network topology used

Traffic Matrix 32 sessions Source/Destination	
From node	To nodes
n1	n9, n19
n2	n18
n3	n4, n11, n17
n4	n3, n10, n13
n5	n12
n6	n14
n7	n16
n8	n15
n9	n1, n19
n10	n4, n13
n11	n3
n12	n5
n13	n4, n10, n17
n14	n6
n15	n8
n16	n7, n18
n17	n3, n13
n18	n2, n16
n19	n1, n9

Fig. 2: Network's traffic matrix

More specifically, if the topology is to be used for simulating a real network, the sessions must be modified to reflect the common case in such networks, where a central node is always the capital of the country, and all other nodes have a connection (direct or via other nodes) to it. Network reliability issues dictate the need of alternative routes for every communicating node pair.

So, a problem of defining the alternative routes arises. This problem is rather complicated as the network manager need not only to define the alternate routes but also guarantee that the network will continue to transmit in the case of more than one link failure. Moreover, the alternate routes must be chosen in a manner that, in case of a failure, they will not pose more traffic in certain links that are already heavy loaded.

V. ISSUES ON LARGE SCALE NETWORK TOPOLOGY DESIGN

A network manager in a major communications provider expanded over a whole country faces many problems. As in real life, a manager cannot start designing from a white sheet, because various constraints usually pre-exist and make the design more complex.

For example, in a network expanded in a whole country (i.e., internet provider network, bank network, universities network), usually (if not always) the major cities are hosting the major network nodes. Moreover, the country's capital usually hosts the central network node (or nodes). Although nobody suggests not do, a manager usually do not pose a network node in the middle of nowhere. So? So, there exists a somewhat predefined network topology and the only design freedom is designing the connections between the "existing" cities-nodes.

One of the first questions to be answered is which type of topology to use. To answer, one must first answer another question: What exactly a network manager expects from a topology?

As serving thousands or millions of customers and/or connections, what one mostly wants from a topology is fault tolerance. Speed and availability may wait a little. So, a large scale network topology for a major communications provider must have alternative routes assuring connectivity even in the event of a failure. By "must have" we mean that the alternative routes have to be specified and standing-by as the network operates. Why? Because in case of a failure, with millions of connections being served, the network does not have time to waste and it would be a small disaster to wait for a routing algorithm to run (again) and calculate new routes.

Another question is how many failures must the topology be able to successively overcome?

As noted before, a common practice is that the network central core node (or nodes) are usually placed in the country's capital, i.e., Athens for Greece, Rome for Italy and so on, following the well known "All roads lead to Rome".

So, usually the central network node is predefined and there exist network nodes which have to connect to the central node. How will the manager do that?

A. Geographical constraints

A known rule in backbone networks is that each network node must have at least two connections, each one connected to a different core node, obviously for reliability reasons. However, sometimes this is not easily achievable. Suppose a city is located high in the mountains or in a somehow isolated island (i.e., Kastelorizo in Greece), having only one major city in nearby distance and all others either far away or geographically difficult to reach and connect.

An alternative to this difficult situation is to use two separate links from city to city. These separate links must preferably follow a totally different route. Why? Because if placed side-by-side they are both vulnerable to the same failure if something goes wrong at their common route. So, one have to connect cities which cannot (due to geographical or economical restraints) have duplicate links with other cities/nodes, with dual or triple links with the same city/node, providing that these links follow different routes. How different? Surface morphology, distance, accessibility and cost will decide.

This technique can "save lives", meaning that can make the ring topology tolerant to single, double or even triple link failures, as it acts like a whole backup network.

B. Ring Topology

Classical ring topology offers a reliability feature over a single failure. If a single link failure occurs, communication between all nodes is still achievable through the remaining active part of the ring. Figure 3 notes that, although for clarity reasons the ring network is shown as a rectangular one.

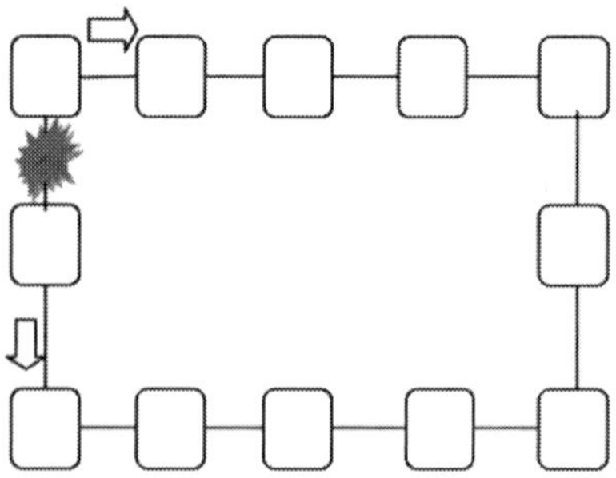

Fig. 3: A ring network experiencing a single link failure can still transmit packets.

But what if two link failures occur? Then you have a big problem, as your ring is separated in two parts, as in Figure 4.

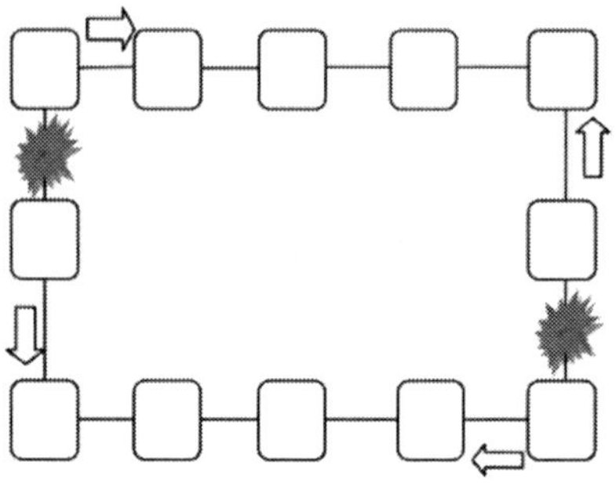

Fig. 4: A ring network experiencing a double link failure is separated in two parts.

This problem can be solved by adding a network node in the middle of the ring. This node, if connected by two other nodes, as shown in Figure 5, technically divides the original ring into two sub-rings. This topology can tolerate two simultaneous network link failures, if each one of them is in different sub-ring. If the two link failures occur in the same sub-ring, the nodes between failures are isolated from the other nodes.

Also, if one (of the two) link failure occurs on the common part of the two sub-rings, communication from every node to every other node will be still achievable.

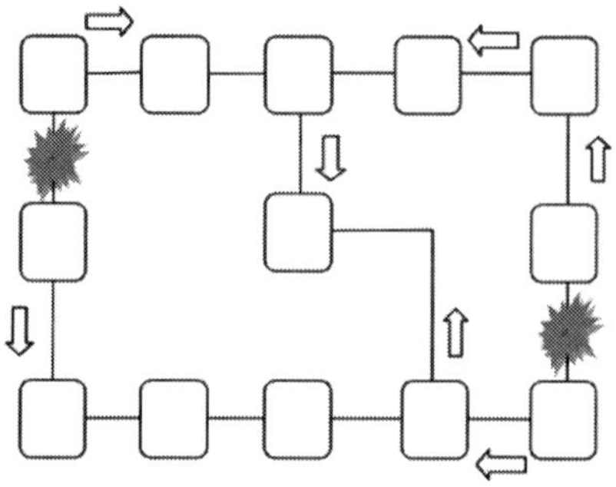

Fig. 5: A ring network divided in two internal rings.

C. Star topology

Naturally, capital's central node is the center of a star topology and all other cities-nodes are directly connected with it. Again, the only freedom one has is to choose the link connections. Fault tolerance reasons dictate the need of at least two links connecting each node with the central node. Also, as noted earlier in the ring topology analysis, it is a safer technique (although obviously more expensive) to use different routes for the links connecting each city-node to the central node.

So, one has to install two or more links between peripheral cities-nodes and the central node/nodes, each one of them preferably following different physical route.

D. Final decisions

So, finally, the topology is chosen and network links are installed. After that, the routing algorithm specifies the optimal and the alternative routes from all sources to all destinations. One big dilemma is whether the alternative routes should be used concurrently with the optimal ones, or should be used only as backup, thus stand-by and be used only in case of a failure.

The concept of using multiple routes to split traffic more efficiently over the available network capacity has been extensively explored by many researchers. One of the most analytical design called mTCP, is presented by Zhang et al in [14] and efficiently faces all problems raised.

Nowadays networks' response and speed are not a major problem. However, if it becomes (not temporarily, but for a long time), adding some high bandwidth links is generally a fair and cheap, in the long run, solution. A network manager except from failures (the frequency of which have to be examined), speed and availability must also merit for simplicity of protocols and algorithms used. So, an easy and "clean" solution would be to choose the second alternative to the big dilemma, which is to let the alternative routes standing by and send traffic to them only in case of a failure.

In this case it would helpful the alternative routes to be as "different" as possible from the optimal ones and, at the same time, do not use links used by other active routes. An interesting and relatively simple approach for finding non-overlapping and disjointed routes is presented at [14].

VI. SIMULATION RESULTS

We conducted various simulations to observe and verify the behavior of the congestion window, the packet loss probability and the total throughput. We used NS2 and the 19 node network topology described in section 4. All links was set to 20 Mbps, links' propagation time was set to 10ms, and drop-tail type of queue was used. Standard NS2 packet size of 1000 bytes was used. As a means to avoid starting the window size from one in a lightly loaded network and the algorithm being slow in gaining bandwidth, we set the initial window size advertised by the receiver to various predefined values at the range from 10 to 100 packets.

Figures 6 and 7 show the window size versus time for TCP Reno and TCP Vegas respectively for initial window size of twenty (20) packets, for six (6), (2, 14, 18, 19, 24, 32) more representative of the topology, sessions. We observe that for TCP Reno the congestion window can reach large values in some flows. Which are these flows? Obviously these are flows that are not using same links with others, or in other words flows operating at a less crowded part of the network.

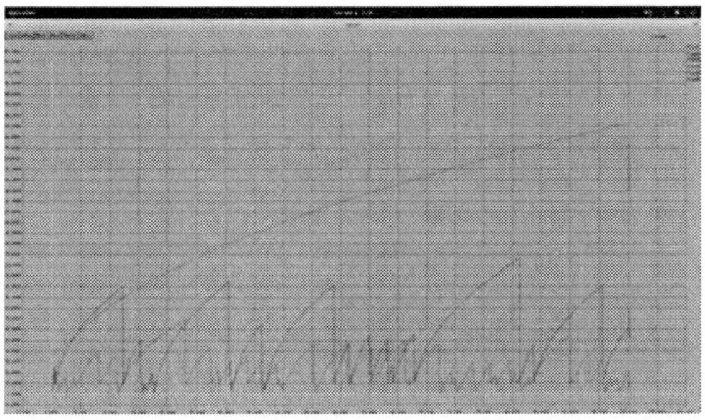

Fig. 6: The congestion window in time, 6/32 flows (TCP Reno)

Let's now focus on Flow 14 (blue colour at Figures 6, 7) which has mode n9 as source node and node n1 as destination. Thus Flow 14 transmits from a "central" node to a peripheral one. If it was a real internet provider's network, node n9 as the central node, would represent the capital of the country, and node n1 a nearby city. As Flow 14 is close to the central node, uses common routes with other sessions, and so, it cannot reach high window values. Why? Because TCP counts for fairness, and so, it divides equally the available bandwidth to the competing users on Flow's 14 links.

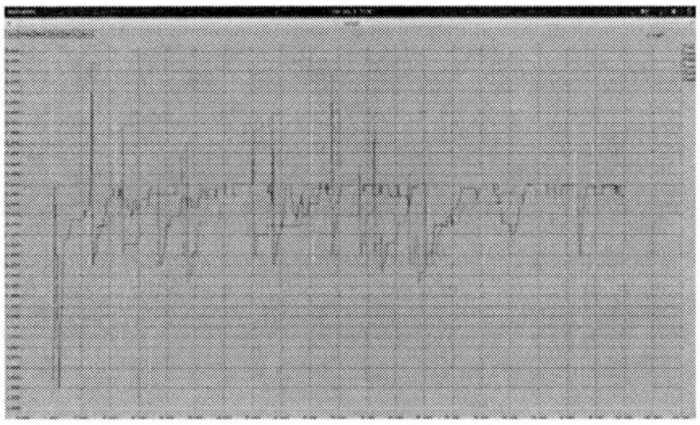

Fig. 7: The congestion window in time, 6/32 flows (TCP Vegas)

Total network statistics for TCP Reno and TCP Vegas, for all tested initial advertised window sizes follow, Tables 1 & 2.

Both TCP Reno and Vegas manage to send approximately the same amount of data packets all over the network. TCP Vegas due to its higher sensitivity manages to keep packet losses lower and so results to lower packet loss probabilities, as shown in Figure 8. One special characteristic of TCP Vegas is that it is hardly affected by the initial window size advertised by the receiver as because of its delay based mechanism it immediately senses network's capacity and adjusts the window size accordingly. TCP Vegas ends with lower packet loss probabilities for the same throughput, and, so, seems a better choice.

We observe that rising the initial advertised (by the receiver) window size beyond a mid-range value (at about 50-60) does not bring any benefits, because in this case we practically pose big loads at the beginning of network's operation. TCP congestion control reacts to these big loads and limits them quickly. So, we end up with higher packet loss probabilities, while the total gain in throughput is marginal.

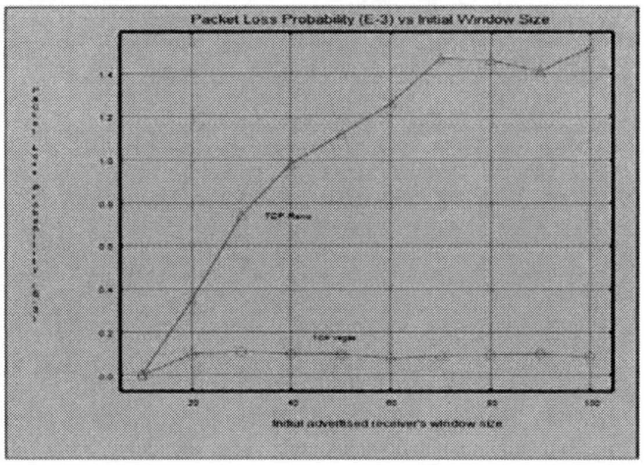

Fig. 8: Packet Loss Probability vs Initial window size for TCP Reno and TCP Vegas.

TABLE 1: TOTAL NETWORK STATISTICS, TCP RENO

TCP Reno					
Init WS	Sent packets	Received_ packets	Lost packets	Packet Loss Prob*10^{-3}	Average Throughput[kbps]
10	3114834	3114834	0	0	124585
20	5635813	5633828	1985	0,352212	225473
30	6904954	6899838	5116	0,740917	276289
40	7801538	7793820	7718	0,989292	311092
50	8368958	8359581	9377	1,12045	333815
60	8810732	8799548	11184	1,269361	351547
70	9016960	9003685	13275	1,472226	359587
80	9264323	9250711	13612	1,469292	370031
90	9304494	9291314	13180	1,41652	371485
100	9291425	9277248	14177	1,525815	371886

TABLE 2: TOTAL NETWORK STATISTICS, TCP VEGAS

TCP Vegas					
Init WS	Sent packets	Received_ packets	Lost packets	Packet Loss Prob*10^{-3}	Average Throughput[kbps]
10	3116546	3116546	0	0	124610
20	5730241	5729683	558	0,097378	229124
30	7177305	7176492	813	0,113274	287016
40	8093051	8092230	821	0,101445	323621
50	8717150	8716294	856	0,098197	348557
60	8883430	8882725	705	0,079361	355232
70	9070137	9069304	833	0,09184	362268
80	9237489	9236605	884	0,095697	369345
90	9220422	9219505	917	0,099453	368156
100	9240714	9239887	827	0,089495	369496

Generally speaking, it is not a good idea to let critical factors take large values in order to gain some benefits in a specific performance measure (with Higher is Better relationship). This policy, due to trade-offs, will probably lead to an equal (if not higher) degradation of another contradicting performance measure and the final result will be worse. This is a "rule" that comes true not only in computer networks but also in many aspects of engineering and life.

VII. CONCLUSION AND FUTURE WORK

We studied TCP Reno and TCP Vegas in a large scale network topology. Both versions prevented severe congestion, while TCP Vegas showed better performance.

Also, we commented on large scale network topologies. A big dilemma faced is whether to use the alternative routes concurrently with the optimal ones, or let them standing-by and use them only in case of a failure. Both options are well used in Greece major telecommunication networks. In either case, algorithms for defining the alternative routes, like the one proposed in [14], must be investigated.

If one chooses to concurrently transmit on alternative-backup routes except from the obvious overhead added, will also, most probably, face packet re-ordering problems. Packet re-ordering in TCP results in major performance degradation [13], and is another area of interest.

We are currently working on the problem of efficiently choosing, using and administrating the alternative non-overlapping backup routes in a large, close to real, network topology.

REFERENCES

[1] V. Jacobson and M. Karels, "Congestion avoidance and control," ACM SIGCOMM 88, 1988.

[2] K. Oyeyinka, et al. "TCP Window Based Congestion Control -Slow-Start Approach," Communications and Network, Vol. 3 No.2, pp 85-98, 2011.

[3] R. King, R. Baraniuk, and R. Riedi, "TCP-Africa: An Adaptive and Fair Rapid Increase Rule for Scalable TCP", Proc. IEEE 24th Annual Joint Conference of the IEEE Computer and Communications Societies, 13-17 March 2005.

[4] H. Jamal and K. Sultan, "Performance Analysis of TCP Congestion Control Algorithms", International Journal of Computer and Communicaitons, Issue 1, Volume 2, 2008.

[5] G. Thaker and J. Cain, "Interactions Between Routing and Flow Control Algorithm" , IEEE Transactions on Communications, March 1986.

[6] L.S.Brakmo and L.L.Peterson, "TCP Vegas: End to End Congestion Avoidance on a Global Internet", IEEE Journal on Selected Areas in Communications, col.13, no 8, Oct. 1995.

[7] A. Afanasyev, N. Tilley, P. Reiher, and L. Kleinrock, "Host-to-Host Congestion Control for TCP", IEEE Communications Surveys & Tutotrials, vol.12, no 3, 3rd quarter 2010.

[8] V. Jacobson, "Modified TCP congestion avoidance algorithm", email to the end2end list, April 1990.

[9] M. Allman, V. Paxson, and W. Stevens, " RFC2581 – TCP congestion control", RFC, 1999.

[10] K. Tan, J. Song, Q. Zhang, and M. Sridharan, "A Compound TCP Approach for High-speed and long Distance Networks", the 4th International Workshop on Protocols for Fast Long-Distance Networks (PFLDNet), 2006.

[11] H.Jamal and K. Sultan, "Performance Analysis of TCP Congestion Control Algorithms", Int. Journal of Computers and Communications, Issue. 1, vol.2, 2008.

[12] K. Paximadis and A. Vasilakos, "A Dynamic Congestion Avoidance Scheme Incorporating A-priori Information for Computer Networks", in Proc. of the 10th International Conference on Computer Communication, ICCC'90, New Delhi, India, 1990.

[13] N. Farrington, "Multipath TCP under Massive packet reording", Technical Report, University of California, San Diego.

M. Zhang, J. Lai, A. Krishnamurthy, L. Peterson, and R. Wang, "A transport Layer Approach for Improving End-to-End Performance and Robustness Using Redyndant Paths", in ATEC '04: Proceedings of the annual conference on USENIX Annual Technical Conference, pp.8-8, Berkely, CA, USA, 2004 Usenix Association.

A Framework for Self-Organized Adaptive Routing in Disaster Scenarios

Thomas Finke*, Silvia Krug†, Sebastian Schellenberg‡, and Jochen Seitz†
*Bosch Engineering GmbH, Abstatt, Germany
Email: thomasroland.finke@de.bosch.com
†Communication Networks Group, Technische Universität Ilmenau, Germany
Email: {silvia.krug, jochen.seitz}@tu-ilmenau.de
‡ADVA Optical Networking SE, Meiningen, Germany
Email: sschellenberg@advaoptical.de

***Abstract*—Routing in Mobile Ad hoc Networks (MANETs) remains challenging after years of research because the network conditions can vary significantly depending on the actual application scenario. This effect is even increased if the external conditions are not stable but rather change during the operation of the network as for example in disaster scenarios. In such a case, one single routing approach is usually not able to perform well because it was optimized for one parameter set only. Hybrid routing protocols usually combine two approaches for better adaptability to multiple use cases but still require a careful selection of the protocols in question. In adaptive routing concepts, nodes can choose from multiple protocols and thus adapt to the given network conditions seamlessly. In this paper, we present our adaptive routing framework allowing easy integration of multiple protocols and discuss its advantages over hybrid and traditional routing concepts as well as the application to disaster scenarios.**

***Keywords*—Mobile Ad Hoc Networks; Adaptive Routing; Hybrid Routing; Disaster Scenarios.**

I. Introduction

When a disaster hits a region, fast and efficient rescue operations are essential to save as many lives as possible. This requires an operational communication network ideally for both the first responders and the affected people. But the disaster will also damage the communication infrastructure, resulting in missing coverage or overloaded networks.

Mobile Ad hoc Networks (MANETs) are one promising option to provide communication under these circumstances, as the network is built based on devices at hand. But due to the structure of the network and the node mobility, routing becomes a challenge and remains challenging even after years of research because the network conditions can be quite different depending on the actual circumstances. In disaster scenarios, where after an initial damage to the whole infrastructure more and more first responders arrive to help and parts of the remaining infrastructure get restored, this effect is even increased because the conditions within the network are not stable but rather change during the operation of the network.

In such a case, a single routing protocol is usually not able to perform well under all conditions because routing protocols are typically optimized for one parameter set only. Hybrid routing protocols try to solve this by combining two approaches for better adaptability to multiple use cases. This shows a better performance, if the protocols in question are carefully selected for the envisioned scenarios. If not, the performance might even decrease.

To overcome the need to preselect the employed routing protocols, adaptive routing has been proposed in the literature. When using such approaches, nodes can choose a currently active routing protocol from multiple options and thus adapt to the given network conditions seamlessly as they are enabled to dynamically switch to a better candidate as needed. In this paper, we present our adaptive routing framework Self-organized Routing in heterogeneous MANETs (SEREMA), which allows easy integration of multiple routing protocols, and show its potential for disaster networks. SEREMA was developed during a dissertation project [1].

The paper is organized as follows. In Section II, we will discuss several related adaptive routing approaches that inspired different features of our framework. Afterwards, we introduce the conceptual design of our framework and discuss its components in detail in Section III and show how this framework can provide robust and reliable communication in disaster scenarios. Then, we prove the feasibility of the concept with simulative evaluations in Section IV. Finally, the paper is concluded in Section V where we also present future planned research studies.

II. Related Work

In this section, we present work that has been done in the field of adaptive routing.

Nada et al. [2] proposed a framework that enables the switching between different routing protocols during runtime. This was realized without any modification to the protocols participating in the framework and thus ensuring that new protocols can be integrated later on. However, the approach comes with the drawback that the whole network has to switch to the same (new) routing protocol if the algorithm decides, hence making the system less flexible and unable to handle different conditions in different parts of the network. Moreover, during such a protocol switch the routing tables of all nodes have to be converted to match the required entry structure of the new protocol. Besides that, the decision mechanism of the whole network is deployed to a single node only. This potentially leads to inefficient routing or a complete failure, if this node is not working or gets corrupted.

Another example for this globally switchable routing is the Chameleon Routing Protocol (CML) proposed by Ramrekha et al. [3]. This approach is also based on a centralized monitoring agent that controls the choice of the routing protocol used by the whole network. Again, the centralized node introduces an undesired single point of failure into the network. However, the monitoring concept described by the authors is quite interesting in order to identify the optimal switching point. The optimal switching point defines when the benefits of changing to another routing protocol out weight the overhead caused by switching. Ideally, the monitoring to determine this point has to be done in a distributed and cooperative way throughout the network.

Hoebeke et al. [4] proposed a strategy, where every node is able to use its own routing protocol depending on the local scenario. Throughout the whole network, multiple routing mechanisms can be activated at the same time and global decision making is no longer needed. Conceptually, this support for multiple active protocols at the same time is desired. However, all envisioned protocols have to be adapted in order to work with the presented framework. Hence, a plug-and-play solution for newly introduced protocols as well as the interaction with unaware nodes is not possible. This limits the usability of the approach in cases where legacy nodes have to be integrated into the network or a flexible extension of the routing framework is needed.

In the Zone Routing Protocol (ZRP) proposed by Beijar et al. [5], participating nodes have two routing zones, a reactive and a proactive one. Depending on the near-field scenario, a node can adapt the radius of these zones dynamically. However, this only changes the size of the regions in which the two protocols are used. Besides that, it is not possible to change the used protocols during runtime, again limiting the adaptability to changing conditions during the operation of the network. While regions with different protocols and dynamic size adaptation are beneficial, the pre-configuration of the active protocols is not, since these might not suit all scenarios.

Besides these approaches, several recent works show the relevance of adaptive routing. Son et al. [6] present a similar approach with different metrics related to the node mobility. Based on the observed mobility, the routing protocol is switched for the whole network only. To achieve this, the scheme requires extensive control information to synchronize all nodes. This has two drawbacks. First, one single switching decision throughout the network might be suboptimal in some parts and second, the additionally introduced traffic should be avoided.

Kaji and Yoshihiro [7] use adaptive routing to identify alternative paths and thus avoid congestion in the network. To enable fast adaptive switching to different paths, they modify the packet structure and require an additional routing table to store alternative paths. Again, the modifications are problematic for legacy node support.

In the next section, we present our new concept that takes the benefits of the presented approaches while eliminating most of the drawbacks.

III. SEREMA FRAMEWORK

A. Conceptual Design Considerations

In order to allow nodes to dynamically select the best routing protocol according to given network situations, several protocols have to be included into the adaptive routing framework. But there are several things that should be considered when designing such a framework.

The network conditions will not be constant throughout the complete network, especially in disaster networks or any other large-scale MANET covering a sufficiently large geographical region. Therefore, the framework should support the *operation of multiple simultaneously active protocols* in different subzones of the same network and allow the *dynamic switching* of the currently active protocol out of a set of protocols based on monitored metrics. This adaptivity mechanism builds the core functionality of any adaptive routing approach.

The operation of multiple protocols in parallel and the switching poses additional challenges that have to be solved in order to build a robust framework. The first point is related to the lifetime of a system running the adaptive routing framework. In case of disaster scenarios, this is important for the first responder devices that are usually employed for longer periods. At the same time, old devices will be constantly replaced by newer ones. The new devices will benefit from recent advances in both technological and software-related enhancements. This will also include more recent routing protocols outperforming the previous ones. Therefore, the framework should be able to integrate additional routing protocol versions without too much extension effort. Hence, the framework should support *easy integration* of additional protocols.

Besides that, it cannot be ensured that the adaptive framework is deployed on all participating nodes. To enable these nodes to communicate with the remaining network, the framework has to *support legacy nodes*. In a region or zone with legacy nodes, the framework should therefore switch to one standard protocol supported by these nodes. This switching, however, does not require all surrounding nodes with adaptive routing to switch to the same protocol, if they are equipped with a more suitable protocol. In this case, one node can act as a *Border Node* [8] bridging the resulting two zones.

In order to enable the support of legacy nodes, the protocol versions integrated into the framework should be standard compliant as far as possible. This can be achieved if the adaptive routing framework does not require any significant changes of the existing protocols. Therefore, we try to avoid modifications for example of the routing table structure, the control packet structure, or the addition of new packet types. The only exception in our approach are standard compliant extensions that are allowed by the protocol specification.

The limitation of modification raises the question whether the framework introduces its own control messages or is able to benefit from the operation principles of the integrated protocols. Ideally, the normal protocol operations are used as far as possible and only few additional control messages or piggy-back extensions to existing control messages should be defined. This is also true for the *routing table structure*. Each protocol comes with its own definition for the routing table it uses and the structure of the corresponding routing entries. An adaptive framework enabling the operation of multiple protocols in parallel has to either define a unified table that is accessed by the forwarding agent or to translate the entries from each table, if multiple tables are used.

Besides that, the framework has to provide a translation mechanism in order to enable seamless communication between the supported protocols. This is needed to exchange routing information between zones using different active protocols, as the format of control messages as well as routing table entries have to be converted into that of the other protocol. For example, the information gathered by one proactive zone should be available in the reactive zone as well. This can be achieved by storing the corresponding routing information in the routing table and use this to respond to corresponding reactive requests. Therefore, the routing information has to be converted or translated from the formats used by the proactive protocol into that of the reactive one and vice versa. To limit the processing overhead introduced by the adaptive routing framework to perform the required translations, the number of the required operations should be minimized.

Finally, the framework has to fulfill multiple performance-related criteria. When employed in a disaster scenario, the framework has to provide *robust* communication and thus reliable packet delivery. For the framework, this requirement results in three crucial design aspects:

- distributed constant *Monitoring* of network conditions,
- distributed *Decision Making*, and
- a high *Decision Quality*.

The first two aspects help to avoid potential single points-of-failure. Besides that, distributed approaches can handle malicious nodes if the surrounding nodes detect apparently contradicting information. A high decision quality is ensured by this because it helps to prevent nodes from switching to a wrong protocol or taking isolated switching decisions. This can be achieved for example by monitoring multiple parameters and integrating them into a weighted scoring function as base for the switching decision.

As mentioned before, the nodes have to monitor the network conditions in their surrounding and take a decision to activate or deactivate specific routing protocols based on the collected data. One of the biggest challenges is the definition of good algorithms realizing such switching decisions.

Based on the points discussed above, the goal of our framework is to provide network-wide adaptive routing which fulfills the following criteria:

- support of an extensible set of routing protocols,
- support of multiple active protocols in different variably-sized zones in parallel,
- support of legacy nodes,
- distributed switching decisions of the active protocol,
- requiring only standard-compliant extensions of the routing protocols, and
- integrating multiple routing tables by building a wrapper component to allow an easy and unified access.

B. Framework Components

Based on the design considerations presented in the previous section, we developed our adaptive routing framework with the following components trying to combine the advantages of previous approaches. In the following, we will introduce the structure of our framework and provide details on how to achieve the mentioned criteria.

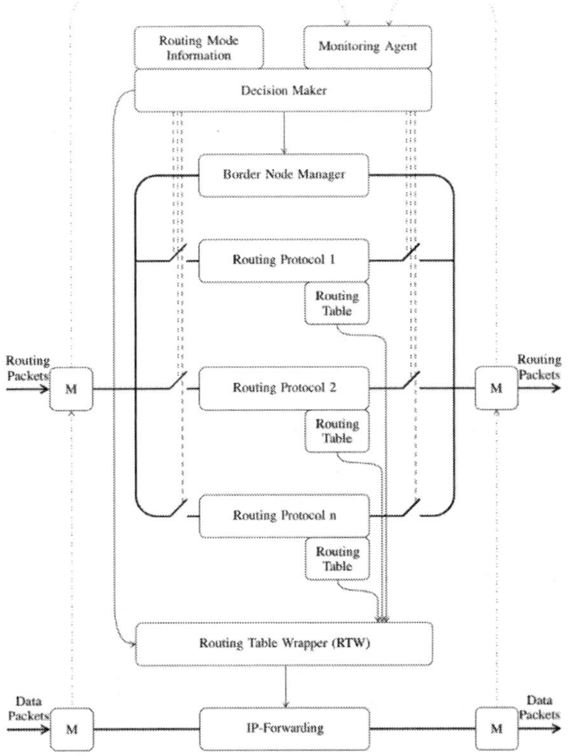

Fig. 1. Architecture of the Adaptive Routing Framework

Our proposed framework has the architecture as shown in Figure 1. The core of the system consists of multiple routing protocols, which can be connected/disconnected from the network via simple switches. Each of the equipped routing protocols can use its own routing table that allows to simply add further protocols without a huge implementation effort or changes to the protocol operation. All of the received and transmitted routing, as well as data packets are monitored locally by probes (M) and all of the gathered information is forwarded to the *Monitoring Agent*. It will calculate relevant statistics on the current traffic, as well as neighboring nodes and provide this information representing the current network situation to the *Decision Maker*. For making a decision about the currently most suitable routing protocol, additional information about the behavior of the protocols is required and provided by the *Routing Mode Information* block. This behavioral information describes the ideal operational parameters of the protocols including the reactions to certain load situations (e.g. increased overhead due to flooding requests). After the *Decision Maker* has used the data from the *Monitoring Agent* and *Routing Mode Information* block to make its protocol decision, it controls the input/output switches of the equipped routing protocols and, therefore, connects/disconnects specific protocols to/from the network. Since the decision is based on the locally observed network conditions at each node including information from its neighbors via received packets, we are able to make a dezentralized decision without requiring additional control traffic.

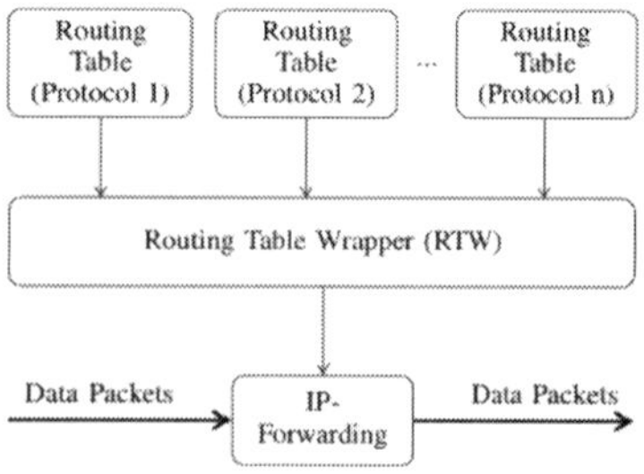

Fig. 2. Routing Table Wrapper

To provide routing information to the forwarding plane, our framework uses a special *Routing Table Wrapper* (c.f. Figure 2) that allows to simply access the information in multiple, different routing tables. With this mechanism, SEREMA is able to use multiple different routing protocols, allowing each protocol to use its own specified routing table. If a route to a specific destination in the network is required, the *Routing Table Wrapper* looks up the destination in all of the equipped routing tables and provides the resulting route to the *IP-Forwarding* module. This mechanism has the big advantage that in the time directly after a routing protocol change, when the new routing protocol has not gathered any new routes yet, the *Routing Table Wrapper* is able to provide the routes from the previously used routing protocol to the *IP-Forwarding*, not interrupting any ongoing data transfers.

If the network uses different routing protocols in different areas at the same time, the *Border Node Manager* (c.f. Figure 1) enables the interconnection of such areas. To achive this, it converts routing information between different protocols and allows to forward routing requests/responses over multiple routing domains. Nodes can freely chose their respective routing protocol in this setup. The interconnection of different routing zones is achieved by Border Nodes, that are able to translate the routing traffic accordingly and thus guarantee the end-to-end consistency of data flows. Any node can act as Border Node, if it detects different routing zones and supports both corresponding routing protocols [8]. Based on this mechanism, we are also able to integrate legacy nodes that support only one protocol as long as a suitable SEREMA node running the required protocol is within range.

The translation also includes a mechanism to enable route discovery across zones with different protocols and possibly different operation principles. This is crucial, if the nodes currently operate with a proactive protocol but are supposed to communicate with nodes in other zones running reactive protocols. In this case, the proactive node has to be enabled to start a reactive-style request. This is achieved by implementing corresponding annotation packets and a passive request mode. All packets needed for this mechanism are designed as standard-compliant packet extensions.

C. Implementation Details

To prove our concept, we implemented an adaptive routing framework that is able to switch between two traditional and well-know routing protocols for our evaluation: Ad hoc On-Demand Distance Vector (AODV) Routing [9] and Optimized Link State Routing Protocol (OLSR) [10].

Core of the implementation is the scoring algorithm employed in the decision maker. It will define which protocol is currently used based on the results of the monitoring agent. Figure 3 shows the implemented scoring algorithm that is used to select the currently active routing protocol.

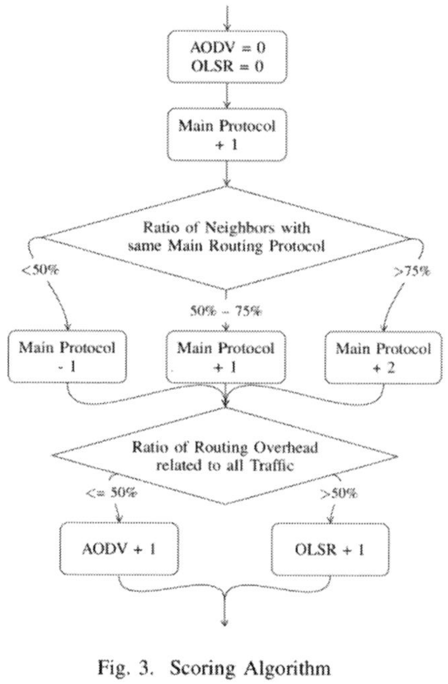

Fig. 3. Scoring Algorithm

To prove the conceptual design of an adaptive switching mechanism, we decided to use simplified criteria to estimate the current conditions in the network that are easy to monitor in simulations. Therefore, the currently implemented algorithm might not take the ideal decisions. However, it is suitable to show the feasibility of our concept in general.

We chose to utilize a score-based mechanism in our algorithm where each protocol can get/lose scoring points depending on the given criteria. This is required because there are several metrics and interactions between them that describe the current conditions in a network. Not all metrics are easy to normalize and afterwards be used in a unified formula which results in a number representing the best protocol.

For example, if we consider the routing overhead on a node related to the data traffic of the node, we get a number between 0 and 100 %. However, if we try to use the number of neighbor nodes for a decision, we do not have a maximum value to use in the formula. Therefore, the scoring algorithm simply adds/removes points to/from a protocol if specific conditions are met. In Figure 3, the notation *Protocol* $\pm$ *1* indicates that either the currently active protocol (main protocol) or the supported variant get an additional scoring point, if the corresponding criteria is fulfilled. Finally, the protocol with the highest score is activated. Depending on the requirements made to the adaptive routing framework, the number of points a protocol gets can be adjusted. In this way the protocol behavior can also simply be adjusted during runtime.

Currently, the algorithm considers three criteria only. These are the network load in terms of an ratio between the overhead introduced by the chosen routing protocol and the actual data traffic, the active protocol, and how many neighboring nodes use the same protocol. The network load in this case is locally observed by each node and relevant metrics are currently not exchanged between neighboring nodes to limit the otherwise introduced signaling overhead. However, the individual decision can propagate through the network, since the protocol selected by neighbors is one criteria. With this subset of criteria, we are able to evaluate our framework in scenarios where the density of nodes varies and should therefore result in adaptive switching decisions.

Future research will be dedicated to the evaluation of more realistic criteria and their corresponding weights in terms of scoring points. This work can be based on previous work on adaptive routing (cf. Lye et al. [11] or Haerri et al. [12]), but should include a thorough evaluation of suitable metrics describing characteristic network situations. Further simulations with our routing framework can help to evaluate the impact of such criteria. Such studies should include the evaluation of routing protocols under the characteristic conditions as well. Besides that, we plan to apply multi criteria decision making principles (e.g., [13]) to enhance our scoring algorithm and thus enable the combination of further relevant criteria. Such approaches allow to consider and optimize multiple criteria even if they have quite different notations. This is based on normalization profiles for each criteria and corresponding weights according to the optimization goals.

D. Application to Disaster Scenarios

Our framework fulfills several points that makes it suitable for disaster communication besides the fact of providing adaptivity. Disaster networks, especially in early stages of any relief mission, are highly heterogeneous and feature intermittent connectivity due to damaged infrastructure or limited communication ranges. At the same time, many users want to communicate either with friends or other affected people, as well as with rescue forces with whatever devices they have available. This adds a high load to the remaining network. In the worst case, this traffic from or to the affected people will however use up valid resources for first responder communication. Therefore, first responders usually provide their own communication network, which is separated from other public communication networks for security reasons.

But affected people can become volunteers, supporting the professional rescuers. In this case, they should have access to the network as well. Besides that, an option to add the devices of affected people for emergency calls is also required, because in this case they are easier to detect and help can be sent faster. Our framework supports both aspects, by allowing legacy nodes to join the network via a suitable *Border Node* acting as gateway. We assume that affected people are equipped with legacy devices, because they most likely did not install any additional software to support our framework just to be prepared for a disaster event.

Using the *Border Nodes* as gateways helps the first responders to become aware of the presence of affected people which might indicate their position and help to rescue them. On the other hand, this gateway can act as traffic shaper to allow the detection of nodes and the placement of emergency calls but limiting other communications to a minimum in order to prevent high traffic by affected people. This could be done by a simple group assignment. Each unauthorized device is assigned to a corresponding group that allows this device to only announce its position and otherwise routes the traffic to the emergency call management. Other destinations are not propagated to these nodes. Once a device has been registered as volunteer, its status changes and it is granted more rights to communicate with further first responders.

With these additional features our framework can ensure reliable and robust communication required during any disaster mission. The core concept here is to provide self-organized adaptivity on the network layer. This ensures the maximum flexibility to various networking conditions, if the selection of any given operation mode is robust.

IV. Simulation and Discussion

In this section, we present simulation results verifing our concept. Simulations were done in the well-known ns-3 [14] in combination with Click [15].

In Figure 4, we show the simulated scenario. We created three subnetworks (routing domains) each with its own active routing protocol. They are connected via Border Nodes translating between the different protocols. In the SEREMA scenario, the first and third routing domain used AODV, while nodes in the second utilized OLSR. Two Border Nodes are used to directly tunnel the reactive control traffic through the OLSR zone [8]. For reason of comparison, we also ran this scenario with AODV and OLSR active on all nodes, respectively.

The simulation was configured to use six data transmissions between areas one and three and in addition one transmission from area one to area two as well as a connection from area two to area three. The rest of the active data transmissions used in the scenarios take place in the proactive routing domain 2.

Each of the simulated routing domains contained 20 nodes with a transmission range of 10 m and a speed of 1-3 m/s. For the movement scenario, we decided to use a Random Waypoint model to not consider special behaviors of specific movement models. The simulated duration of the scenario was 300 s and the results were averaged over ten simulation runs.

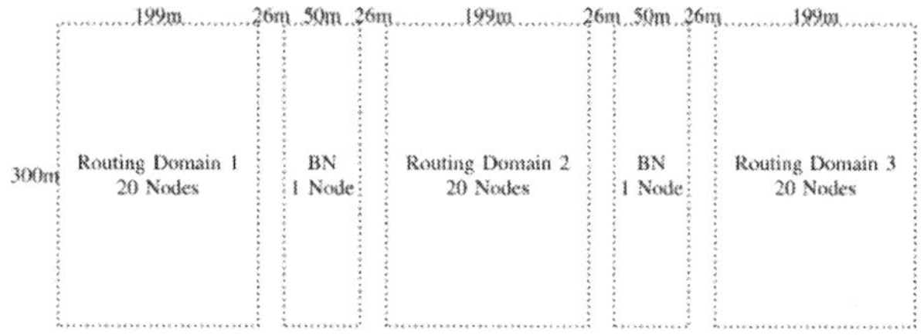

Fig. 4. Simulated Scenario

The first measured parameter is the Packet Delivery Ratio (PDR), showing how successful routes could be established for communication. Figure 5 shows that the gradient of the PDR graph decreases with an increasing number of active data transmissions in the network. This behavior is because in a scenario with a lower number of active data transmissions, the number of received packets increases with the number of sent packets, but if the traffic in the network increases, the percentage of received packets, related to sent packets, decreases. In the simulated scenario, most of the data transmissions take place in routing domain two, which is used by the data transmissions between routing domain one and three for transit. This means that such data packets have to pass a network area with a higher traffic load. Furthermore, it can be seen that in the AODV-only scenario, the PDR is highest, as the reactive routing searches for routes on-demand and therefore delivers the most up-to-date routing information. In this scenario, SEREMA has a higher PDR than OLSR, because of the reactive part of SEREMA which provides better routes than OLSR-only. However, SEREMA cannot reach the performance of AODV in this scenario, because of SEREMA's proactive behavior which produces additional routing traffic in the network.

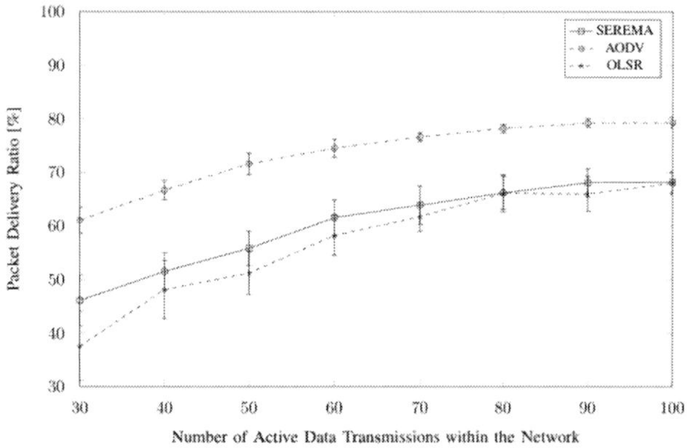

Fig. 5. Comparison between Packet Delivery Ratios

The last parameter we evaluated is the routing overhead related to the overall traffic introduced by the routing protocols as shown in Figure 6. For networks with lower traffic, AODV outperforms OLSR and behaves comparable to SEREMA. However, as soon as the number of active data transmissions in the network increases, AODV generates more routing traffic because of its reactive behavior that emits packets on demand. In this case, the routing overhead ratio of OLSR decreases as the overall traffic in the network increases while the OLSR routing overhead stays more or less constant because of the proactive protocol behavior. SEREMA can outperform both protocols since it benefits from both routing protocols (AODV and OLSR). In routing domain two with a high traffic, it behaves like OLSR and limits the produced routing overhead, while in routing domain one and three which only have a few data transmissions it uses AODV to avoid the periodical static load to the network caused by OLSR. It can be seen that the network benefits from our adaptive routing framework as the routing overhead stays lower, compared to AODV-only as well as OLSR-only networks.

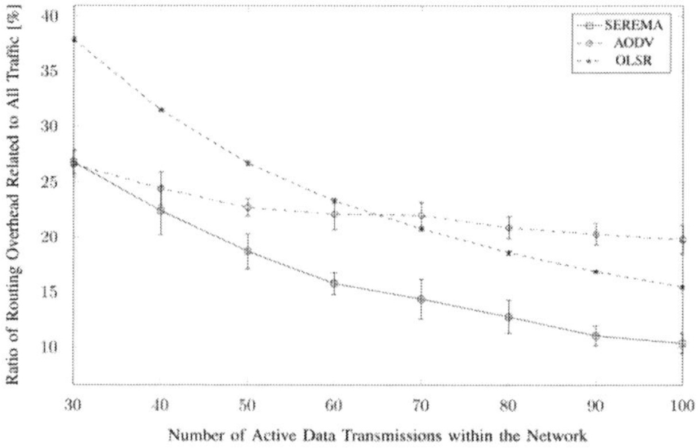

Fig. 6. Comparison between the Routing Overhead

Finally, we evaluated the switching performance of our scoring algorithm (cf. Figure 3). To do that, the resulting decision was evaluated analytically for both protocols. Tables I and II present the corresponding switching matrices. The criteria used are the overhead ratio between routing traffic and data traffic and the neighbor ratio indicating which subset of all neighboring nodes runs the same protocol (cf. Section III-C). In both tables '1' denotes the decision to switch the protocol and '0' to keep the current protocol.

It should be noted that the number of neighboring nodes running the same routing protocol is a ratio here and does not reflect the node density in the network. This commonly used metric for the utilization of reactive or proactive routing schemes will be considered in future versions of our algorithm.

Based on the two metrics currently considered, both tables show that our approach is able to switch the routing protocol under given network conditions. Here, the switching is in general done when few neighboring nodes run the same protocol and depending on the current overhead introduced by the routing protocol, AODV is favored for low overhead cases and OLSR for cases with higher overhead.

TABLE I
SWITCHING DECISION UNDER OLSR

Neighbor Ratio	Overhead Ratio									
	10	20	30	40	50	60	70	80	90	100
0	1	1	1	1	0	0	0	0	0	0
10	1	1	1	1	0	0	0	0	0	0
20	1	1	1	1	0	0	0	0	0	0
30	1	1	1	1	0	0	0	0	0	0
40	1	1	1	1	0	0	0	0	0	0
50	0	0	0	0	0	0	0	0	0	0
60	0	0	0	0	0	0	0	0	0	0
70	0	0	0	0	0	0	0	0	0	0
80	0	0	0	0	0	0	0	0	0	0
90	0	0	0	0	0	0	0	0	0	0
100	0	0	0	0	0	0	0	0	0	0

TABLE II
SWITCHING DECISION UNDER AODV

Neighbor Ratio	Overhead Ratio									
	10	20	30	40	50	60	70	80	90	100
0	0	0	0	0	1	1	1	1	1	1
10	0	0	0	0	1	1	1	1	1	1
20	0	0	0	0	1	1	1	1	1	1
30	0	0	0	0	1	1	1	1	1	1
40	0	0	0	0	1	1	1	1	1	1
50	0	0	0	0	0	0	0	0	0	0
60	0	0	0	0	0	0	0	0	0	0
70	0	0	0	0	0	0	0	0	0	0
80	0	0	0	0	0	0	0	0	0	0
90	0	0	0	0	0	0	0	0	0	0
100	0	0	0	0	0	0	0	0	0	0

If a node detects that it should act as border node, this decision matrix is obsolete as both protocols have to be active in this case.

V. CONCLUSION AND FUTURE WORK

In this paper, we presented our adaptive routing framework SEREMA and discussed relevant design choices required for a common solution in highly dynamic scenarios. Our framework is able to fulfill the resulting requirements by providing distributed decision making and support of legacy nodes.

The framework was implemented and evaluated using ns-3 and click. Simulations showed that adaptive routing in MANETs is an interesting solution if conditions are not constant network wide. Even though we use simplistic scoring criteria, our solution is able to outperform single routing protocols with respect to the analyzed metrics. To overcome the reduced PDR in comparison to pure OLSR, further research is required to identify both the ideal switching point and the relevant metrics.

Future work will therefore include a thorough evaluation of further more realistic metrics and criteria that are characteristic for given network conditions, as well as the impact of these parameters on different routing protocols in order to enhance the performance of our adaptive routing framework. We also plan to incorporate further relevant routing protocols into our framework to enhance the adaptivity to additional conditions and exploit the combination of adaptive routing and Delay Tolerant Networks (DTNs) principles in an hybrid DTN-MANET scenario. Finally, the adaptive approach could be combined with address resolution and service discovery mechanisms as presented by Finke et al. [16]. Such combination of different approaches could provide benefits in terms of lower delay for name resolutions and robustness to node failures.

REFERENCES

[1] T. Finke, "SEREMA Self-Organized Routing in Heterogeneous Mobile Ad Hoc Networks," Dissertation, Technische Universität Ilmenau, 2016.

[2] S. Nanda, Z. Jiang, and D. Kotz, "A Combined Routing Method for Ad Hoc Wireless Networks," Dept. of Computer Science, Dartmouth College, Tech. Rep. TR2009-641, Feb. 2009.

[3] T. Ramrekha and C. Politis, "A Hybrid Adaptive Routing Protocol for Extreme Emergency Ad Hoc Communication," in *19th International Conference on Computer Communications and Networks (ICCCN)*. Zurich, Switzerland: IEEE, Aug. 2010, pp. 1–6.

[4] J. Hoebeke, I. Moerman, and P. Demeester, "Adaptive routing for mobile ad hoc networks," *EURASIP Journal on Wireless Communications and Networking*, no. 2012:216, Mar. 2012.

[5] N. Beijar, "Zone Routing Protocol (ZRP)," *Networking Laboratory Helsinki University of Technology Finland*, vol. 9, no. 4, pp. 427–438, 2001.

[6] T. T. Son, H. Le Minh, and N. Aslam, "MSAR: A metric self-adaptive routing model for Mobile Ad Hoc Networks," *Journal of Network and Computer Applications*, vol. 68, pp. 114–125, Jun. 2016.

[7] K. Kaji and T. Yoshihiro, "Adaptive Rerouting to Avoid Local Congestion in MANETs," in *Wireless Communications and Networking Conference (WCNC)*. San Francisco, CA, USA: IEEE, Mar. 2017, pp. 1–6.

[8] S. Schellenberg, S. Krug, T. Finke, P. Begerow, and J. Seitz, "Inter-Domain Routing and Name Resolution using Border Nodes," in *International Conference on Computing, Networking and Communications (ICNC)*. Anaheim, CA, USA: IEEE, Feb. 2015, pp. 950–956.

[9] C. Perkins, E. Belding-Royer, and S. Das, "Ad hoc On-Demand Distance Vector (AODV) Routing," RFC 3561 (Experimental), Internet Engineering Task Force, Jul. 2003.

[10] T. Clausen and P. Jacquet, "Optimized Link State Routing Protocol (OLSR)," RFC 3626 (Experimental), Internet Engineering Task Force, Oct. 2003.

[11] P. G. Lye and J. C. McEachen, "A Comparison of Optimized Link State Routing with Traditional Ad-hoc Routing Protocols," in *5th Workshop on the Internet, Telecommunications and Signal Processing (WITSP)*. Hobart, Australia: IEEE, Dec. 2006.

[12] J. Haerri, F. Filali, and C. Bonnet, "Performance Comparison of AODV and OLSR in VANETs Urban Environments under RealisticMobility Patterns," in *5th Annual Mediterranean Ad Hoc Networking Workshop (MED-HOCNET)*. Lipari, Italy: IFIP, Jun. 2006.

[13] Y. Yeryomin and J. Seitz, "Enhanced multi-criteria-based path selection algorithm for heterogeneous networks," in *8th International Conference on Ubiquitous and Future Networks (ICUFN)*. Vienna, Austria: IEEE, Jul. 2016, pp. 804–809.

[14] Network Simulator 3 (ns-3). (visited 2017-08-16). [Online]. Available: http://www.nsnam.org/

[15] E. Kohler, R. Morris, B. Chen, J. Jannotti, and M. Kaashoek, "The Click Modular Router," *ACM Transactions on Computer Systems*, pp. 263–297, Aug. 2000.

[16] T. Finke, J. Schroeder, S. Schellenberg, M. Hager, and J. Seitz, "Address Resolution in Mobile Ad Hoc Networks using Adaptive Routing," in *International Conference on Systems and Networks Communications (ICSNC)*. Lisbon, Portugal: IARIA, Nov. 2012, pp. 7–12.

On a Fuzzy AHP Weight for Partial Inner Dependence Structure

Shin-ichi Ohnishi, Takahiro Yamanoi
Faculty of Engineering
Hokkai-Gakuen University
Sapporo, Japan
email: {ohnishi, yamanoi}@hgu.jp

***Abstract* - In a field of decision making for systems that contains human beings, the Analytic Hierarchy Process (AHP) is widely employed. It elicits weights of criteria and alternatives that are independent enough of each other. For cases in which criteria are not independent enough, an extended inner dependence AHP is useful. In this paper, we investigate "partial inner dependence" structure, i.e., only some elements (proper subset) of the criteria are independent. For the partial inner dependence AHP, we propose a new kind of fuzzy weight representation that is valid even if a data matrix is not consistent or reliable enough. Although lots of kinds of fuzzy weight for AHP have been proposed, our new representation can be defined by using the results of two kinds of the sensitivity analyses and they are useful for partial inner dependence structure. We finally show a numerical example of the fuzzy weight for partial inner dependence AHP.**

Keywords* - *AHP; fuzzy set; sensitivity analysis.

I. INTRODUCTION

The Analytic Hierarchy Process (AHP) proposed by T.L. Saaty in 1977 [1] is widely used in decision making because it reflects humans feelings naturally. The normal AHP assumes independence among all criteria, although it is difficult to choose enough independent elements. The inner dependence AHP [2] is used to solve this kind of problem when criteria have dependency. However, inner dependence method requires dependency matrix for all elements even if some criteria are independent. In this research, we employ "partial inner dependence" structure. Our method divides a set of criteria to two subsets, such as a dependent part and an independent part, and then we can easily understand a relation among elements.

On the other hand, the comparison data matrix may not have enough consistency when AHP is applied, because, for instance, a problem may contain too many criteria to make decision. It means that answers from decision-makers, i.e., components of the matrix, do not have enough reliability. They may be too ambiguous or too fuzzy [3][5]. To avoid this issue, we usually have to revise again, but it takes a lot of time and costs. Then, we consider that weights should also have ambiguity or fuzziness. Therefore, it is necessary to represent these weights using fuzzy set.

In our research, we first apply sensitivity analysis to normal AHP to analyze how much the components of a pairwise comparison matrix influence the weight and/or consistency indices of the matrix. Next, we define new fuzzy weight representation of criteria for partial inner dependence AHP using L-R fuzzy numbers [4][6][7][8]. At last, we then propose overall fuzzy weight of alternatives when a comparison matrix among elements does not have enough consistency. Though a main idea of representing fuzzy weight for inner dependence structure was proposed by authors several years ago, we extend this representation to partial inner dependence.

In Sections 2 and 3, we introduce the partial inner dependence AHP, consistency index and sensitivity analyses for AHP. Then, in Section 4, we define fuzzy weight for partial inner dependence structure, Section 5 is a numerical example, and Section 6 is a summary.

II. CONSISTENCY AND INNER DEPENDENCE

In this section, we introduce the processes of the normal AHP, its consistency and inner dependence extension.

A. Normal AHP

Usually, the AHP consists of following 4 processes.

(Process 1) Representation of structure by a hierarchy. The problem under consideration can be represented in a hierarchical structure. At the middle levels, there are multiple criteria. Alternative elements are put at the lowest level of the hierarchy.

(Process 2) Paired comparison between elements at each level. A pairwise comparison matrix A is created from a decision maker's answers. Let n be the number of elements at a certain level, the upper triangular components of the matrix a_{ij} ($i< j = 1,\ldots,n$) are 9, 8, .. , 2, 1, 1/2, ..., or 1/9. These denote intensities of importance from element i to j. The lower triangular components a_{ji} are described with reciprocal numbers, for diagonal elements, let $a_{ii} = 1$.

(Process 3) Calculations of weight at each level. The weights of the elements, which represent grades of importance among each element, are calculated from the pairwise comparison matrix. The eigenvector that corresponds to a positive normalized (so as sum of components is 1) eigenvalue of the matrix is used in calculations throughout in the paper.

(Process 4) Priority of an alternative by a composition of weights. With repetition of composition of weights, the overall weights of the alternative, which are the priorities of the alternatives with respect to the overall objective, are finally found.

B. Consistency

Since components of the comparison matrix are obtained by comparisons between two elements, coherent consistency is not guaranteed. In AHP, the consistency of the comparison matrix A is measured by the following consistency index (C.I.)

$$\text{C.I.} = \frac{\lambda_A - n}{n-1}, \tag{1}$$

where n is the order of comparison matrix A, and λ_A is its maximum eigenvalue (Frobenius root).

If the value of C.I. becomes smaller, then the degree of consistency becomes higher, and vice versa. It is said that the comparison matrix is consistent if $\text{C.I.} \leq 0.1$.

C. Partial Inner Dependence Method

The normal AHP ordinarily assumes independency among criteria, although it is difficult to choose enough independent elements in practice. The dependency means some kind of interaction among the elements. Inner dependence AHP [2] is used to solve this type of problem even for the case that criteria have dependency.

In the inner dependence method, using a dependency matrix $F=\{ f_{ij} \}$, we can calculate modified weights $w^{(n)}$ as follows,

$$w^{(n)}=Fw \tag{2}$$

where w represents weights from independent criteria, i.e., normalized weight of normal AHP and dependency matrix F consists of eigenvectors of influence matrices that represent dependency among criteria. However, inner dependence method requires dependency matrix for all elements even if some criteria are independent. In this research, we employ "partial inner dependence" structure, and then we can easily understand a relation among elements.

In a partial inner dependence AHP, we can divide a criteria set $C=\{X_1, X_2, ..., X_n\}$ to two subsets, dependent part $C_a=\{X_1^{(a)}, X_2^{(a)}, ..., X_{n1}^{(a)}\}$ and independent part $C_b=\{X_1^{(b)}, X_2^{(b)}, ..., X_{n2}^{(b)}\}$, $n_1+n_2=n$, they are determined whether the element is independent criterion or not. Let weights of C_a be $w^{(a)}=(w_{i_1}^{(a)}),\ i_1=1,\dots,n_1$, and weight of C_b be $w^{(b)}=(w_{i_2}^{(b)}),\ i_2=1,\dots,n_2$.

First, we calculate modified weight of dependent criteria subset $w^{(an)}=(w_{i_1}^{(an)})$, using dependency matrix F as follows:

$$w^{(an)}=Fw^{(a)}. \tag{3}$$

Then, the partial crisp (i.e. not fuzzy yet) weight $w^{(pn)}=(w_i^{(pn)}),\ i=1,\dots,n$ is made by the following connection.

$$w^{(pn)}=(w_1^{(an)},\dots,w_{n_1}^{(an)},w_1^{(b)},\dots,w_{n_2}^{(b)}) \tag{4}$$

Using this modified criterion weight, we can easily calculate the priority of alternatives, i.e., overall weight of alternatives with respect to overall objective.

III. SENSITIVITY ANALYSES

When we use AHP in some applications, it often occurs that a comparison matrix is not consistent or that there is not great difference among the overall weights of the alternatives. In these cases, it is very important to investigate how components of the pairwise comparison matrix influence its consistency or the weights. In this study, we use a method that some of the present authors have proposed before. It evaluates a fluctuation of the consistency index and the weights when the comparison matrix is perturbed. It is useful because it does not change the structure of the data.

Since the pairwise comparison matrix is a positive square matrix, Perron-Frobenius theorem holds. From Perron-Frobenius theorem, the following theorem about a perturbed comparison matrix holds.

Theorem 1 *Let $A=(a_{ij})$, $(i, j = 1,\dots, n)$ denote a comparison matrix and let $A(\varepsilon) = A+\varepsilon D_A$, $D_A=(a_{ij}d_{ij})$ denote a matrix that has been perturbed. Let λ_A be the Frobenius root of A, w be the eigenvector corresponding to λ_A, and v be the eigenvector corresponding to the Frobenius root of transposed A'. Then, a Frobenius root $\lambda(\varepsilon)$ of $A(\varepsilon)$ and a corresponding eigenvector $w(\varepsilon)$ can be expressed as follows*

$$\lambda(\varepsilon)=\lambda_A+\varepsilon\lambda^{(1)}+o(\varepsilon), \tag{5}$$

$$w(\varepsilon)=w+\varepsilon w^{(1)}+o(\varepsilon), \tag{6}$$

where

$$\lambda^{(1)}=\frac{v' D_A w}{v' w}, \tag{7}$$

$w^{(1)}$ is an n-dimension vector that satisfies

$$(A-\lambda_A I)w^{(1)}=-(D_A-\lambda^{(1)}I)w, \tag{8}$$

where $\boldsymbol{o}(\varepsilon)$ *denotes an n-dimension vector in which all components are* $o(\varepsilon)$.

About a fluctuation of the consistency index, the following corollaries hold.

Corollary 1 *Using appropriate* g_{ij}, *we can represent the consistency index* C.I.(ε) *of the perturbed comparison matrix* $A(\varepsilon)$ *as follows*

$$\text{C.I.}(\varepsilon) = \text{C.I.} + \varepsilon \sum_i^n \sum_j^n g_{ij} d_{ij} + o(\varepsilon). \quad (9)$$

To see g_{ij} in (9) in Corollary 1, we can determine how the components of a comparison matrix impart influence on its consistency.

Corollary 2 *Using appropriate* $h_{ij}^{(k)}$, *we can represent the fluctuation* $\boldsymbol{w}^{(1)}=(w_k^{(1)})$ *of the weight (i.e., the eigenvector corresponding to the Frobenius root) as follows*

$$w_k^{(1)} = \sum_i^n \sum_j^n h_{ij}^{(k)} d_{ij}. \quad (10)$$

Then, we can evaluate how the components of a comparison matrix impart influence on the weights, to see $h_{ij}^{(k)}$ in (10).

Proofs of these corollaries are shown in [4].

IV. Fuzzy Weight Representation

When a comparison matrix has poor consistency (i.e., 0.1<C.I.<0.2), components of the comparison matrix are considered to be fuzzy because they are results from human fuzzy judgment. Therefore, weight should be treated as fuzzy numbers [4][6].

Definition 1 (fuzzy weight) Let $w_k^{(pn)}$, $k=1,\dots,n$, be a crisp weight of criterion k of partial inner dependence model, and g_{ij} | $h_{ij}^{(k)}$| denote the coefficients found in Corollary 1 and 2. If 0.1<C.I.<0.2, then a fuzzy weight of partial inner dependence criteria $\tilde{\boldsymbol{w}}^{(pn)} = (\tilde{w}_k^{(pn)}), k=1,\dots,n$ can be defined by

$$\tilde{w}_k^{(pn)} = (w_k^{(pn)}, \alpha_k, \beta_k)_{LR} \quad (11)$$

where

$$\alpha_k = \text{C.I.} \sum_i^n \sum_j^n s(-, h_{ij}^{(k)}) g_{ij} \mid h_{ij}^{(k)} \mid, \quad (12)$$

$$\beta_k = \text{C.I.} \sum_i^n \sum_j^n s(+, h_{ij}^{(k)}) g_{ij} \mid h_{ij}^{(k)} \mid, \quad (13)$$

The definition above is an extension of fuzzy weight representation for independent structure [4]. Therefore, we can use this definition for dependent and independent elements part both.

Using the above definition, the overall fuzzy weight of alternative l ($l=1,\dots,m$) can be calculated as follows:

$$\tilde{v}_l = \sum_k^n \tilde{w}_k^{(pn)} u_{kl} \quad (14)$$

where u_{kl}, $k=1,\dots,n$, $l=1,\dots,m$ is weight of the l-th alternatives with only respect to the criterion k.

V. Numerical Example

In this section, we show an example of "Leisure in holiday with family" having 4 criteria and 4 alternatives. Criteria are {popularity, good for rain (rain), fatigue, expense} and alternatives are {theme park (park), indoor theme park (indoor), cinema, zoo}.

Table I shows a comparison matrix of criteria and normal weight, where its consistency is not so good (C.I. >0.1). Then using results of sensitivity analyses of consistency and weights, we can calculate fuzzy weights. There is a partial inner dependence between only 2 criteria (popularity and expense). Dependency matrix between popularity and expense is shown in Table II. Therefore, using a dependency matrix of criteria (TABLE II) and results of sensitivity analyses, modified fuzzy weight are obtained as shown in TABLE III. For partial inner dependence structure, centers of popularity and expense are changed.

TABLE IV shows weights of alternatives with only respect to criteria and consistency index. There is consistency in all criteria. Finally, using composition (14), we evaluate overall fuzzy weights of alternatives in TABLE V.

TABLE I. Comparison Matrix

	popularity	rain	fatigue	expense	*weight*
popularity	1.000	0.500	5.000	0.333	0.214
rain	2.000	1.000	2.000	0.333	0.226
fatigue	0.200	0.500	1.000	0.333	0.092
expense	3.000	3.000	3.000	1.000	0.469

C.I.= 0.134

TABLE II. Dependency Matrix of Criteria F

	popularity	excpense
popularity	0.800	0.400
expense	0.200	0.600

TABLE III. Modified Fuzzy Weight of Criteria.

	Center	*Spread(L)*	*Spread(R)*
popularity	0.358	*0.0079*	*0.0080*
rain	0.226	*0.0072*	*0.0071*
fatigue	0.092	*0.0052*	*0.0024*
expense	0.324	*0.0014*	*0.0043*

TABLE IV. LOCAL WEIGHT OF ALTERNATIVES AND ITS CONSISTENCY

	popularity	rain	fatigue	excpense
park	0.333	0.206	0.112	0.134
indoor	0.105	0.165	0.305	0.313
cinema	0.154	0.499	0.517	0.435
zoo	0.408	0.130	0.067	0.113
C.I.	0.032	0.69	0.012	0.039

TABLE V. OVERALL FUZZY WEIGHT OF ALTERNATIVES

	Center	*Spread(L)*	*Spread(R)*
park	0.219	*0.0007*	*0.0007*
indoor	0.204	*0.0005*	*0.0005*
cinema	0.357	*0.0011*	*0.0011*
zoo	0.218	*0.0006*	*0.0006*

From overall weight of alternatives, we can make fuzzy decision in partial inner dependence structure.

VI. CONCLUSION AND FUTURE WORK

There are many cases in which data of AHP does not have enough consistency or reliability and structure of a problem does not contain complete independent criteria. For these cases, we propose a fuzzy weight representation and compositions for incomplete inner dependence structure using results of sensitivity analyses and fuzzy set. Although lots of kinds of fuzzy weight for AHP have been proposed, our new representation can be defined by using the results of two kinds of the sensitivity analyses and they are useful for partial inner dependence structure. Our example can not only show how to represent weight of criteria and alternatives, but also makes it possible to investigate how the result of AHP has fuzziness even if data are not consistent or reliable enough.

In the next step, we will compare the partial inner dependence AHP and the normal AHP with real data.

REFERENCES

[1] T. L. Saaty, The Analytic Hierarchy Process. McGraw-Hill, New York, 1980.

[2] T. L. Saaty, Inner and Outer Dependence in AHP, University of Pittsburgh, 1991

[3] D. Dubois and H. Prade, Possibility Theory An Approach to Computerized Processing of Uncertainty, Plenum Press, New York (1988)

[4] S. Ohnishi, H. Imai, and M. Kawaguchi, "Evaluation of a Stability on Weights of Fuzzy Analytic Hierarchy Process using a sensitivity analysis," J. Japan Soc. for Fuzzy Theory and Sys., 9(1), Jan. 1997, pp.140-147.

[5] S. Ohnishi, D. Dubois, H. Prade, and T. Yamanoi, "A Fuzzy Constraint-based Approach to the Analytic Hierarchy Process," Uncertainty and Intelligent Information Systems, June 2008, pp.217-228.

[6] S. Ohnishi, T. Yamanoi, and H. Imai, "A Fuzzy Weight Representation for Inner Dependence AHP," Journal of Advanced Computational Intelligence and Intelligent Informatics, Vol.15, No.3, June 2011, pp. 329-335.

[7] S. Ohnishi and T. Yamanoi, " Applying Fuzzy weights to Triple Inner Dependence AHP," DBKDA2015, June 2015, pp. 104-106.

[8] S. Ohnishi and T. Yamanoi, " Fuzzy Weight Representation for Double Inner Dependence Structure in 4 Levels AHP," MODOPT2016, May 2016, pp. 70-72.

A Mobile Learning Combinative Application for Comparing Educational Techniques

Kiriakos Patriarcheas
School of Sciences and Technology, Computer Science
Hellenic Open University
Patras, Greece
e-mail: k.patriac@eap.gr

***Abstract*—This article focuses on the e-learning fora of with the purpose of comparing educational techniques widely used in the fields (such as Snowballing and Brainstorming) in a combined environment both via mobile and computer devices, in the framework of a training course in advanced technologies integration skills computer instructors. For the purpose of this study, modeling in formal language was used to classify the messages in the Moodle forum, as well as a respective system to automate this procedure.**

***Keywords-** e-learning; mobile learning; education ;educational techniques; modelling; advanced technologies integration skills*

I. Introduction

Over recent years, the rapid development of mobile devices has made possible the support of educational applications in e-learning to the extent that the term m-learning (mobile learning) has now been established as a relatively autonomous field with distinct features as to the means used compared to e-learning in general. The main feature of e-learning is that there is physical distance between the trainee and the instructor. Therefore, communication is important for the success of an e-learning course. Extremely useful tools used by e-learning are the fora that provide the opportunity for asynchronous communication not only between the instructor and the trainees, but also between trainees themselves. During the past twenty years, a multitude of systems that offer the critical service of asynchronous fora for e-learning have been developed, such as: Manhattan Virtual Classroom (MVC), Moodle, Claronline, Online Learning and Training (OLAT), Cisco Networking Academy Management System (CNAMS), Pioneer (Microelectronics Educational Development - University of Paisley), AulaNet, etc. Furthermore, over the recent years, the development of mobile devices has made possible the support of educational applications (MSN Messenger, Gmail, etc.) to the extent that the term m-learning (mobile learning) is now a significant field of e-learning with distinct features as to the means used.

Moreover, field researchers have been interested in a basic issue during these past twenty years: how they can have, at each given moment, an overall picture of the situation in a number of discussion threads in a e-learning forum, not just at a quantitative level of participation, but at the quality level of what is discussed and whether the desirable learning climate is achieved through the discussion in the fora. This paper presents a study that compares educational techniques (Snowballing and Brainstorming), in the asynchronous forum Moodle through the use of a combined environment, both via computer and mobile devices in a training course in in advanced technologies integration skills computer instructors. It is worthy to note here that, for this study, the previous practical and research experience was utilized within the framework of Hellenic Open University (HOU) and concerns, among other things, previous projects related to the attitude of HOU students [1][2], as well as fora modeling as a methodology for the interpretation of messages [3].

The structure of this article is the following: Section II, where a brief literature review is presented. In section III, the study methodology is presented. In section IV, the data analysis is presented. In section V, the respective discussion takes place and the results are presented, which are combined with the conclusions of relative studies and finally section VII, where the major conclusions and the future goals are presented.

II. Literature Review

There are a number of studies about the use of mobile devices in e-learning. Indicatively, Nonyongo, Mabusela, & Monene [4] studied the reliability and effectiveness of communication through messages, as a complementary form of communication for the students of the distance education University of South Africa (UNISA), as an opportunity in communicating and providing support for their students who in their majority live in rural areas and informal settlements with limited infrastructure, while Nakahara et al. [5] study the encouragement provided to collaborative learning environments through mobile technology. Gerosa et al. [6] focused on the improvement of coordination support in educational forums using mobile devices through patterns in discussion groups, while Wang et al. [7] researched the impact of mobile learning on students' learning behaviours and performance. Rekkedal & Dye [8] present an in depth presentation of the pedagogical dimension of mobile distance learning, while Kukulska-Hulme [9] studied mobile usability in educational environments and discovered that it is dependent on human factors. These indicative studies show the ever growing importance of mobile learning and demarcate a distinct role in the broader framework of e-learning. Gikas & Grant [10] focus on exploring teaching and learning when mobile computing devices, such as mobile phones and smartphones, have been applied to higher education. Lai et al. [11] investigates the differences between mobile learning environmental preferences of high school teachers and students. Bannan, Cook, & Pachler [12] examine how the intersection of mobile learning and design research, prompts the reconceptualization of research and design individually as well as their integration appropriate for current, complex learning environments.

In the field of fora in e-leraning, a subject researchers have been focusing on in the past years (as well as coordinators and tutors) is how we can have, at any given moment, an overall picture of the situation in a number of threads about what is being discussed and whether the creation of the desirable learning climate is achieved through discussion in the fora [13]–[16]. Dringus & Elis [17] seek to intersect the information an instructor may wish to extract from the forum, with viewable and useful information that the system could produce from the instructor's query. Romero, Ventura & Garcia [18] describes the full process for mining e-learning data, as well as, how to apply the main data mining techniques used, such as statistics, visualization, classification, clustering and association rule mining of Moodle data. Furthermore, Romero & Ventura [19] describes the different groups of user, types of educational environments, and the data they provide, as well as, the most typical/common tasks in the educational environment, that have been resolved through data-mining techniques.

There are numerous studies on educational techniques used in e-learning fora some of which concern educational techniques such as Snowballing and Brainstorming. Indicatively, concerning Brainstorming technique Pinsonnealt et al. [20] adopt the term Electronic Brainstorming (EBS) addressing that "it has been proposed as a superior approach to both nominal Brainstorming (working alone) and face-to-face Brainstorming (verbal)". There are studies that try to particularise in subcategories the Brainstorming technique, namely Camacho & Paulus [21], refer to solitary Brainstorming, while Helquist et al. [22] to "very large groups" of Brainstorming, and studies which examine the creativity [23] or the productivity [24] in a web-based context of asynchronous electronic Brainstorming groups. Offner et al. [25] explored the unblocking Brainstorming. Finally, Dugosh et al. [26] examine the potential of cognitive stimulation in Brainstorming technique.

With regard to the Snowballing technique Thomas & Carswell [27] use it in their effort to assess the role of collaborative learning in a distributed education environment within the framework of a relative research of the Open University of London, highlighting that it offers essential support for students studying at a distance. Kember & Gow [28] also evaluate it when studying the action research as a form of staff development in higher education, in attempting to improve their own teaching through cycles of planning, acting, observing and reflecting.

In summary, it is concluded that despite the fact that there is a multitude of studies on the mobile dimension of e-learning, and other studies referring to educational techniques, such as Snowballing and Brainstorming that are widely used in e-learning fora, a void is detected however in the comparison of educational techniques through processes that use a combined environment with a computer and mobile devices.

III. Methodological Framework

A. *Sample*

This research was conducted from October 2016 to February 2017, in 8 training computer instructors' centers of Greece. The sample consisted of 144 instructors-trainees', at the areas of Attica (3 Centers), Central Greece, Thessaly, Western Greece, Peloponnesus and Crete within the framework of a training course in advanced technologies integration skills computer instructors. All trainees were of the same level of knowledge. Evaluated were the discussion threads on forum (in all 2498 messages).

B. *Method*

The trainees were grouped in 8 groups of 18 people; there was an effort to form all groups absolutely uniform as far as the members' education profile was concerned (age, sex, experience, etc.) Supporting material with the concepts to be presented, as well as a manual with the commands of the 5 modules of the course (IHMC Cmap tools, Edison for the creation of electrical circuits, Java Virtual Machine, Scratch and Java applets for Ph.E.T.) were available via Internet before the beginning of the course. Training was based upon the Moodle forum, with the use of a combined environment via internet and mobile devices. Furthermore, after the end of each of the 5 modules of the course, a self-evaluation test was completed by the trainees. The aforementioned educational procedure is mainly applied by HOU in Greece.

At this point, it should be noted that the standard instructions for designing applications for Mobile devices were followed, as described in the mobile best web practice document of the World Wide Web Consortium (W3C).

C. *Activities*

The lesson plans distributed to the trained to be developed, should comprise: a) title for the hourly module b) the goals of the course (as for knowledge, skills, attitudes), c) sub-units, (parts into which teaching shall be divided) and time used for each one, d) educational techniques and teaching aids to be used for each sub-unit and e) justification of the above choices. The lesson plans concerned the creation of 5 exercises of each object IHMC Cmap tools, Edison for the creation of electrical circuits, Java Virtual Machine, Scratch and Java applets for Ph.E.T).

D. *Procedure*

During the asynchronous discussion on the forum it was decided to use the educational techniques of Snowballing and Brainstorming. More specifically the Snowballing technique was used in four groups while the Brainstorming was used in the other four.

In the case of the Snowballing technique, it was chosen so that views were exchanged in order to advance and expand the trainees' consideration as far as the advanced technologies integration skills is concerned. In particular, the procedure which took place exclusively through the Moodle forum and was repeated in each course of the program was the following: a) The trainees had the opportunity to comment on the issues of the concepts' teaching approach in advanced technologies integration skills they faced b) Then each trained person compared their comments to another (by creating threads of 3 people) c) The same procedure was repeated in groups of six and d) At the end of the procedure all the trainees of the group participated (18) presenting all the views in a plenary session and they tried to compose their views and to reach conclusions, as they did in Brainstorming technique. At this point it is advisable to present the modeling used.

As for the Brainstorming, the procedure intended to the exposure of numerous sides of the issue of advanced technologies integration skills, the knowledge enrichment of the trained and finally the consolidation or change of their opinions. In particular, the procedure which took place exclusively through the Moodle forum and was repeated in each course of the program was the following: a) They all participated in the same thread and each one was stimulated to express her/his own ideas in a spontaneous way even if their ideas seemed unrealistic at a first level without being necessary (at this phase) to explain them and without criticizing any of them b) The tutor codified all ideas and presented them in a uniform manner c) Each trainee was asked to explain or even modify (if they wanted) their initial placement d) At the end of the procedure, it was stimulated to compose the opinions and to reach conclusions as for the compilation of lesson plans.

E. Modelling

Based on observations at the HOU fora, the following became evident: a) There are two categories of communication actors: Tutors and Students. For brevity, tutors will be symbolised with a *T* and students with an *S* b) As regards message types, these are distinguished into questions and answers. Hereinafter, symbolised with *q* and *a* respectively c) As to their content, messages are distinguished into those relating to (the respective symbols are given in brackets): i) study of educational material (*M*), ii) questions/answers for exercises – assignments (*X*), iii) presentation of sample assignments by tutors (*P*), iv) instructions (*I*), v) assignment comments, corrections (*C*), vi) student comments on assignments (*D*), vii) sending – receiving assignments (*J*), viii) sending - receiving grade marks (*G*), ix) notification of advisory meeting (*V*) and x) pointless message (*L*).

Finally, the order in which the above symbols will be written is: a) message carrier b) message type and c) the content of the category to which the message belongs. A message concerning a student's question for an assignment is represented as: *SqX* (where *S* for student, *q* for question and *X* for the fact that this message is about an assignment). An indicative example is presented that contains a series of messages represented by the sequence *SqVMTaVMSqMXSaXM*, which represent a discussion thread as follows: in the beginning is a message whose sender is student *S* who is asking a question *q* referring to forthcoming advisory meeting *V* and also concerning the study of educational material *M*. This message is replied to by tutor *T* who is answering *a* referring to forthcoming advisory meeting *V* and also about the study of educational material *M*. This message is replied to by student *S* who is asking a question *q* concerning the study of educational material *M* and also about the forthcoming assignment *X*. This message is replied to by another student *S* who is answering *a* about the forthcoming assignment *X* and also about the study of educational material *M*. As it is obvious this modeling uses a formal language. Additionally, it should be noted that for this Language syntax check algorithm was used, as well as a respective system to automate this procedure by inserting threads from discussion fora and exporting the respective strings.

According to this approach, a system of automatic classification [29]-[33] was used, which comprised the following steps: Data filtering, Storage of roots files and Strings' production. In data filtering process, an algorithm was used, that would input a file containing one or more discussion threads in their original form and output a file of documents containing the following information (User name, date, message content). In the second stage (Storage of roots files) an algorithm of roots export of words was used, that produces the result with one parsing and removes the endings based on the Quick Fitting (QF) principle. In Strings' production stage, was used a process that inputs: a) the records file containing useful information (User name, date, message content); b) the file containing pairs of word/phrase roots or symbols and terminal symbols relating to the type of message; and c) the file containing the pairs of words/phrases and terminal symbols referring to the content category of the message. This system was tested experimentally using a combination of algorithms, such as: AdaBoost, Naive Bayes, 1-Nearest, and WINNOW. Subsequently, was followed a calibration process of repeated readjustment, and the results was deemed satisfactory (98.92% correct message interpretation in present case).

IV. Data Analysis

In groups 1, 2, 3 and 4, where the Snowballing technique was used, we received 1119 messages; 81 from the instructors and 1038 from trainees while, as far as content categories are concerned we had 1685 appearances in all. In groups 5, 6, 7 and 8, where the Brainstorming technique was utilized, we received 1379 messages; 115 were from the instructors and 1264 from the trainees. Given that, according to the above modeling, more than one category of content may be included in each message (e.g. the same message may be a question on the study of educational material as well as a project too), 2788 such questions were confirmed. The above information is presented in Table I.

TABLE I. APPEARANCES NUMBER (AN) PER MESSAGE CONTENT CATEGORY (CC)

Content Category	Groups 1, 2, 3 and 4 (Snowballing)	Groups 5, 6 , 7 and 8 (Brainstorming)
M	288	652
X	356	781
P	44	47
I	41	59
C	201	272
D	256	380
J	357	360
G	37	36
V	33	32
L	72	169
Total	**1685**	**2788**

It is obvious "Figure 1" that there is a respective uniformity per message content category but with a different intension.

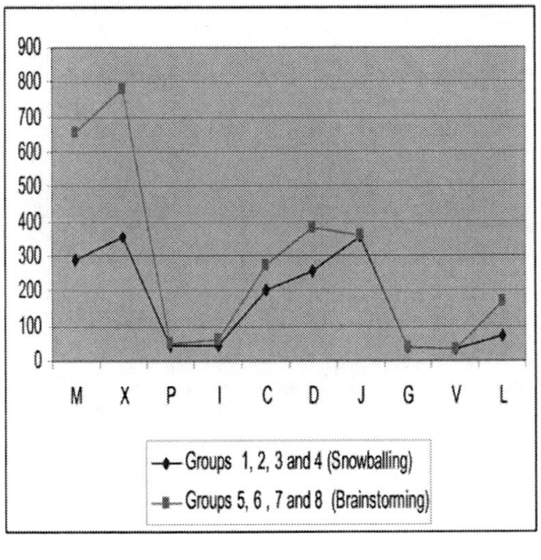

Figure 1. Graphic representation of Snowballing and Brainstorming techniques.

If we take into account only interventions of trainees, then we have 879 appearances for Snowballing groups. This arises from the deduction the tutor's interventions and the said "service type" of interventions, i.e. the categories presentation of sample assignments by tutors (P), assignment comments, corrections (C), sending – receiving assignments (J), sending - receiving grade marks (G), notification of advisory meeting (V) which function as separate variables according to the initial plan, as well as the tutor's interventions appearing on the remaining content categories. The respective numbers of appearances for Brainstorming groups are 1889. The above information is presented in Table II.

TABLE II. APPEARANCES NUMBER (AN) PER MESSAGE CONTENT CATEGORY (CC) WITHOUT THE TUTOR'S INTERVENTIONS

Content Category	Groups 1, 2, 3 and 4 (Snowballing)	Groups 5, 6 , 7 and 8 (Brainstorming)
M	241	605
X	311	735
D	255	380
L	72	169
Total	**879**	**1889**

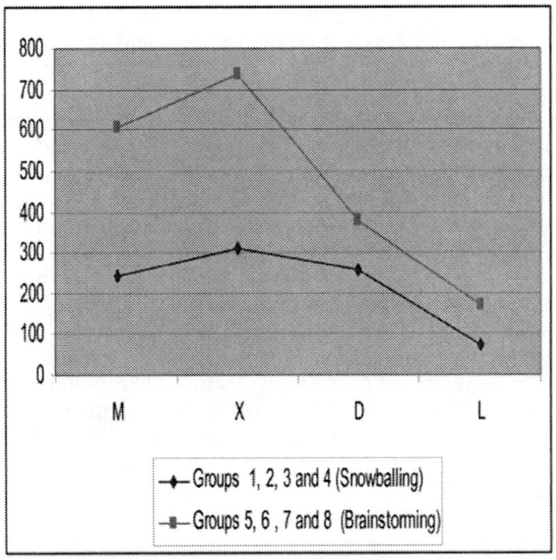

Figure 2. Graphic representation of the distributions of Snowballing and Brainstorming techniques containing only the trainees interventions.

It is obvious "Figure 2" that the difference in participation increases when the tutor's intervention reduces.

V. DISCUSSION

According to the data analysis, in groups where Brainstorming was used, higher participation at forum is noted, compared to Snowballing in both as for messages (1379 against 1119) and range of content categories (2788 against 1685). Furthermore, if from this number the content categories P, J, G, V are deducted, as well as the tutor's interventions, which in our case constitute separate variables, then the discrepancy (respectively) increases even more (1889 against 879). Moreover, even if we deduct the needless messages (L), then the discrepancy of participation (in educationally substantial categories) is 1720 against 807.

In the case of the Brainstorming in relation to the Snowballing, enforcement of the creativity and the participants' experiences is noted; this finding arises from practical experience and messages' texts analysis as well as from the fact that we have 605 against 241 and 735 against 311 for the categories: study of educational material (M) and questions/answers for exercises assignments (X) respectively. In addition, improvement of critical thinking is noted (category: student comments on assignments (D): 380 against 255).

On the other hand, in Brainstorming technique the phenomenon of more needless messages arises, i.e., off topic interventions (169 against 72). Despite the fact that it can be quantitatively proven, meanwhile the observation and study of messages' contents offers (in a quite small extent) a show of imagination by a smaller percentage of participants in Brainstorming technique, in contradiction to Snowballing technique. This may be explained given the fact the Snowballing technique is more "disciplined".

As it can also be seen in Tables I and II, a slightly uniform distribution to both techniques is noted, as far as where the attention is during the forum discussions, both throughout all the messages and also to those remaining if we deduct the messages functioning as separate variables. It becomes thus obvious that *(X)* category: questions/answers for exercises – assignments comes first (781 and 735 against 356 and 311), followed by the *(M)* category: study of educational material (652 and 605 against 288 and 241).

Even though, as mentioned above, there is a void regarding the comparison of the educational techniques of Snowballing and Brainstorming through processes that use a combined environment with computer and mobile devices for e-learning, yet there are relevant studies referring to these techniques individually. When studying the results of this study, we had in mind that the educational practices are regarded as social practices to be changed through collaborative action [28]. On the high percentage of participation in Brainstorming, despite seeming presumable, at first it is not always so, given that "a poorly crafted Brainstorming input creates a cognitive load that consumes attention resources and may stifle the Brainstorming process" [22], while according to Michinov and Primois [23] participation is encouraged "only when participants have access to a shared table facilitating the comparison among group members". As for the ascertainment of educational participation of Brainstorming in this study, it is at first, in contrast to a respective study [20] where it is highlighted that "the prevailing popularity of group Brainstorming (verbal or electronic) in organizations may be explained by the perceived productivity" and that "these perceptions, which are at odds with reality, create the illusion of productivity"; but Camacho & Paulus [21], who, despite ascertaining the same, however explain that "part of the productivity loss observed in interactive Brainstorming groups may be due to the inhibited performance of individuals who are uncomfortable with group interaction"; Michinov and Primois [23] are of similar opinion. This conclusion is also reached by a respective study [26] where it is noted that "the attentional set of the participant and the content of the exposure manipulation (number of ideas, presence of irrelevant information) affected its effectiveness". To the above, we must add that similar results regarding the increased participation of Brainstorming compared to Snowballing appear in a relevant study on training of programming didactics for informatics high schools teachers [34].

VI. Conclusion & Future Goals

The development of a plethora of systems that provide the service of asynchronous e-learning fora the development of mobile devices and their use in education creates a new landscape the recent years in education, which needs to be studied from many aspects. This paper focuses on the comparison of educational techniques that are widely used in the e-learning fora (such as Brainstorming and Snowballing) through a combined environment via computer and mobile devices, in the framework of a training course in the advanced technologies integration skills of computer instructors. As is deduced, both from data analysis, as well as from the study of the text messages in the Moodle forum, the groups where Brainstorming technique was utilized show higher participation at the forum than those utilizing the Snowballing technique. Additionally, a better enforcement of the participants' critical thinking is noted. On the other hand, in Snowballing technique it is noted that quite less time is spent and there are no off topic interventions in relation to Brainstorming.

Among other things, future goals are the comparison of the remaining educational techniques that are used in e-learning as well as the study of dimensions that affect the effectiveness of asynchronous fora, such as the size of the group of participants through relevant environments.

References

[1] M. Xenos, C. Pierrakeas, and P. Pintelas, "A Survey on Student Dropout Rates and Dropout Causes Concerning the Students in the Course of Informatics of the Hellenic Open University", Computers & Education, vol. 39, pp. 361-377, Dec. 2002.

[2] M. Xenos, "Prediction and Assessment of Student Behaviour in Open and Distance Education in Computers using Bayesian Networks", Computers & Education, vol. 43, pp. 345-359, Dec. 2004.

[3] K. Patriarcheas and M. Xenos, "Modelling of distance education forum: Formal languages as interpretation methodology of messages in asynchronous text-based discussion", Computers & Education, vol. 52, pp. 438-448, Feb. 2009.

[4] E. Nonyongo, K. Mabusela, and V. Monene, "Effectiveness of SMS communication between university and students" The 4th World Conference on Mobile Learning (M-Learn), Cape Town, 2005. [Online]. Available: http://iamlearn.org/mlearn-archive/mlearn2005/CD/papers/Nonyongo%26%20Mabusela.pdf

[5] J. Nakahara, Y. Kazaru, H. Shinichi, and Y. Yamauchi, "iTree: Does the mobile phone encourage learners to be more involved in collaborative learning?" In T. Koschmann, T. Chan, D. Suthers (Eds), Proc. CSCL 2005, pp. 470–478, LEA editions, USA.

[6] M. A. Gerosa, D. Filippo, M. Pimentel, H. Fuks, and C. J. P. Lucena, "Is the unfolding of the group discussion off-pattern? Improving

coordination support in educational forums using mobile devices", Computers & Education, vol. 54, pp. 528-544, Feb. 2010.

[7] M. J. Wang, R.M. Shen, D. Novak, and X. Y. Pan, "The Impact of Mobile Learning on Learning Behaviors and Performance: Report from a Large Blended Classroom", British Journal of Educational Technology, vol. 38, pp. 294-311, Mar. 2007.

[8] T. Rekkedal and A. Dye, "Mobile Distance Learning with PDAs: Development and Testing of Pedagogical and System Solutions Supporting Mobile Distance Learners", International Review of Research in Open and Distance Learning, , vol. 8, pp. 1-21, Jun. 2007.

[9] A. Kukulska-Hulme, "Mobile Usability in Educational Contexts: What Have We Learnt?" The International Review of Research in Open and Distance Learning, vol. 8, p. 1-16, Jun. 2007.

[10] J. Gikas and M. M. Grant (2013). "Mobile computing devices in higher education: Student perspectives on learning with cellphones, smartphones & social media", The Internet and Higher Education, vol. 19, pp. 18-26, Oct. 2013.

[11] C. L. Lai, G. J. Hwang, J. C. Liang, and C. C. Tsai, "Differences between mobile learning environmental preferences of high school teachers and students in Taiwan: a structural equation model analysis", Educational Technology Research & Development, vol. 64, pp. 533-554, Jun. 2016.

[12] B. Bannan, J. Cook, and N. Pachler, "Reconceptualizing design research in the age of mobile learning,", Interactive Learning Environments, vol. 24, pp. 938–953, Jul. 2016.

[13] L. M. Harasim, Global Networks: Computers and International Communication. Cambridge, MA:MIT Press, 1993.

[14] R. Benbunan-Fich and S. R. Hiltz, "Impacts of asynchronous learning networks on individual and group problem solving: A Weld experiment", Group Decision and Negotiation, vol. 8, pp. 409–426, Sep. 1999.

[15] J. Hewitt, "How habitual online practices affect the development of asynchronous discussion threads", Journal of Educational Computing Research, vol. 28, pp. 31–45, Jan. 2003.

[16] R. M. Marra, J. L. Moore, and A. K. Klimczak, "Content analysis of online discussion forums: a comparative analysis of protocols", Education Technology Research and Development, vol. 52, pp. 23–40, Jun. 2004.

[17] L. P. Dringus and T. Ellis, "Using data mining as a strategy for assessing asynchronous discussion forums", Computers & Education, vol. 45, pp. 141-160, Aug. 2005.

[18] C. Romero and S. Ventura, and E. Garcia, "Data mining in course management systems: Moodle case study and tutorial", Computers & Education, vol. 51, pp. 368-384, Aug. 2008.

[19] C. Romero and S. Ventura, "Educational Data Mining: A Review of the State of the Art", IEEE Transactions on Systems, Man, and Cybernetics, Part C (Applications and Reviews), vol. 40, pp. 601-618, Nov. 2010.

[20] A. Pinsonneault, H. Barki, R. B. Gallupe, and N. Hoppen, "Electronic Brainstorming: The Illusion of Productivity", Information Systems Research, vol. 10, pp. 110-133, Feb. 1999.

[21] L.M. Camacho and P. B. Paulus, "The role of social anxiousness in gr oup brainstorming", Journal of Personality and Social Psychology, vol. 68, pp. 1071-1080, Jun. 1995.

[22] J. H. Helquist, J. Kruse, and M. Adkins, "Group support systems for very large groups: A peer review process to filter brainstorming input", in 12th Americas Conference on Information Systems, Association for Information Systems, Atlanta., 2006.

[23] N. Michinov and C. Primois, "Improving productivity and creativity in online groups through social comparison process: new evidence for asynchronous electronic brainstorming", Computers in Human Behavior, vol. 21, pp. 11-28, Jan. 2005.

[24] B. Mullen, C. Johnson, and E. Salas, "Productivity loss in brainstorming groups: a meta-analytic integration", Basic and Applied Social Psychology, vol. 12, pp. 3-23, 1991.

[25] A. K. Offner, T. J. Kramer, and J. P. Winter, "The effects of facilitation, recording, and pauses on group brainstorming", Small Group Research, vol. 27, pp. 283-298, Apr. 1996.

[26] K. L. Dugosh, P. B. Paulus, E. J. Roland, and H. Yang, "Cognitive stimulation in brainstorming", Journal of Personality and Social Psychology, vol. 79, pp. 722-735, Nov. 2000.

[27] P. Thomas and L. Carswell, "Learning through collaboration in a distributed education environment", Educational Technology and Society, vol. 3, pp.373-382, 2000.

[28] D. Kember and L. Gow, "Action research as a form of staff development in higher education", Higher Education, vol. 23, pp. 297-310, Apr. 1992.

[29] K. Patriarcheas, S. Papaloukas, and M. Xenos, "Analyzing the fora: An algorithms combination for the representation of messages", Proc. of the 15th Panhellenic Conference on Informatics with international participation (PCI 2011), IEEE Computer Society Press, Oct. 2011, pp. 353-357, ISBN: 978-1-61284-962-1, doi: 10.1109/PCI.2011.1.

[30] K. Patriarcheas and M. Xenos, "Integration of a System for Discussions Study in Text-Based Computer-Mediated Communication", Proc. of the 16th Panhellenic Conference on Informatics with international participation (PCI 2012), IEEE Computer Society Press, Oct. 2012, pp. 381-386, ISBN: 978-1-4673-2720-6, doi: 10.1109/PCi.2012.44

[31] K. Patriarcheas and M. Xenos, "Fora for Distance Education: Another Way for Analysis of Discussions", The Second International Conference on Social Eco-Informatics (SOTICS 2012), IARIA, Oct. 2012, pp. 70-75, ISBN: 978-1-61208-228-8.

[32] K. Patriarcheas, S. Papaloukas, and M. Xenos, "The Text-Based Computer-Mediated Communication in Distance Education Fora: A Modelling Approach Based on Formal Languages", in T. Daradoumis et al. (Ed.): Intelligent Adaptation and Personalization Techniques in Computer-Supported Collaborative Learning, Series "Studies in Computational Intelligence" (SCI), Springer, vol. 408, pp.239-266, 2012.

[33] K. Patriarcheas and M. Xenos, "The complexity of text-based computer mediated communication: a system for automated representation of discussion threads' messages in asynchronous distance education fora", International Journal of Innovation and Regional Development, vol. 6, pp. 285-309, 2015.

[34] K. Patriarcheas and M. Xenos, "Asynchronous Distance Education Forum - Brainstorming vs. Snowballing: A Case Study for Teaching in Programming Didactics", Proc. 8th International Conference on Web-based Learning (ICWL 09), LNCS Springer, Aug. 2009, pp. 322-331.

SGASDP: Smart Glasses Application Software Development Platform

Jing Chen
Department of Electrical Engineering
National Cheng Kung University
Tainan City, Taiwan ROC
e-mail: jchen@mail.ncku.edu.tw

Yu-Chieh Pai* Jian-Hong Liu
Institute of Computer and Communication Engineering
National Cheng Kung University
Tainan City, Taiwan ROC
e-mail: {q36031203*, liuken}@rtpc06.ee.ncku.edu.tw

***Abstract*—Smart glasses have inspired a variety of applications with innovation in many areas ranging from personal life to industry. However, owing to some uncertainties in application trends, which raise the issues concerning security and privacy, and the difference in the human-computer interaction between smart glasses and popular smart phones, not only consumers hesitate, but also the makers do not seem to invest much in supporting application software development. Therefore, the developers of smart glasses applications mostly could only rely on traditional Google Android application development tools and suffer from cost in terms of work load and time. This paper presents an application software development platform for smart glasses, namely SGASDP (Smart Glasses Application Software Development Platform), which is intended to increase the productivity and the efficiency in building smart glasses applications, as well as to help enhance the user experience of developers during the development process. The development of SGASDP adopts as its base the original application development platform of Google Android systems. This work extends the part of software development kit (SDK) by integrating, as built-in components, an SDK for live streaming and an SDK for voice recognition. In addition, development aids are added into the platform, which include a smart glasses display layout design tool and an expandable API usage helper. SGAPDP has been tested via developing application software for products of two local smart glasses makers. The success in the development demonstrates the contribution of this work.**

Keywords- smart glasses; wearable computing; application development; Android; application launcher

I. INTRODUCTION

Smart glasses or smartglasses is a wearable computer equipped with a near-eye display or optical head-mounted display (OHMD) [1]. It is considered as one of the latest innovations among wearable computing devices, which has emerged to address the limitation of mobile devices, such as requiring dedicated attention, hand-held and operating, etc. Since Google Glass was introduced, smart glasses products quickly prevailed [2][3], and many applications, not only in personal daily life, but also in many areas which range from education to industry have been inspired [4]-[8]. However, not only consumers appear to hesitate but also makers do not invest much effort in supporting development of application software. The main reasons might include the uncertainty in application trends with concerns of security and privacy, and the difference in human-computer interaction between smart glasses and popular smart phones [9][10]. Further, Google Inc. enforced a policy that is very different from the one for Android system in developing application software [2][11]. Consequently, in developing applications for Android-based smart glasses products, the developers could only rely on the traditional Android application development tools [12] and might suffer from more work load and cost of time.

Despite that the production of Google Glass is ceased [2], applications of smart glasses in many areas, such as health care and medical field [13][14], automotive industry [15], and those in which in-field hands-off operating is required [16], can be seen quite flourishing. A software development platform that helps build smart glasses applications thus is highly desirable. For example, two scenarios of smart glasses applications in medical field are shown in Figure 1. In (1), smart glasses is used in an operating room for live streaming, which transmits or broadcasts the process of a surgery operation, so that other physicians can offer advices in real-time [17]; or to make it a teaching or training aid for medical courses. The scenario in (2) shows that smart glasses, with its particular features, can cast information on the lens and can provide the doctor an intuitive way to consult patient's medical records or other information while voice recognition is used to help operate smart glasses; the doctor's hands thus are free for other needs. The application functionality of smart glasses required in these scenarios calls for a software development platform which can help develop application software for smart glasses efficiently and conveniently.

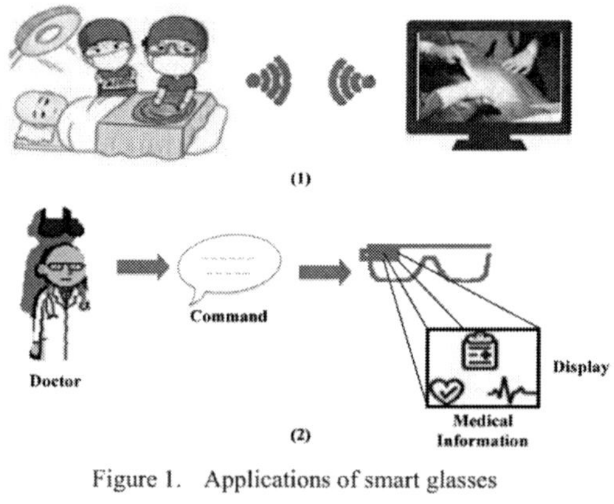

Figure 1. Applications of smart glasses

This paper presents the development of SGASDP, which is an application software development platform intended to

TABLE I. COMPARISON OF SMART GLASSES PRODUCTS

Maker	Google [2][18]	Chipsip [19]	Jorjin [20]	Sony [21]	Epson [22]	Lenovo/Vuzix [23]
PRODUCT	Google Glass	SiME Smart Glasses	Jorjin Smart Glasses Solutions	SmartEyeglass	Moverio	Lenovo Vuzix Smart Glasses
MODEL	X1	SiME	JGK-S101	SED-E1	BT-200	M100
DATE	2014/04	2015/03	N/A	2014/09	2014/12	2014/09
CPU	OMAP 4430	Newton32 SiP (Dual Cortex-A9)	OMAP 4460	N/A	OMAP 4460	OMAP 4460
RAM	1 GB	1 GB	1 GB	N/A	1 GB	1 GB
DISPLAY	Monocular	Monocular	Monocular	Binocular	Binocular	Monocular
RESOLUTION	640 × 360	800 × 480	800 × 480	419 × 138	960 × 540	400 × 240
WIRELESS	1. Wi-Fi 2. Bluetooth 4.0 3. GPS	1. Wi-Fi 2. Bluetooth 4.0 3. GPS	1. Wi-Fi 2. Bluetooth 4.0 3.GPS	1. Wi-Fi 2. Bluetooth 3.0	1. Wi-Fi 2. Bluetooth 3.0 3. GPS	1. Wi-Fi 2. Bluetooth 4.0 3. GPS
O/S	Glass OS / Android 4.4	Android 4.4.2	Android 4.2.2	Android 4.1 or later	Android 4.0.4	1. Android 4.0.4 2. Customized Android
SDK	1. Android SDK 2. GDK	1. Android SDK 2. SiME SDK	1. Android SDK 2. Jorjin SDK	1. Android SDK 2. SmartEyeglass SDK	1. Android SDK 2. MOVERIO BT-200 SDK	1. Android SDK 2. Vuzix SDK
SUPPORT	Developer Web site	Company team	Company team	1. Stackoverflow 2. Developer Web site	Developer Web site	Developer Web site
NOTES	1. Developer is Google X 2. H/W maker is Foxconn 3. Discontinued 2015/01		Jorjin provides BSP as the maker SDK	1. Developer Edition 2. H/W spec. are not all publicly shared.		Cobranded by Lenovo and Vuzix

help increase the efficiency and the productivity in building smart glasses applications. The goals of this development include the following desirable achievements on SGASDP:

- The platform would take Android-based system as the target of applications. This is because that Android not only has been very popular in mobile devices, but also is the base system of Google Glass. In addition, it can allow experienced developers to avoid the learning curve in adapting to a new development platform.
- The platform should support the common features and requirements of smart glasses user interfaces, such as horizontal display and voice control.
- The platform should support functionalities commonly required in building various smart glasses applications, such as the flexibility in integrating suitable SDK.
- The platform would, through integrating useful and handy tools or development aids, provide convenience and help enhance the user experience of developers in the development process.

In addition, this platform would be targeted on developing user space application software. By adopting Android system to be its base, the impact from system level dependency and hardware variety would not cause much difficulty.

The rest of this paper is organized as follows. Section II discusses briefly the background and related works. Section III presents the development of SGASPD, from the design to implementation while Section IV discusses and evaluates the current implementation. Section V concludes this paper.

II. BACKGROUND AND RELATED WORKS

This section gives a summary on developing application software for smart glasses products, which forms the basis of this work.

Smart glasses and portable devices (e.g., smart phones and tablet computers) have similar hardware components, such as processor, memory and sensor modules. The main differences, however, are the operating methods and the horizontal display which relate to user interfaces (UI) or human-computer interaction. To cope with these differences, Google Glass comes with new UI called timeline cards [24] and Glass Development Kit (GDK) [18]. The timeline is the main user interface that is composed of 640×360 pixel cards. Users can scroll through different sections of the timeline so as to reveal cards in the past, present, and future. Figure 2 is Google Now weather card which shows relevant information of current weather [24]. GDK is an add-on to Android SDK and supports the functions of voice control, gesture detector, cards, and others. GDK makes existing Android SDK work on Google Glass and allows developers to build applications that directly run on Google Glass. However, GDK is only available for Google Glass and those applications developed using GDK can only run on Google Glass [11].

Due to space limit and to in order to focus on the main theme of this paper, the details of smart glasses products cannot be included here. Table I presents a brief comparison on Google Glass and smart glasses products of other known makers. This comparison is by no means exhaustive but it can be observed from the table that Android system is quite popular. Therefore, the software developers of smart glasses applications in general can leverage the development tools and environment of Android SDK.

Figure 2. Example of Google Live Card [24]

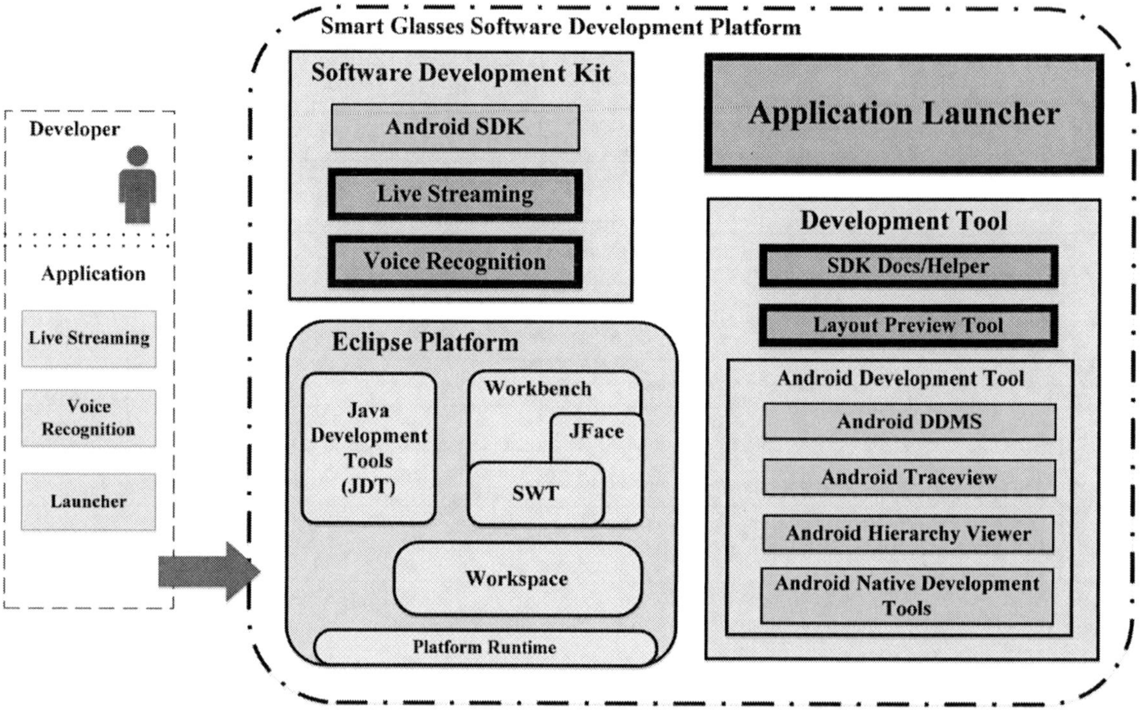

Figure 3. The architecture overview of Smart Glasses Application Software Development Platform (SGASDP)

As shown in Table I, the makers of smart glasses provide their proprietary SDK, as a supplement to Android SDK, to help access maker-specific devices as well as enable the third party application development. This, mostly, is not the same case as the GDK of Google Glass, because these maker SDK do not, if any, support all the functions provided in GDK. An example is the UI of timeline and cards, as mentioned earlier. Developing applications for these smart glasses products thus would have to handle extra work load in addition to coping with application logic.

III. THE DEVELOPMENT

This section describes the development of SGASPD, which includes the design, its architecture and its implementation. SGASPD was conceived with the application development platform of Android systems in mind. The reason is not only that Android system has a large, and is still growing, market share in the arena of mobile platforms, but also it is relatively stable such that hardware variety in smart glasses products would not impose impact upon developing application software. In addition, for experienced Android software developer, the burden of learning and becoming used to a new development platform or environment can be greatly reduced. Of course, the reasons of open source and free availability both have shares in making the decision.

A. The Design

Figure 3 depicts the architecture overview of SGASDP and shows the main design consideration. The dotted boxes at the left-hand side in the figure shows some functionalities that might be commonly desirable in applications of smart glasses, such as live streaming and voice recognition. These functional requirements and other potential ones, such as gesture-based control, might suggest that a mechanism of this platform to support implementing functionality specific to smart glasses applications is helpful and desirable. SDK would be suitable to serve as package of functionality while an SDK manager is designed to harness the flexibility in adding and removing SDK.

The launcher box below the box of voice recognition in Figure 3 stands for a customized application launcher which is intended to replace the native Android Launcher (also known as Android launcher app.) because the user interfaces of smart glasses are very different from those of Android smart phones or tablet devices. A new application launcher is thus necessary and therefore it is included in the design.

B. The Architecture

Based on the design described above, the big chain block in Figure 3 shows the main architecture of SGAPSPD, which is composed of four main parts:

- Software Development Kits: These components include not only the SDK required to develop Android apps [25], but also the SDKs pertinent to implementing desirable functionality of smart glasses applications.
- Eclipse Platform: Eclipse [26] is adopted as the base of SGASDP. The components are Java Development Tools, Workbench, Workspace, and Platform Runtime.
- Application Launcher: This a light weight UI included specifically for smart glasses applications. It takes as reference the concept of "timeline cards" [24] from GDK to fit the horizontal view of smart glasses.

- Development Tools: These components are intended to provide handy assistance to developers, which include a design aid for the display layout of application, preview utility, usage guide and other Android development tools.

With the built-in capability of Eclipse [27], components can be added or removed as needed. SGASDP therefore features expandability as well as flexibility.

C. The Implementation

SGASDP is implemented taking as its base the original application development platform for Android system [25], of which the core components are Eclipse platform and Android SDK. SGASDP extends the part of SDK with an SDK for live streaming and an SDK for voice recognition. The part of development aids is realized by porting an open source display layout design tool, namely DroidDraw [28], and implementing an Eclipse plug-in module to serve the role of the SDK Docs/Helper [27]. The application software launcher, namely SGASDP Launcher, is built as a user-space program which supports landscape view of smart glasses and can be configured to replace the native Android launcher. All the implementation work was done on an Intel x86 computer running Windows 7 operating system. The components were created using Java programming language.

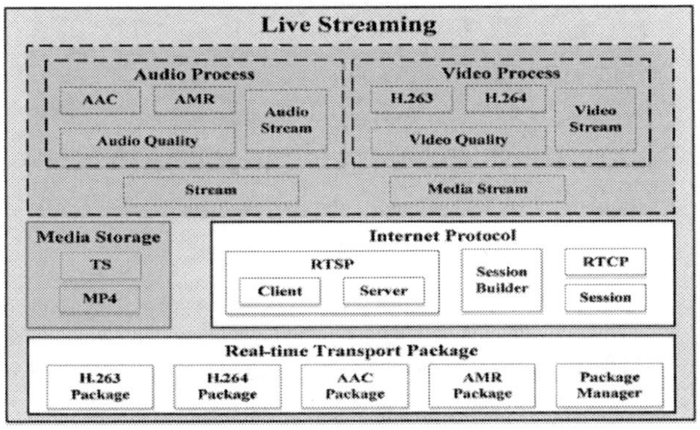

Figure 4. The composition of Live Streaming SDK

(1) Live Streaming SDK: This SDK is realized through porting and rebuilding the libstreaming package [29]. Figure 4 shows the structure of Live Streaming SDK. It can stream data from the camera or microphone of an Android device using Real-time Transport Protocol (RTP) [30] over User Datagram Protocol (UDP) [31] and can achieve 1080p. It has five parts, namely Audio Process, Video Process, Real-time Transport Package, Internet Protocol, and Media Storage.

(2) Voice Recognition SDK: This SDK is implemented by rebuilding the PocketSphinx package of Sphinx project, an open source project to build toolkit for speech recognition [32][33]. The rebuilding work includes compiling the Linux version of the package into the format of dynamic linking library, and then building into Android SDK using Android NDK [34]. This SDK supports off-line voice recognition and developer can customize it with different dictionary files to be integrated into the application.

(3) SGASDP Launcher: This launcher is implemented to fit the horizontal display layout for smart glasses and can be used to replace the native Android launcher app. It provides a horizontal list view of icons and supports voice-operating capability to handle application triggering behaviors from the user. This launcher should be configured into Android App Manifest [35] of the target system in order to make it the first program to run when target Android system starts. Figure 5 shows an example display of this SGASDP Launcher.

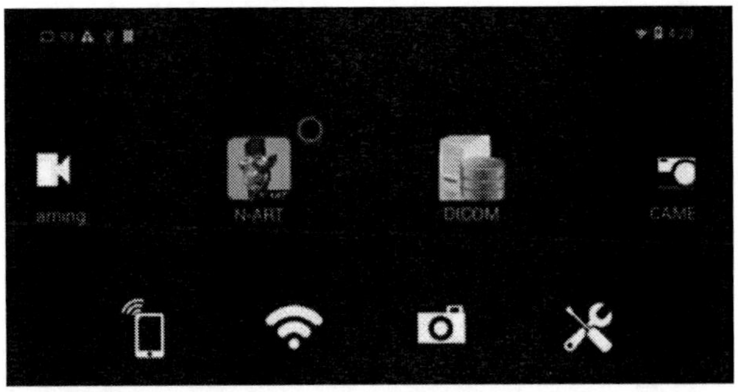

Figure 5. The landscape view of SGASDP Launcher display

(4) SDK Docs/Helper: The function of SDK Docs/Helper is to help developers in using SGASDP and the integrated SDKs. In order to be easily integrated as well as managed in SGASDP, it is implemented using the Plug-in Development Environment (PDE) [27] and the Standard Widget Toolkit (SWT) [36] of Eclipse.

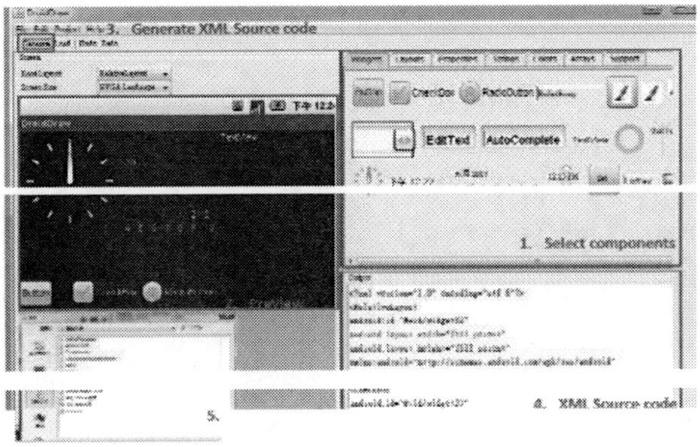

Figure 6. The GUI of the layout design aid and preview tools of SGASDP

TABLE II. RESOLUTIONS SUPPORTED BY THE LAYOUT PREVIEW TOOL

Standard	Resolution	Aspect Ratio
QVGA	320 × 240	4:3
HVGA	480 × 320	3:2
nHD	640 × 360	16:9
VGA	640 × 480	4:3
SVGA	800 × 600	4:3
WVGA	800 × 480	5:3
FWVGA	854 × 480	~16:9
qHD	960 × 540	16:9

(5) Display layout design tool: The implementation of this tool adopts and extends DroidDraw open source project [28]. DroidDraw is intended to be a graphical user interface (GUI) builder for the Android platform, which can help developers to design the display layout of their applications.

An example is shown in Figure 6. In addition, as listed in Table II, more display resolutions are implemented to cope with product variety of smart glasses. The functions of this tool help design including preview a display layout, and convert a layout design to source code in XML format to be imported to the target application.

IV. EVALUTIONS

To demonstrate the functionality and the effectiveness, the current implementation of SGASDP was used to develop example application software for the scenarios mentioned in Section I. The developed software features real-time live streaming using Wi-Fi connection, as shown in Figure 7, and voice control via the SGASDP Launcher. It runs well on the smart glasses products of two local makers, namely ChipSip [19] and Jorjin [20]. The smart glasses from ChipSip, namely SiME Smart Glasses, is equipped with Newton 32 SiP of Dual Cortex-A9 processors [19], while that from Jorjin, Jorjin Smart Glasses, is equipped with OMAP4460 processor [20]. Both are operating at the clock rate of 1.2 GHz. A test case of real-time live streaming on SiME smart glasses is shown in Figure 8.

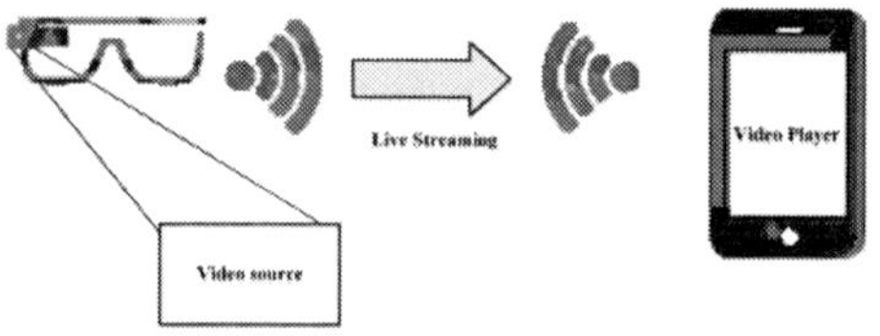

Figure 7. Real-time live streaming using Wi-Fi connection

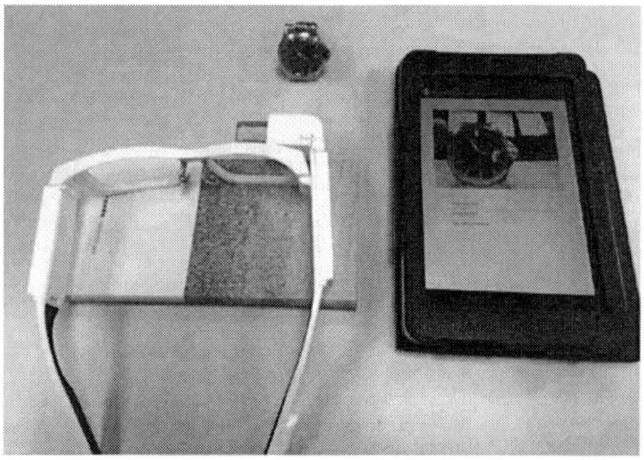

Figure 8. Testing real-time live streaming on SiME smart glasses

During the process of developing the example application software, two handy tools provided by SGASDP, namely the layout design tool and SDK Docs/Helper, are used as shown in Figure 6 and Figure 9 respectively. Figure 6 demonstrates the typical five-step procedure from selecting components to saving the generated XML code defining the display layout. Figure 9 is a snapshot of screen display during the software development and the window located in the lower part of the main view is the SDK Docs/Helper UI which demonstrates the functionality of querying API usage.

Figure 9. Using SDK Docs/Helper

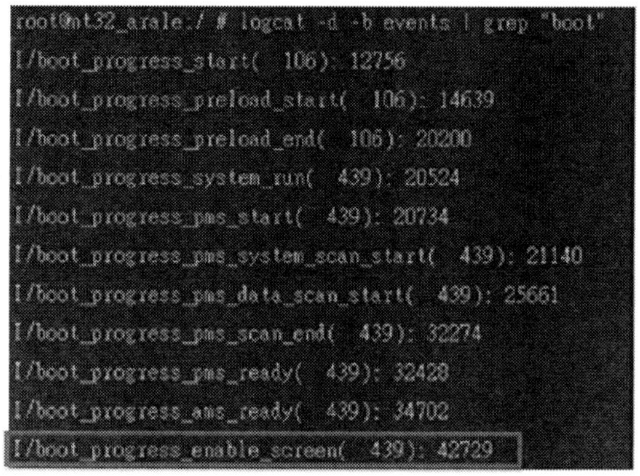

Figure 10. Using Android ADB to retrieve log data

TABLE III. COMPARISON OF SMART GLASSES LAUNCHERS

Launcher	Startup Speed	Operating	Display
Native Launcher	Slow	Touch	Portrait
SGASDP Launcher	Fast	Touch & voice	Landscape

TABLE IV. COMPARISON OF LAUNCHER STARTUP TIME

Launcher	Average	Max.	Min.	Std. dev.
Native Launcher	44.463	47.352	42.102	1.760
SGASDP Launcher	43.712	46.145	42.132	1.283

Unit: second

For evaluating application launcher of SGASDP, listed in Table III are the characteristics of two launchers in which the Native Launcher is the default Android application launcher that is built in the Android system of SiME Smart Glasses. Table IV compares the performance in terms of startup time from cold-start state, which can be obtained via measuring the booting time as the typical launching activity is included in the cold-start booting process. So the booting time can be calculated from the time interval between the timestamps of "boot_progress_start" and "boot_progress_enable_screen" recorded in system log file. The results listed in Table IV are obtained from booting each launcher 10 times and retrieved the timestamps using Android Debug Bridge (ADB) [37] as shown in Figure 10. It is seen that the SGASDP Launcher with voice control capability incurs no significant loading.

V. CONCLUSIONS

This paper presents SGASDP, smart glasses application software development platform, which is aimed to increase the productivity as well as the efficiency in building smart glasses applications. SGASDP features the following main beneficial characteristics: (1) live streaming SDK which helps implement the functions of video or audio streaming in applications; (2) customizable voice recognition SDK which supports off-line voice recognition capability; (3) application launcher which provides user interface of horizontal display and voice-control operating functions; (4) a display layout design tool which helps design and preview the layout of application display. Besides, SGASDP can be transplanted easily through directly copying the relevant files to the new environment when needed, and developers can customize or enhance its capability by integrating their own development kits or tools to make this platform more fit and powerful.

Test results demonstrate that SGASDP works properly and there is no burden, for developers with little experience, in learning to operate this platform. The main contribution of this work is a software development platform that effectively helps developers in building smart glasses applications.

Acknowledgment

This work is partially sponsored by Ministry of Science and Technology (MOST) of Republic of China (ROC) under the contract MOST106-3011-E-006-001.

References

[1] Wikipedia contributors, "Smartglasses", http://en.wikipedia.org/wiki/Smartglasses, accessed on 2017-07-28.

[2] Wikipedia contributors, "Google Glass", http://en.wikipedia.org/wiki/Google_Glass, accessed on 2017-08-16.

[3] P. Lamkin, "The best smartglasses 2017: Snap, Vuzix, ODG, Sony & more", July 10, 2017, https://www.wareable.com/headgear/the-best-smartglasses-google-glass-and-the-rest, accessed on 2017-07-30.

[4] Google Glass, "Google Glass: What Is It and How Can It Change Our Lives", CreateSpace Independent Publishing Platform, March 9, 2014, ISBN 978-1497301719.

[5] E. Butow and R. Stepisnik, "Google Glass for Dummies", For Dummies, 1st Edition, April 21, 2014, ISBN 978-1118825228.

[6] M. Wells, "How Google Glass Can Be used in Education", http://www.gettingsmart.com/2014/07/google-glass-can-used-education/, July 19, 2014, accessed on 2017-07-24.

[7] M. C. O'Connor, "Smart Glasses Finding Work Across Industries", Jan. 6, 2015, http://www.iotjournal.com/articles/view?12576, accessed on 2017-08-05.

[8] M. Margolis, "Smartglasses: Industrial Applications And Now In Retail", July 2, 2015, https://seekingalpha.com/article/3299785-smartglasses-industrial-applications-and-now-in-retail, accessed on 2017-08-05.

[9] A. Oreskovic, S. McBride, and M. Nayak, "Google Glass future clouded as some early believers lose faith", Nov. 14, 2014, http://www.reuters.com/article/us-google-glass-insight-idUSKCN0IY18E20141114, accessed 2017-07-26.

[10] M. Swider, "Google Glass Review", Feb. 21, 2017, http://www.techradar.com/reviews/gadgets/google-glass-1152283/review, accessed on 2017-07-30.

[11] Google Inc., "Google Developer Policies", https://developers.google.com/glass/policies, accessed on 2017-07-01.

[12] Android Developers, "Android Studio," https://developer.android.com/studio/index.html, accessed on 2017-08-01.

[13] N. Wrzesińska, "The use of smartglasses in healthcare - review", Medtube Science, Vol. III (4), Dec. 2015.

[14] E. Bostancı, "Medical wearable technologies: Applications, Problems and Solutions", 2015 Medical Technologies National Conference (TIPTEKNO), Bodrum, 2015, pp. 1-4.

[15] M. Neuner, "How can the car industry benefit from Wearables", August 16, 2016, https://www.wearable-technologies.com/2016/08/how-can-the-car-industry-benefit-from-wearables/, accessed on 2017-08-13.

[16] J. Dutschke, "Enhancing the Maintenance Vision", http://www.mromagazine.com/features/enhancing-the-maintenance-vision/, accessed on 2017-08-18.

[17] D. F. Carr, "Google Glass Enables Surgeons To Consult Remotely", Nov. 29, 2013, http://www.informationweek.com/healthcare/mobile-and-wireless/google-glass-enables-surgeons-to-consult-remotely/d/d-id/1112837?, accessed on 2017-08-15.

[18] Glass Explorer Edition, "Glass Development Kit (GDK)", https://developers.google.com/glass/develop/gdk/, accessed on 2017-05-31.

[19] ChipSip Technology Co., "SiME Smart Glasses", http://www.chipsip.com/computing/index.php?mode=data&id=126, accessed on 2017-08-17.

[20] Jorjin Technologies Inc., "Jorjin Smart Glasses Solution", http://www.jorjin.com/solution_content.php?id=28, accessed on 2017-07-26.

[21] Sony Developer World, "Develop SmartEyeGlass App", https://developer.sony.com/develop/wearables/smarteyeglass-sdk/, accessed on 2017-08-18.

[22] Epson Inc., "Epson Moverio BT-200", https://www.epson.com/Support/Wearables/Moverio/Epson-Moverio-BT-200/s/SPT_V11H560020, accessed on 2017-07-31.

[23] Vuzix Inc., "M100 Smart Glasses", https://www.vuzix.com/Products/m100-smart-glasses, accessed on 2017-08-15.

[24] Glass Explorer Edition, "User Interface", https://developer.google.com/glass/design/ui, accessed on 2017-08-01.

[25] Wikipedia contributors, "Android Software Development", http://en.wikipedia.org/wiki/Android_software_development, accessed on 2017-08-13.

[26] Eclipse, "Eclipse Platform Technical Overview", http://www.eclipse.org/articles/Whitepaper-Platform-3.1/eclipse-platform-whitepaper.html, accessed on 2017-08-17.

[27] Eclipse, "PDE", http://www.eclipse.org/pde/, accessed on 2017-08-15.

[28] L. Meyer, "DroidDraw", https://github.com/sosiouxme/DroidDraw, accessed on 2017-08-16.

[29] Simon (fyhertz), "libstreaming", https://github.com/fyhertz/libstreaming, accessed on 2017-08-02.

[30] "RTP: A Transport Protocol for Real-Time Applications", https://tools.ietf.org/html/rfc3550, accessed on 2017-08-15.

[31] "UDP: User Datagram Protocol", https://tools.ietf.org/html/rfc768, accessed on 2017-08-15.

[32] CMUSphinx, "Open Source Speech Recognition Toolkit", https://cmusphinx.github.io, accessed on 2017-08-19.

[33] CMUSphinx, "Overview of CMUSphinx toolkit", http://cmusphinx.sourceforge.net/wiki/tutorialoverview, accessed on 2017-08-12.

[34] Android Developers, "Android NDK", https://developer.android.com/ndk/index.html, accessed on 2017-08-09.

[35] Android Developers, "App Manifest", https://developer.android.com/guide/topics/manifest/manifest-intro.html, accessed on 2017-08-09.

[36] Eclipse, "SWT: The Standard Widget Toolkit", https://www.eclipse.org/swt/, accessed on 2017-08-15.

[37] Android Studio, "Android Debug Bridge (adb)", https://developer.android.com/studio/command-line/adb.html, accessed on 2017-08-01.

A Call Procedure Design for Underwater Celluar Networks

Hee-won Kim, Junho Cho, Ho-Shin Cho
School of Electronics Engineering
Kyungpook National University
Daegu, Republic of Korea
e-mail: {hwkim, jh_cho, hscho}@ee.knu.ac.kr

***Abstract*—In this paper, we design a call procedure between underwater base station controller (UBSC) and underwater base station (UBS) in cellular-type underwater networks. For reliability and stability, the procedure is initiated by UBSC. Then, data is transferred in three distinctive modes so that data can be collected in more efficient way according to the application services.**

Keywords-underwater cellular networks; call procedure; initialization; medium access control.

I. INTRODUCTION

In recent years, research on underwater wireless networks has been actively conducted for many applications, such as disaster prevention, tactical surveillance, and ocean exploration [1]. Since signals suffer from high propagation delay, severe multipath fading, and narrow bandwidth in the underwater channel, systematic resource management is highly required. Depending on the presence or absence of infrastructure, we can categorize the underwater wireless networks into two types: cellular networks and sensor networks, respectively. Although constructing the infrastructure in underwater is expensive, the cellular-type networks have very efficient resource management [2] compared to the sensor networks. In this paper, we design a call procedure between underwater base station controller (UBSC) and underwater base station (UBS) in underwater cellular networks.

Figure 1 shows an architecture of underwater cellular network. On the seabed, UBSs are installed and communicate with a UBSC buoyed on the surface. The UBSC manages the UBSs by disseminating downlink (DL) data and gathers uplink (UL) data from the UBSs. Similarly, each UBS takes charge of multiple user equipment (UE) and delivers UL data from the UEs to the UBSC.

In Sections 2 and 3, we explain the proposed call procedure between the UBSC and the UBSs and conclude the paper, respectively.

II. CALL PROCEDURE

The call procedure consists of initialization and data transfer phases as shown in Figure 2. The initialization phase is divided into two sub-phases—UBS search and system configuration.

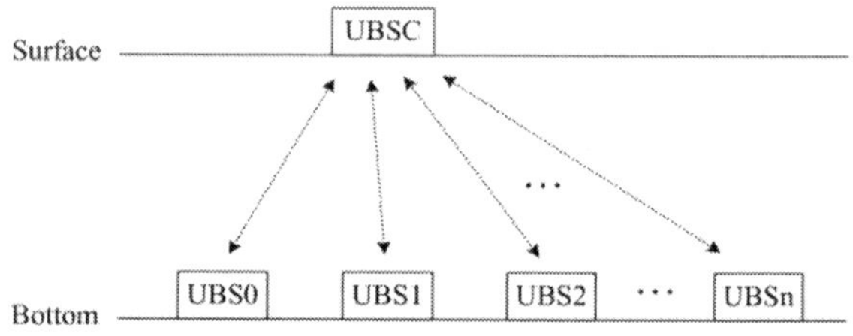

Figure 1. Network structure.

A. *Initialization phase*

In the UBS search sub-phase, the UBSC broadcasts an *echo request* (ERQ) packet to search for UBSs, and the UBSs respond with an *echo response* (ERP) packet. Since the UBSs do not have their own dedicated UL frequency band, they send the ERP using a shared band. To prevent packet collision, each UBS defers the ERP transmission for a certain time. Through the ERQ–ERP exchange, the UBSC knows the number of available UBSs and distances from each of them. During the system configuration sub-phase, based on aforementioned knowledge, the UBSC allocates dedicated UL bands of the UBSs in such a way that a nearer UBS gets a higher frequency band and then notifies them of this information using a *system parameter configure* (SPC) packet in the next system configuration phase. Since the SPC contains system parameters, such as data transfer mode as well as the allocated UL band, the UBSs can configure the system for a subsequent data transfer phase. As a response to the SPC, the UBSs send a *system parameter configure complete* (SPCC) packet to the UBSC. The UBSs use their dedicated UL band from the moment they complete the system configuration.

Note that both sub-phases are initiated by the UBSC while the UBSs wait for UBSC's request packets such as ERQ and SPC. Additionally, only the successfully recognized UBSs by UBSC during the UBS search can transit to the system configuration phase.

B. *Data transfer phase*

In this phase, based on the previous system parameter setting, UL or DL data is exchanged between the UBSC and the UBSs. Once the network initialization is completed, the UBSC broadcasts a *data transfer start* (DTS) packet to announce the move to the data transfer phase. When the

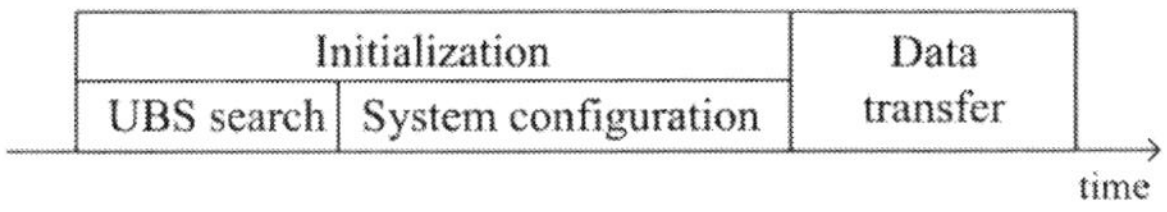

Figure 2. Call procedure between UBSC and UBS.

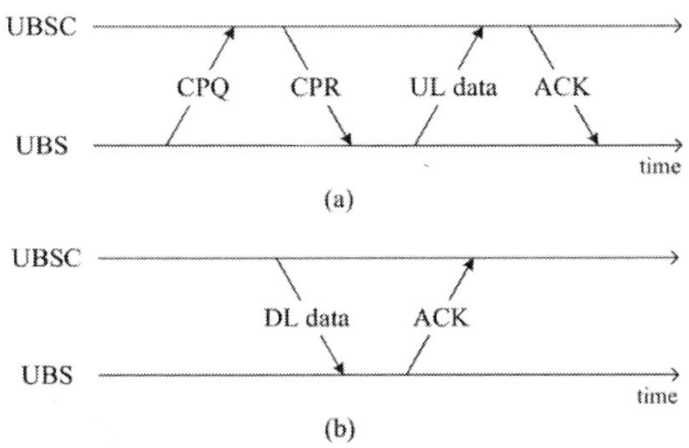

Figure 3. Procedures of data transfer: (a) UL data, (b) DL data.

UBSs receive the DTS, they recognize transition to the data transfer phase and then respond with a *data transfer start complete* (DTSC) packet. As mentioned earlier, only the successfully recognized UBSs by the UBSC during the system configuration phase can transit to the data transfer phase. Therefore, even though a UBS sends a SPCC to the UBSC after system configuration, it may not join the data transfer phase if the SPCC is lost.

The protocol has three different data transfer modes 1, 2, and 3. The modes 1 and 2 are normal mode but they are distinct from each other, depending on whether the UBSs sleep or not. On the other hand, the mode 3 is ad hoc mode where the UBSC establishes a direct link and communicates with a mobile UE (e.g., a diver).

In modes 1 and 2, a session for UL or DL data comprises a 4-way or 2-way handshake, respectively, as shown in Figure 3. In the case of UL session, the UBS and the UBSC first exchange channel probe request (CPQ) and channel probe response (CPR) packets. On receiving the CPQ, the UBSC measures the UL channel quality and responds with the CPR that carries the most appropriate modulation and coding scheme (MCS) level for UL data. Then, the UBS sends the UL data using the corresponding MCS level and are acknowledged by the UBSC. A large amount of UL data can be transmitted with a chain of consecutive data packets (packet train) within a single UL session. Meanwhile, note that there is no CPQ–CPR handshake in DL data session, thus reducing the delay caused by channel quality estimation. Instead, since the DL data normally carry important control information, the lowest MCS level is applied by default. As an automatic repeat request (ARQ) method, the UL session employs the selective ARQ. When UL data are erroneous, the UBSC selectively requests retransmission of the erroneous data by sending a negative acknowledgment (NACK) packet to the UBS. Referring to this NACK, the UBS resends the corresponding packets only. On the other hand, the simple stop-and-wait ARQ is used in the DL session.

Compared to the mode 2, the mode 1 additionally introduces UBS's sleep for energy saving. The UBSC calculates the sleep time for each UBS at the end of every UL session and includes it in the ACK packet. Then, the UBS sleeps during the specified time, which means that no UL and DL sessions can be established until the sleeping ends. Depending on application type or traffic pattern, the sleep time can be fixed or variable.

In the mode 3, the UBSC makes conversation directly with a UE, without passing through the UBSs. The UE does not have a dedicated UL band but borrows one of the UBS's UL bands. Throughout the mode 3, all of the UBSs keep silence not to interfere with UE's communication. This mode consists of three procedures: call setup, conversation, and call termination. To set up a call, the UBSC sends a *call setup* (CS) packet to the UE, which responds to this with a *call setup complete* (CSC) packet. After the CS–CSC exchange, the UBSC and the UE can talk to each other until the call is terminated. If the conversation is over, the UBSC requests call termination to the UE by sending a *call terminate* (CT) packet. When receiving the CT, the UE acknowledges with a *call terminate complete* (CTC) packet and disconnects the link. Note that the call setup and call termination procedures are also initiated by the UBSC.

III. Conclusion

In this paper, a call procedure between the UBSC and the UBS of underwater cellular networks was proposed. The procedure is centralized by the UBSC to achieve reliability and stability. In addition, the data transfer phase has three distinctive modes so that the network can adaptively choose one according to the application. For further work, we will design a UBS–UE call procedure and then combine it with the UBSC–UBS call procedure. Additionally, we will conduct field experiments to verify the proposed procedure.

Acknowledgment

This research was a part of the project titled "Development of Distributed Underwater Monitoring & Control Networks," funded by the Ministry of Oceans and Fisheries, Korea.

References

[1] I. F. Akyildiz, D. Pompili, and T. Melodia, "Underwater acoustic sensor networks: research challenges," Ad Hoc Netw., vol. 3, pp. 257–279, May 2005, doi: 10.1016/j.adhoc.2005.01.004.

[2] M. Stojanovic, "Design and Capacity Analysis of Cellular-Type Underwater Acoustic Networks," IEEE J. Oceanic. Eng., vol. 33, pp. 171–181, Oct. 2008, doi: 10.1109/JOE.2008.920210

An Implementation of MAC Protocol for Underwater Cellular Networks

Junho Cho, Hee-won Kim and Ho-Shin Cho
School of Electronics Engineering, Kyungpook National University
Daegu, Republic of Korea
e-mail: {jh_cho, hwkim, hscho}@ee.knu.ac.kr

Abstract—**In this paper, we propose a communication system that implements a Medium Access Control (MAC) protocol for underwater acoustic cellular networks. To evaluate the network's performance between the underwater base station controller (UBSC) and the underwater base stations (UBS), we implemented a protocol stack on the commercial ARM Linux based hardware platform. We implemented the physical layer interface considering underwater channel characteristics and designed underwater MAC protocol on the data link layer. By testing the implemented system, we can evaluate the network performance and eventually can optimize the protocol performance.**

Keywords- Medium Access Control Protocol; Underwater Networks; Underwater Acoustic Communication.

I. INTRODUCTION

For reliable underwater communications, acoustic waves are preferred over Radio Frequency (RF) waves owing to the extensive attenuation and fading losses experienced by the RF waves imposed by the unique underwater channel characteristics [1]. However, underwater acoustic channel is limited in operational bandwidth, higher Bit Error Rate (BER), and introduce a relatively large propagation delay compared to terrestrial RF channel [2]. Therefore, to achieve better performance in underwater acoustic network, it is pertinent to consider the underwater channel characteristics in the design of an efficient underwater Medium Access Control (MAC) protocol [3].

In this paper, we present a commercial-platform based communication system to implement an underwater MAC protocol designed for underwater acoustic cellular networks.

II. PROTOCOL DESIGN

We consider an underwater cellular network which consists of an underwater base station controller (UBSC) and underwater base stations (UBS). Figure 1 shows the network architecture. The UBSC is deployed on the surface of the ocean while the UBSs are deployed underwater. UBSC registers and controls the UBSs and thus, each UBS is connected through acoustic wireless links to the UBSC. That is, the network has a UBSC centric cellular network configuration.

The proposed MAC protocol comprises of the three phases— network initialization, parameter setting, and data-transfer. In the network initialization phase, UBSC discovers the UBSs and estimates the distance by exchanging control messages. This is followed by the parameter setting phase where the UBSC, based on UBS information and following data transfer mode, allocates the suitable up/down link frequency channels for each UBSs and forwards system parameters that are used to specify the communication between UBSC and UBS.

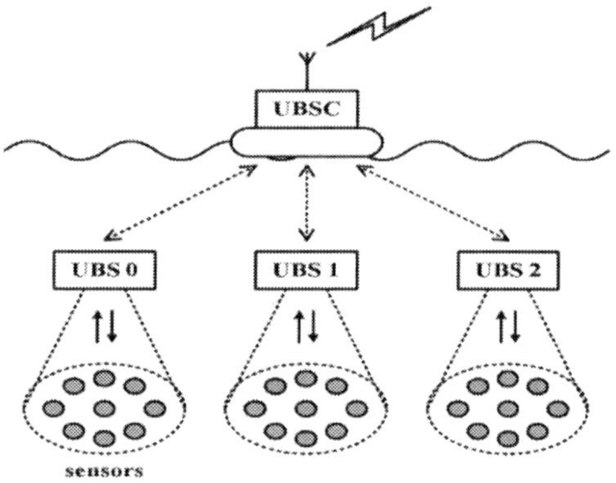

Figure 1. Underwater cellular network architecture.

On the completion of the parameter setting phase, the data-transfer phase begins immediately. Data-transfer phase consists of three modes: mode 1, 2, and 3, depending on call procedure. Data-transfer mode 1 uses a 4-way handshaking method to start the uplink or downlink session and delivering data frames. In this mode, if there are no uplink and downlink sessions for a period of time, the UBSC orders UBS to enter the sleep mode in order to save energy consumption. UBS which enters the sleep mode, cannot receive or transmit any frames during that time duration. Data-transfer mode 2 operates similar to mode 1, however there is no procedure for sleep mode setting. Thus, all the UBS remain in the active mode, allowing them to deliver the data immediately. Data-transfer mode 3 creates an ad-hoc communication between the UBSC and an underwater mobile node (e.g., diver, Autonomous underwater vehicle). In this mode, the UBSC and the mobile node transmit the data frames continuously and simultaneously through the uplink and downlink channel after call setup procedure.

III. PROTOCOL IMPLEMENTATION

To evaluate the performance and verify the operation of underwater MAC protocol, we implemented the protocol on the commercial platform. Xilinx Zynq 7000 series DSP board based on ARM Linux system was used as the hardware platform.

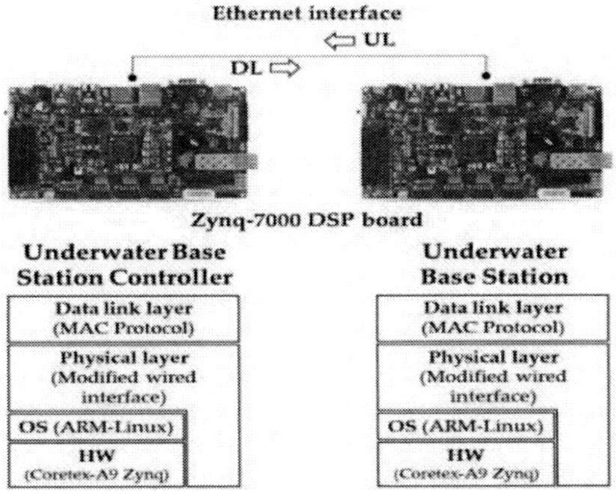

Figure 2. Architecture of the system

Figure 2 shows the architecture of the system. We implemented the protocol stack, which consists of physical and data link layer, on the Linux operating system. As a physical layer, a modified wired interface was used to replicate the underwater acoustic channel characteristics. To apply the realistic underwater channel such as available bandwidth and propagation delay depending on internodal distance, we modified the frame transmission time and the propagation delay by using a delay function. This physical layer interface is designed to be replaced by OFDM based underwater acoustic modem, which will be our final version of the implementation.

As a data link layer, we implemented the proposed MAC protocol mentioned in section 2. Data link layer operates on one downlink and multiple independent uplink channels. Each channel is separated in the frequency domain; hence, there are no inter channel interference or collision and it supports full duplex communication.

A node plays a role as one of UBSC, UBS, or mobile node according to user's input parameters that include node type, unique node ID and underwater channel specification. As a data traffic for testing, we used an image on both up- and downlinks. And, as a way of diagnosing the procedure, we made every event happening during the call procedure displayed on the monitor. In addition, for the purpose of further examination later, all events along with timing information are logged.

IV. Performance Evaluation

System parameters used for performance evaluation are listed in Table I. We tested communication scenario between UBSC and mobile node which sends 51.4kb size image data to each other by using data transfer mode 3. Considering underwater acoustic OFDM PHY frame, transmission time of control and data frames are set to 7s.

Figure 3 shows the call procedure diagram and event time figured out based on the event log. By analyzing the event log, we can verify that it takes 30s for network initialization and parameter setting. In data transfer phase, it takes 287s for the call setup procedures, 102.8kb data transfer and call terminates.

TABLE I. System Parameters

Parameter	Value
Iinternodal distance	1km
Propagation speed	1500m/s
Data rate	214.29bps
Payload size	1500bits

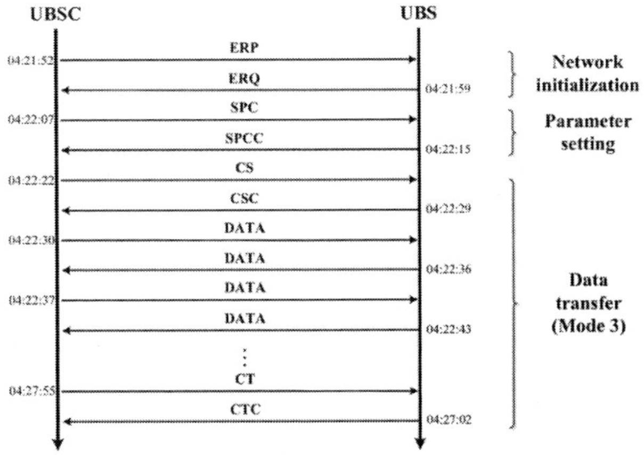

Figure 3. Protocol procedure of data-transfer mode 3

Thus, total network throughput is 358.2bps.

V. Conclusion

In this paper, we presented a commercial platform based communication system to implement an underwater MAC protocol designed for underwater acoustic cellular networks. By using the proposed system, we evaluated the network's performance, such as throughput or latency, which can be used to improve or optimize the protocol performance.

For further work, we will verify the designed protocol operation and measure the network performances in real underwater environment by using an underwater OFDM based modem physical layer interface.

Acknowledgment

This research was a part of the project titled "Development of Distributed Underwater Monitoring & Control Networks," funded by the Ministry of Oceans and Fisheries, Korea.

References

[1] I. F. Akyildiz, P. Dario, and M. Tommaso, "Underwater acoustic sensor networks: research challenges." Proc. Ad Hoc Networks, Elsevier, May 2005, pp. 257-279, doi: 10.1016/j.adhoc.2005.01.004.

[2] M. Stojanovic and J. Preisig, "Underwater Acoustic Communication Channels: Propagation Models and Statistical Characterization," IEEE Commun Mag., vol. 47, pp. 84-89, Jan. 2009, doi:10.1109/MCOM.2009.4752682.

[3] X. Lurton, An Introduction to Underwater Acoustics: Principles and Applications. London, UK; Springer Science & Business Media, 200

5G Network Resources Requirements for Mobile Immersive Digital Environments

Experimental Validation of Mobile Virtual Reality Network Requirements in Unity 3D

Danaisy Prado-Álvarez, David Garcia-Roger, Jose F. Monserrat
iTEAM Research Institute
Universitat Politècnica de València, Camino de Vera, s/n
46022 Valencia, Spain
email: dapraal@teleco.upv.es, dagarro@iteam.upv.es, jomondel@iteam.upv.es

***Abstract*—The accelerated increase in the adoption of immersive digital technologies like virtual reality and 360-degree video escalates the pressure on mobile cellular networks. Its higher bandwidth demands and minimum latencies are crucial for enjoying the contents with a satisfactory quality and comfort. This paper describes a study that estimates the minimum critical bandwidth, and latency prerequisites, as well as video resolutions and bitrate needed in a mobile network so as to support immersive applications with a specific subjective quality of experience, using the consumer-ready hardware platforms Oculus Rift and Samsung Gear VR. One of the main conclusions is that the strict requirements of around 20 milliseconds of minimum latency highlights the important challenge that must be addressed by future 5G mobile cellular networks, but this is far from some target values discussed in the literature.**

Keywords-immersive technology; virtual reality; 5G networks; latency; quality of experience.

I. Introduction

In recent years, the improved technological development has made the dream of immersive digital environments like virtual reality (VR) and 360-degree video come true. In fact, VR headsets are now a tangible, consumer-ready visualization platform option available for PCs (Oculus Rift, HTC Vive), video game consoles (Sony Playstation VR) and smartphones (Samsung Gear VR, Google Cardboard, Google Daydream). VR is a computationally created environment that mimics reality, where the user enjoys an immersive experience and interacts with the virtual world that surrounds her/him as if it were real.

VR has three key characteristics: i) immersion, in which the user is only able to perceive the stimuli generated by the virtual environment; ii) interaction, in which the user is able to interact with the virtual environment in real time; iii) responsiveness, in which the user is able to sense simulated realities reacting quickly and positively. VR as a concept initially popularized by video games has gained relevance in sectors, such as medicine, archeology, artistic creation, military training, flight simulation, or virtual offices, among others.

On the go, wireless, cloud-powered VR via mobile cellular networks could be a future emerging trend, where the VR image is transmitted to the viewer from a remote entity in the cloud. In such scenarios, it is imperative to guarantee a superb user experience. Bandwidth demands in VR are remarkable because of the responsiveness trait. With tens of cameras capturing a scene, not even dynamic caching and multicast would be able to reduce the load. Because users should be able to select their individual point of view dynamically delivering content to thousands from a single feed is an unfeasible approach. Therefore, the feed from all of the cameras needs to be available almost instantly and the cellular network might be overwhelmed.

Together with bandwidth bottlenecks, coding artifacts, resolution degradation, and latency spikes are enough to trigger motion sickness. While VR technologies can handle slight impairments, many users will feel motion sick if they spend too much time in the headset perceiving a degraded experience [1]. With VR-induced motion sickness, the effect starts subtle, but is cumulative. What begins as slight discomfort or even a feeling of unease will progress into full-blown nausea. It is not something that the users can push through or become acclimated to. Once it starts, their discomfort will not end until they remove the headset.

Therefore, in order to guarantee a good user experience in the abovementioned scenarios, it is vital to consider which requisites need to be fulfilled by the oncoming the future fifth-generation (5G) mobile cellular network, and the quantitative values for such parameters.

As a subject of research, cloud-powered VR is pushing the limits of current mobile cellular networks, and there is the need of specifying measurable bounds for the magnitude of enhanced capabilities of 5G that are required for VR to reach their full potential. 5G is expected to deliver a high speed network that will allow 10 Gb/s transmission speeds per device, as well as below 1 ms, both specs, 10 to 100 times better than current 4G/LTE networks [2]. Anticipating the impact of such technology on VR, well-known surveys on mobile and wireless technologies for VR like [3] on low bandwidth and high round-trip times in 3G networks have given way to the significant plethora of reviews of current trends towards 5G performed very recently. For example, the authors of [4] review the state of the art in virtual and augmented reality communications and highlights efforts for an operative, universal 5G network in niche markets like telepresence, education, healthcare, streaming media, and haptics. In addition, [5] describes the 5G low-latency applications business case and the potential market benefits for operators on other vertical industries such as automotive, public transport, infrastructure, entertainment, and manufacturing.

The purpose of this paper is describing a study that estimates the minimum critical bandwidth and latency prerequisites, as well as video resolutions and bitrate needed in a 5G mobile network to support immersive applications with a specific subjective Quality of Experience (QoE). This is made by using the consumer-ready hardware platforms Oculus Rift and Samsung Gear VR, with the objective of statistically ascertaining the weight that network induced effects can have on an adequate VR experience under such conditions of latency and bandwidth.

The remaining sections of the paper are structured as follows. Section II describes the relevant features of the immersive technologies addressed in the present work. Section III explains the set of specific performance goals that are evaluated. Section IV gives an overview of the experimental virtual reality testbed used. Section V presents the results of the performance assessment. Finally, Section VII draws the main conclusions of this work.

II. Immersive Technologies and 5G

On the go, wireless, cloud-powered VR via mobile cellular networks has only just started to be developed as a concept. Conceived as a solution to the substantial local storage demands of traditional VR applications, cloud-powered VR streams the contents from storage resources located in a cloud, and playbacks it directly in the headset without the requirement of a previous download.

Prominent research initiatives on 5G like METIS-II European project [6] mention cloud-powered applications of telepresence like VR as a specific use case. Bidirectional flows with sustained transmission rates of 1 Gb/s, in addition to synchronization flows at 5 Gb/s and packet loss rates less than 5% are discussed. In this sense, there is a current application, 360-degree video, that although may be experienced in a VR headset, it is not technically VR. 360-degree video is recorded from every direction and users may observe all aspects of the virtual world that surrounds her, but cannot interact with it. It is expected that 360-degree video may escalate up to bandwidth demands similar to VR, if resolutions beyond 4K are considered in the future, but also research is being done at ways of minimizing the amount of data through user orientation prediction and transmitting only a given subset of cameras [7].

With respect to latencies, 60 ms has been mentioned as the absolute upper-bound, but uncomfortable delays are reported with technologies such as Oculus Rift when latency is larger than 40 ms [8][4]. Stringent requisites for 5G in 0, state that average packet-to-packet latency should less than 10 ms, and further extremely low latencies of 8 ms are desired in [4], or 15 ms to 7 ms application to application delay, i.e., action to reaction, is the threshold to provide a smooth action-reaction experience in [5]. Other studies claim that latencies less than 20 ms are imperceptible [9], and still several related works provide different estimations [1][10][11] With respect to latencies. Network latencies may be solved through processing at the edge or the user's device [12][13]. However, it must be taken into account that latencies in VR arise not only from the restrictions imposed by current mobile network technology but also from several sources, e.g., CPU-intensive tasks inherent to VR like real time capture and video stitching, and also sensing time (although recently reduced to an amount that is imperceptible by humans [4]), USB data speed delays, data crosschecking, game code execution time, frame rendering delay, video output delay, pixel switching time of a LCD, and frame buffering. Furthermore, individual VR experiences have unidirectional latency, but in games and telepresence latency is bidirectional, actually doubling the network infrastructure requirements [4].

Bandwidth and latency limitations still prevent current networks from achieving smooth telepresence and collaborative virtual and augmented reality applications [4]. Specifically, 4G/LTE is not able to support services requiring big data sizes, where the transmission of the gigabytes of data comprising a 3D model at a reasonable cost is a necessity. 4G/LTE networks also exhibit typical latencies of 50 ms [14] and are not able to satisfy instantaneous access to future cloud services.

Still, some argue that even 5G could face latency and bandwidth challenges in more remote or crowded locations [4], or 5G is unlikely to deliver the resolution and responsiveness requirements of some high-end applications of VR [12]. A detailed list of potential solutions in RAN and core network is [16], including software defined network (SDN), network function virtualization (NFV), caching, and mobile edge computing (MEC), will allow 5G networks to meet latency and other 5G requirements. Consequently, it is essential to evaluate the QoE of available VR applications over current mobile networks to find out if the limiting factor is the network or video processing in real-time.

There are previous works that address network latency in immersive applications, but either only non-VR cloud-gaming [16], or actual VR but without taking into account the network effects [17]. However, so far, to the best of the authors' knowledge, there has been no exhaustive study of a cloud-VR network scenario in 5G, ascertaining the value of the limiting latency for a sample of population.

The purpose of the work described in this paper is to create a VR testbed assisted by the 3D game engine Unity 3D, to experimentally determine the critical values of bandwidth and latency for a mobile cellular network supporting immersive applications, expressed with respect to the QoE perceived by its users, with the main goal of statistically profile the ratio of users that will enjoy a satisfactory VR experience under such conditions of latency and bandwidth.

III. Virtual reality Testbed

The VR testbed is shown in Figure 1. It consists of a Samsung Gear VR headset and a Samsung Galaxy S7 (4 GB of RAM, Android Nougat 7.0, and a screen resolution of 2560x1440 pixels at 60 frames per second). There is also an Oculus Rift consumer version (headset with resolution 2160x1200 pixels, 1080x1200 per eye at 90 fps, sensor, Xbox controller and Oculus Remote controller), and workstation with the following specs: graphics card GeForce GTX 1070 G1 Gaming 8GB GDDR5, Intel i7-6700K 4.0Ghz processor, 32 GB of RAM, Windows 10 Enterprise.

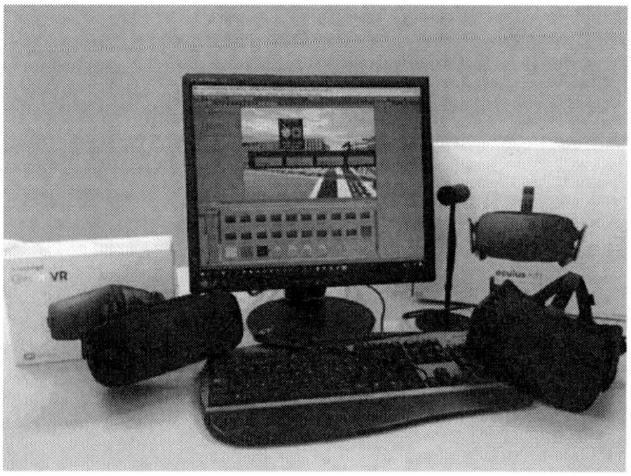

Figure 1. Virtual reality testbed.

The VR was used to carry two experiments on latency and display resolution QoE, experiment I and experiment II, respectively. Experiment I consists of evaluating the QoE perceived by a random group of persons enjoying a VR experience with respect to different values of latency. Experiment II uses the same population sample and several 360-degree test videos with known bitrate and resolutions to estimate the minimum bandwidth required for the satisfactory transmission of the 360-degree video.

During experiment I, the volunteer used the Oculus Rift headset to visualize a 3D rendering of Madrid with increasing degrees of latency. The planning of Experiment I made use of the Unity 3D game engine and required building on the code of the Madrid Grid visualization tool of METIS-II [18]. This platform simulates the shortcomings of 4G and introduces candidate 5G solutions for improved network traffic in a typical urban environment.

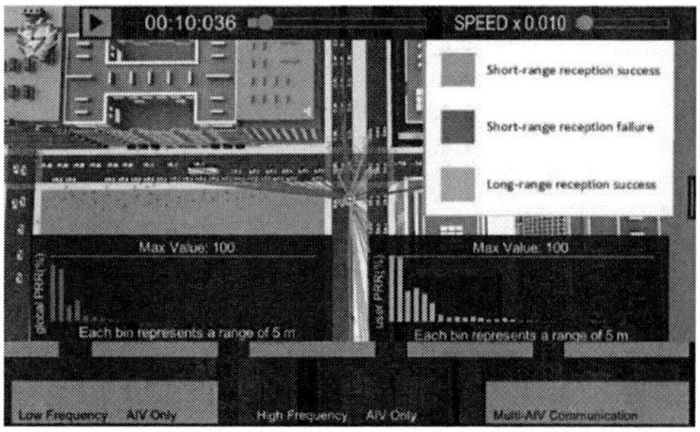

Figure 2. METIS-II Madrid Grid visualization platform.

The Madrid Grid visualization platform interface, is shown in Figure 2. which depicts a scenario with multi air interface variant communications for V2V. The interface includes the street traffic simulation and an overlay layer that provides information to the and allows interaction through a flexible, but traditional, mouse-based, graphical user interface (GUI).

The visualization platform required an extension to so as to enable VR output compatible with the Oculus Rift headset. However, the traditional GUI could not be easily translated in to a VR-friendly paradigm and therefore it was necessary to create also a proper VR GUI as well as the definition of a set of ways to interact with the GUI through the Oculus Remote controller instead of the mouse. The status bar was relocated as a head-up display (HUD) inside world-space and the lack of mouse in VR was solved with a fixed reticle assisted by the buttons of the Oculus Remote as shown in Figure 3.

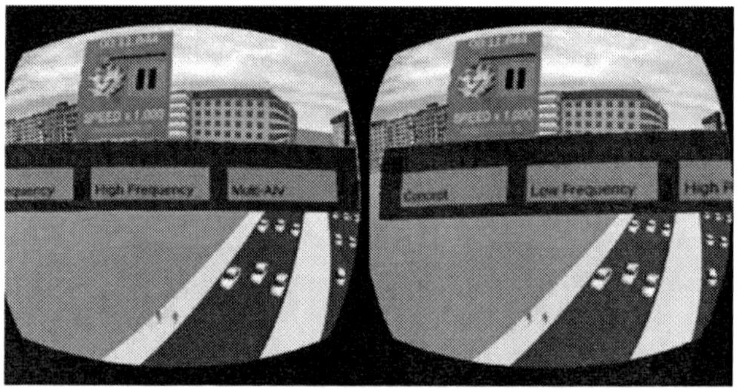

Figure 3. Visualization platform VR GUI reticle and head-up display.

Experiment I also required the configuration of the Oculus Debug Tool to force a range of different latency values. This is a debugging tool provided by Oculus that allows the study of real-time performance of a VR experience in runtime. By using the performance HUD, and selecting the option *latency timing*, the performance in ms of several contributions to delay may be observed, as shown in Figure 4. Specifically, the parameter *App Tracking to Mid-Photons* summarizes all the contributions to latency, and it may be impacted by changing the *Pixels per display pixel override* parameter in the Oculus Debug Tool.

Specifically, the parameter App Tracking to Mid-Photons summarizes all the contributions to latency, and it may be impacted by changing the Pixels per display pixel override parameter in the Oculus Debug Tool as shown in Figure 5.

Increasing the pixel density from 1.0 to 2.0 improves in the image resolution but after 2.0 there is no discernable effect and further increasing comes at a cost: latency increase, which may be handily used to adjust the latency experienced during the experiment as shown in Table I.

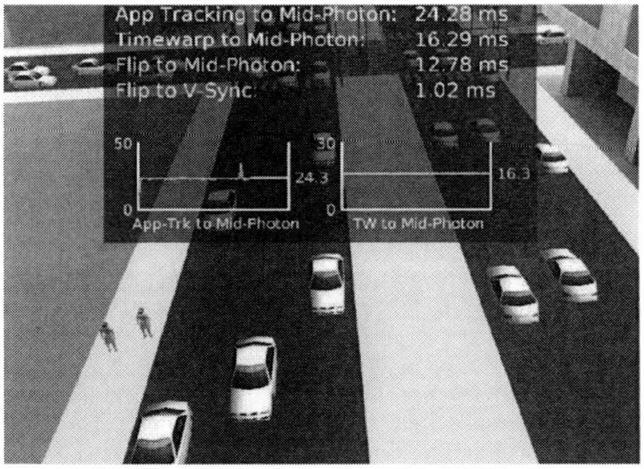

Figure 4. Oculus Debug Tool, displaying latency contributions.

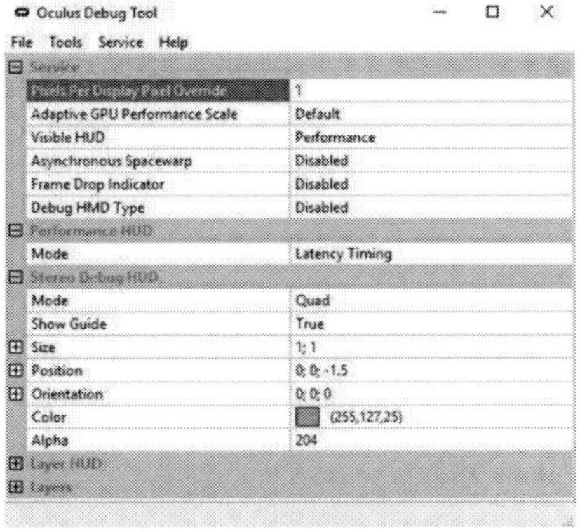

Figure 5. Oculus Debug Tool, Pixels per display override.

TABLE I. LATENCIES PRODUCED BY SEVERAL PIXEL DENSITIES

Pixel density	Associated latency
0	22
1	22
2	25
3	30
4	40
5	50
5.2	60

During experiment II, the volunteer used the Samsung Gear VR to watch a 360-degree video depicting a location surrounded by African wild elephants. The preparation of Experiment II required the selection and download of a 4K 360-degree video of excellent quality from Youtube [19]. The video was re-encoded with the FFmpeg tool [20] to generate 2K, 1080p, 720p, 480p, 360p, 240p, and 144p versions of the same video to deduce estimations of the required streaming bandwidth required to transmit them, as shown in Table II, assuming that 8 camera rigs have been used for the recording of the video. The FFmpeg tool *ffprobe* was used to analyze and may be also used to live-stream the videos to the Samsung Galaxy S7 smartphone inside the Samsung Gear VR headset.

IV. PERFORMACE ASSESSMENT

The experiments were performed on 25 volunteers, a typical value similar to previous studies [18][21]. Participants ranged from 25 to 40 years old, and were initially surveyed about their previous experiences with VR headsets just in case that would bias their opinion about the experience; 20% of them had tested either Samsung Gear VR or Oculus Rift.

A. Experiment I

During experiment I on latency, the Oculus Rift headset was used. The experimental results are shown in Figure 6. It should be noted that QoE rating by users was worsened if they were subjected to degraded quality for too much time. Evaluation criteria are linked to the tolerance of the subjects. The latency achieved with the best configuration is 22 ms, and is used as the reference value. The rating method is based in degradation category rating (DCR), which evaluates the QoE according to a metric mean opinion score (MOS) [22]. As shown, 22 ms of latency seems to be imperceptible for 76% of the subjects; it seems reasonable that reducing latency by some seconds would achieve almost 100% of agreement on its imperceptibility. At 25 ms the noticeable effect of latency is not only perceptible for someone but unpleasant for 32% of the subjects. At 30 ms latency is clearly perceptible for 84% of the subjects. As latency is increased, subjects agree on the distressing nature of the experience, and at 60 ms 80% of the surveyed persons expressed their intention to stop the experiment.

TABLE II. 360-DEGREE VIDEO DETAILS

Video ID	Resolution	Bitrate (kb/s)	Bandwidth (Mb/s)
1	3840x2048	12672	101.7
2	2560x1440	8217	65.7
3	1920x1080	3458	27.7
4	1280x720	1572	12.6
5	854x480	767	6.2
6	640x360	459	3.7
7	426x240	296	2.4
8	256x144	161	1.3

The percentage of surveyed persons that report motion sickness for different latencies is shown in Figure 7.

As shown, the percentage of subjects that report motion sickness with respect to latency follows an exponential law. Note that subjects reported 60 ms of latency as unbearable, because they were visually exhausted and dizzied.

B. Experiment II

During experiment II on display resolution, the Samsung Gear VR headset with a Samsung Galaxy S7 smartphone was used and eight 360-degree videos coded at diminishing resolutions were displayed in succession. The rating method is based in absolute category rating (ACR), which evaluates with simple stimuli the QoE according also to a MOS metric

[22]. The QoE rating of each of the eight videos is shown in Figure 8. The subjects had to stand while evaluating all videos with audio enabled except the one at 2K which was watched while sitting on a chair with audio at minimum. Note that although the video coded at 4K has the best resolution the resolution of the Samsung S7 used in the experiment is limited to 2K.

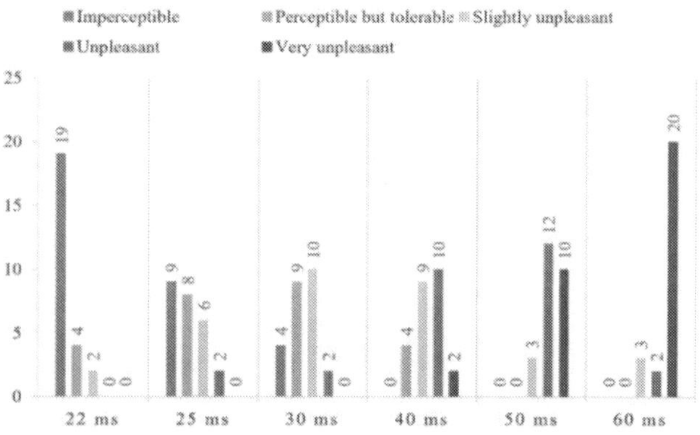

Figure 6. Experiment I on latency: QoE results.

As shown, reducing the display resolution negatively affects QoE. Even at 4K, 52% of the subjects did not considered the video quality to be excellent, and 36% of them were able to detect the pixelization on the smartphone screen. At 1080p, 64% of the users expressed their disagreement (average, poor) with the quality of the visualized video. Compared to conventional applications, VR requires higher resolution in order to perceive a similar QoE mainly because of the magnification optics lenses that bend the light inside the headset in a way that helps the user to see clearly.

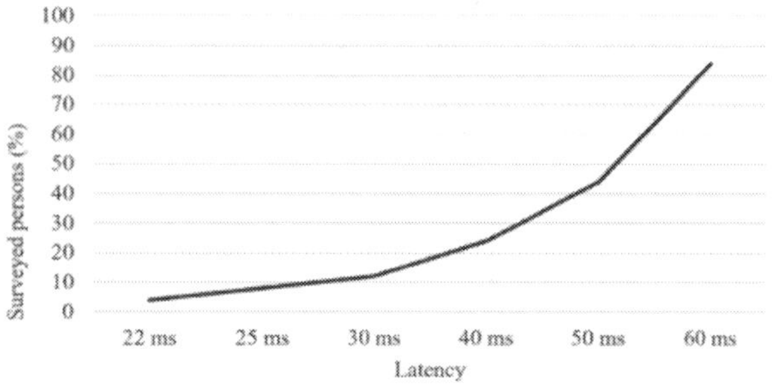

Figure 7. Experiment I on latency: motion sickness results.

The percentage of surveyed persons that report motion sickness for different display resolutions is shown in Figure 9. As shown, as resolution is reduced, the extra visual effort required to distinguish the features in the video yields motion sickness. From 720p to lower resolutions, motion sickness increases logarithmically. At 480p, 52% of the subjects report vertigo, and 60% at 144p. Subjects that did not experienced dizziness reported that were forcing themselves to tell apart the objects in the video.

The percentage of surveyed persons that report the experience as immersive is shown in Figure 10. The surveyed persons reported that as resolution decreased, the scene depicted was less immersive because of the degrading visual depth perception, and turned into an unpleasant experience. Also of note is the fact that although the view shown was all a straight capture from a GoPro Omni camera, even the 2K resolution induced certain participants to wonder whether the elements where real or computer-generated imagery. In addition, the video at 2K, received lower rates than the 2K resized version of the 4K video even though both had the same resolution. A reason could be that the lack of audio and the sitting position worsens the immersive experience, as notified by most of the subjects. This hypothesis is confirmed because the 1080p video (again with audio) produces better perception for the viewers than the 2K version. When resolution is 480p video quality is unacceptable and 92% of the participants thought that the experience was not immersive. Note finally that in order to transmit 360-degree 4K videos, it would be necessary a bandwidth of roughly 11 Mbps, but it is foreseeable that for future applications, even 8K per eye would not be enough for a perfect VR experience.

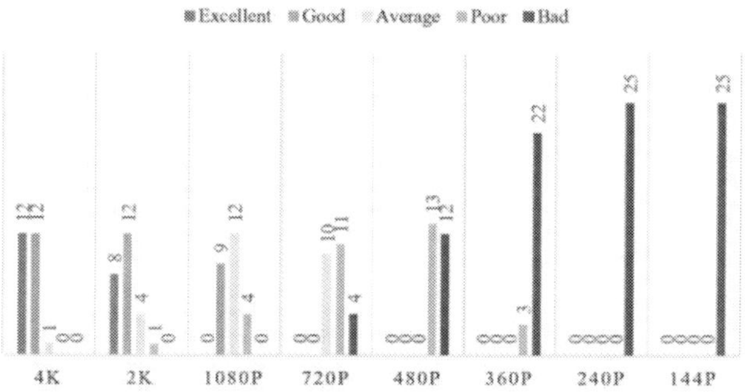

Figure 8. Experiment II on display resolution: QoE results.

Experiment I on latency shows that, by default and without taking into account communication network effects, the baseline latency of a consumer-ready headset like Oculus Rift is 22 ms. Since up to 25 ms is a tolerable latency, there is only 3 ms of buffer for network induced latency for a cloud-powered VR experience. Although reduced latencies are expected from headsets yet to come, current LTE networks have a latency of 50 ms, and therefore reducing latency by an order of magnitude in upcoming 5G cellular networks is also of utmost importance.

Experiment II demonstrates that even 360-degree videos at the 2K native resolution of smartphones do not satisfy 50% of the participants. Consequently, to enhance the VR experience, future devices should have screens with higher resolutions. In this sense, Samsung has announced a 11K smartphone in 2018; with such higher resolutions, network capacity demands for cloud-based VR are expected to climb sharply.

V. Conclusions

The higher bandwidth demands and minimum latencies of wireless, cloud-powered VR will escalate the pressure on future 5G mobile cellular networks. This paper provides estimates of the minimum critical bandwidth (4K great quality lossy compression at 80 Mb/s), and latency prerequisites (less than 25 ms) needed in a mobile network to support immersive applications with a specific subjective quality of experience Potential solutions that will allow 5G networks to meet the requirements in RAN and core network, include SDN, NFV, caching, and MEC.

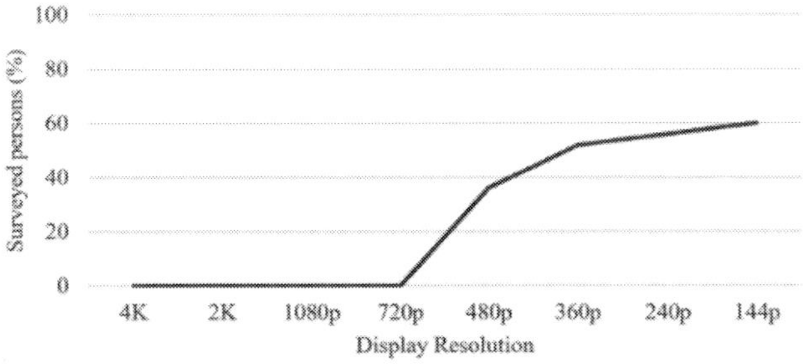

Figure 9. Experiment II on display resolution: motion sickness results.

Acknowledgments

Part of this work has been performed in the framework of the H2020 project METIS-II (H2020-ICT-2014-2, topic ICT-14-2014) co-funded by the European Commission. The authors would like to acknowledge the contributions of their colleagues. The views expressed are those of the authors and do not necessarily represent the project. Part of this work has been also supported by the Ministerio de Economía y Competitividad, Spain (TEC2014-60258-C2-1-R), by the European FEDER funds.

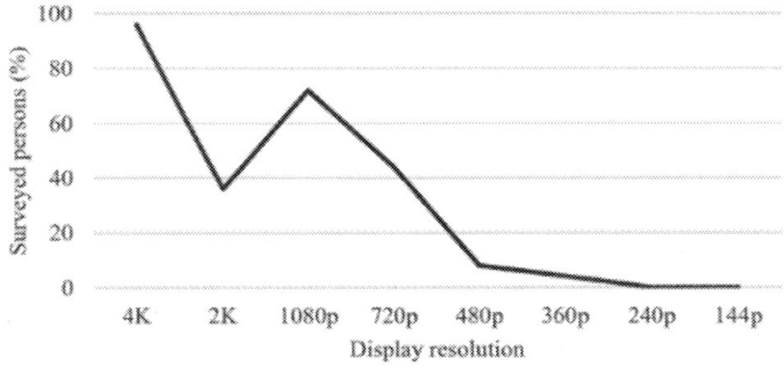

Figure 10. Experiment II on display resolution: degree of immersiveness.

References

[1] M. Meehan, S. Razzaque, M. C. Whitton and F. P. Brooks, "Effect of latency on presence in stressful virtual environments," IEEE Virtual Reality, 2003 pp. 141-148.

[2] H. Tullberg et al., "The METIS 5G system concept: Meeting the 5G requirements", IEEE Communications Magazine, vol. 54, no. 12, pp. 132-139, 2016.

[3] G. Papagiannakis, G. Singh, and N. Magnenat-Thalmann. "A survey of mobile and wireless technologies for augmented reality systems." Comput. Animat. Virtual Worlds, 19(1), pp. 3-22, Feb. 2008.

[4] J. Orlosky, K. Kiyokawa, and H. Takemura, "Virtual and Augmented Reality on the 5G Highway", Journal of Information Processing, vol 25. pp. 133-141, 2017.

[5] M. A. Lema et al., "Business Case and Technology Analysis for 5G Low Latency Applications," in IEEE Access, vol. 5, no. , pp. 5917-5935, 2017.

[6] S. E. El Ayoubi, F. Pujol, and M. Fallgren (ed.), METIS-II/D1.1 Refined scenarios and requirements, consolidated use cases, and qualitative techno-economic feasibility assessment. (2016).

[7] F. Qian, B. Han, L. Ji, and V. Gopalakrishnan, "Optimizing 360 video delivery over cellular networks". In ACM MobiCom All Things Cellular Workshop, pp. 1-6, Oct. 2016.

[8] S. LaValle, "The latent power of prediction", *Oculus Developers Blog*. 2013.

[9] J. Carmack, "Latency mitigation strategies," *Twenty Milliseconds*, 2013.

[10] B. D. Adelstein, T. G. Lee, and S. R. Ellis, (2003, October). Head tracking latency in virtual environments: psychophysics and a model. In *Proceedings of the Human Factors and Ergonomics Society Annual Meeting* (Vol. 47, No. 20, pp. 2083-2087). Sage CA: Los Angeles, CA: SAGE Publications.

[11] K. Mania, B. D. Adelstein, S. R. Ellis, and M. I. Hill, "Perceptual sensitivity to head tracking latency in virtual environments with varying degrees of scene complexity." In *Proceedings of the 1st Symposium on Applied perception in graphics and visualization* (pp. 39-47). ACM, August 2004.

[12] C. Westphal, "Challenges in networking to support augmented reality and virtual reality", ICNC 2017, Silicon Valley, California, USA, 26-29 January, 2017.

[13] P. Mach, and Z. Becvar, "Mobile Edge Computing: A Survey on Architecture and Computation Offloading," in IEEE Communications Surveys & Tutorials, vol. 19, no. 3, pp. 1628-1656, thirdquarter 2017.

[14] 3GPP TR 36.913, "Requirements for further advancements for E-UTRA (LTE-Advanced)".

[15] I. Parvez, A. Rahmati, I. Guvenc, A. I. Sarwat, and H. Dai, "A Survey on Low Latency Towards 5G: RAN, Core Network and Caching Solutions," arXiv:1708.02562v1 Aug 2017.

[16] T. Kämäräinen, M. Siekkinen, A. Ylä-Jääski, W. Zhang, and Pan Hui, "A Measurement Study on Achieving Imperceptible Latency in Mobile Cloud Gaming", *Proceedings of the 8th ACM on Multimedia Systems Conference,* MMSys'17, pp. 88-89, 2017.

[17] M. Nabiyouni, S. Scerbo Siroberto, D. A. Bowman, and T. Höllerer, "Relative Effects of Real-world and Virtual-World Latency on an Augmented Reality Training Task: An AR Simulation Experiment", Frontiers in ICT, vol 3, pp 34, 2017.

[18] M. Maternia, and J. F. Monserrat (ed.), METIS-II/D2.1 Performance evaluation framework.

[19] IM360, "Surrounded by Wild Elephants in 4k 360" goo.gl/NdP1WN [retrieved: Sep. 2017]

[20] FFmpeg.org [retrieved: Sep. 2017]

[21] R. Schatz, A. Sackl, C. Timmerer, and B. Gardlo, "Towards subjective quality of experience assessment for omnidirectional video streaming," QoMEX, Erfurt, 2017, pp. 1-6.

[22] Recommendation ITU-T P.913 Methods for the subjective assessment of video quality, audio quality and audiovisual quality of Internet video and distribution quality television in any environment, 03/201

Network Functions Evaluation of Hardware Accelerated NFV Platform in View of 5G Requirements

Athanasia-Nancy Alonistioti
Department of Informatics & Telecommunications
National Kapodistrian University of Athens
Athens, Greece
email: nancy@di.uoa.gr

***Abstract*— Network Function Virtualization (NFV) enables the implementation of "softwarized" network functions, using a shared hardware substrate. However, such functions are expected to offer performances comparable to native hardware environments. Therefore, increasing the performance of "software-based" Network Functions (NFs) that are executed on commodity hardware servers is an emerging challenge that should be addressed to fulfill the vision of NFV. Hardware accelerators, such as Many Integrated Core Architectures (MICs), Graphic Processor Units (GPUs) and Field Programmable Gate Arrays (FPGAs) are a valuable asset that can be paired with commodity servers to boost up network services performance. In this paper, we present an analysis of two commonplace network functions: a) Routing, b) Firewall and evaluate their implementation in an NFV middlebox combining software based network functions along with hardware accelerated ones in view of their applicability for 5G and interworking with Broadband Forum (BBF) network segments. Finally, we present detailed experimental results of CPU, GPU and FPGA solutions for these functions (routing, firewall and DPI) in order to evaluate their performance and verify their suitability for incorporation in hardware-accelerated NFV platforms.**

Keywords- 5G; Network Function Virtualization; Network services.

I. INTRODUCTION

Virtualization is the ability to implement a functionality separated from the hardware and simulated as a "virtual instance". Modern networks increasingly rely on advanced network processing functions for a wide spectrum of crucial functions ranging from security (firewalls, Intrusion Detection Systems (IDS), etc.), traffic shaping (rate limiters, load balancers), dealing with address space exhaustion (Network Address Translation (NAT)) or improving the performance of network applications (traffic accelerators, caches, proxies), to name a few.

Middleboxes are defined as intermediary boxes performing these network functions and represent the defacto approach for network evolution in response to changing performance, security, and policy compliance requirements. NFV brings a new era in network virtualization by involving the implementation of software-based middleboxes that implement such NFs in software and can run on standard server hardware. Such NFV middleboxes are suitable nodes for implementing a virtualization scheme in the basis of "Network Function as a Service (VNFaaS)" as defined in the NFV standardization process [1]. ICT research community seeks to address this issue [2] by shifting software solutions running on top of modern multi-core systems that have good flexibility and programmability, but they inherently lack high parallelism and quickly become the performance bottleneck for more compute-intensive applications, to a decoupling from dedicated hardware solutions. For example, even the best multi-core software algorithms today for routing and firewall can only achieve a rate of up to 30 Gbps [6], which is an order of much less than the widely deployed 100 Gbps links used in large Internet Service Provider backbones and Data Center networks. Moreover, taking into consideration that the performance vision in the era of 5G wireless networks is to achieve a 10Gbps individual user experience [3], the Internet Service Provider backbones and Data Center networks will boost their bandwidth needs in the scale of Tbps. Therefore, increasing the performance of "software-based" network services that are executed on commodity hardware servers is an emerging challenge that should be addressed to fulfill the vision of "software-based" network services through NFV. Modern commodity servers can be paired with hardware accelerators (Many Integrated Core Architectures (MICs), Graphic Processor Units (GPUs) and Field Programmable Gate Arrays (FPGAs) to boost up their performance. Such accelerators are a valuable asset and can be exploited to offload on demand the "software-based" network services that cannot comply with high performance demanding NFV environments. In this direction, the work presented in this paper explores the pairing of modern hardware accelerator (MICs, GPUs, and FPGAs) with commodity hardware to build a scalable hardware accelerated NFV platform to speed up NFs and support NF reallocation to different accelerators on demand. Important NFs to be considered in this paper are a) Routing and b) Firewall. These are very important NFs in view also of the needs for Broadband Forum (BBF) and 5G 3GPP interworking for the seamless application provision and QoS requirements between the involved network segments [14].

The rest of this paper is organized as follows. Section II presents related work and in parallel examines the considered NFs, their characteristics, their challenges and the applicability of hardware acceleration on them. Section III presents experimental results to evaluate and compare the performance of software and hardware assisted implementations of these use cases. Finally, Section IV concludes this paper.

II. Network Functions: Related work Identification and NFV challenges

In this section, we present the two aforementioned NFs a) Routing, b) Firewall. An overview of algorithmic schemes, applicability of hardware acceleration, advantages, related work and NFV tradeoffs are discussed for each use case.

A. Routing

IP Router functionalities are grouped into two categories, packet processing and packet forwarding. Routing table lookup is the most critical packet processing algorithm and has been extensively discussed in the literature, as it is considered the main bottleneck in router performance [4]. Therefore, we focus on routing table lookup process, which is the main performance bottleneck and we omit discussing updating process. Key metrics used to evaluate routing table lookup performance are searching time, dynamic updates and memory requirements. In software routing table lookup schemes [4], tries are the dominant solution for the organization of IP Router Forward Information Base (FIB) and the service of IP lookup requests in virtualized environments [5]. Multibit tries are a subcategory of tries that achieve a speedup of the lookup process as multi-bit tries examine strides of bits at a time and lower total memory accesses, as shown in Fig. 1.

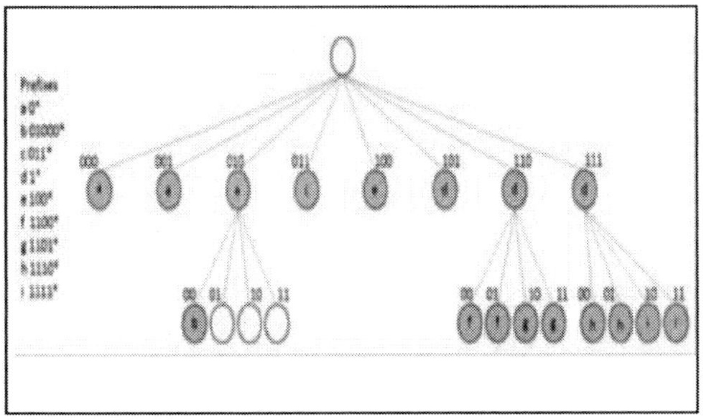

Figure 1. Multi-bit trie representation of a FIB.

Moreover, further speedup can be achieved by the processing of "IP request" in large batches if parallelism in lookup process can be implemented. Towards this direction, GPUs can instantiate thousands or threads in parallel that can be exploited to boost performance in trie lookup process. In addition, there are three characteristics in IP table lookup process that make GPU implementations a tempting alternative [6], [7].

•IP requests in large batches: In real routers, IP requests can form batches of more than 216 concurrent requests. However, the bigger the size of a batch, the better is the utilization of GPU computing capabilities.

•IP requests locality: In real traffic conditions, IP requests present repetition (e.g., UDP flows, TCP bursts). This feature boosts performance in GPU, since accessing adjacent memory positions is extremely fast in GPU oriented implementations.

•GPU memory coalescence: extremely large FIBs (i.e., more levels in a trie) do not always mean more references in memory and thus lower lookup speed. Due to coalescence in GPU memory, the size of each level of the trie also affects the performance in parallel lookup.

On the other hand, one of the deficiencies of GPU is that host memory and GPU are separate units and thus transfer of data between host and device memory is inevitable. In order to alleviate time consuming I/O transactions, batch of requests can be divided into several groups executed on independent kernels on different streams in order to achieve I/O transactions pipelining [8]. Hardware-based routing table lookup schemes [9] fall in two categories: TCAM-based (TernaryContent Addressable Memory) and SRAM-based (Static Random Access Memory) solutions.

B. Firewall

Firewalls usually respond in synergy with IP routers. Firewall architectures have the same unique scope; to examine packet headers under a hierarchical set of rules and either discard or accept them. An indicative example of firewall policy rules is presented in Fig. 2. Without loss of generality, we will focus on the most used but simplest architecture of firewalls, the stateless firewall, to present the algorithmic schemes for purely software and hardware accelerated approaches along with their advantages and tradeoffs.

RuleNo.	Protocol	Type	Source IP	Source Port	Destination IP	Destination Port	Action
1	TCP	-	140.192.37.2	*	161.120.33.5	1433	ACCEPT
2	TCP	-	140.192.37.1	*	161.120.33.*	22	DENY
3	UDP	-	142.192.*.*	*	161.121.33.43	69	ACCEPT
4	ICMP	8	141.192.*.*	*	*	*	ACCEPT

Figure 2. Firewall Rules.

The main pitfall in software-based firewall solutions is the linear search of the ruleset for every packet (ruleset may exceed 1K rules in many cases). Even though, linear search is a non-sophisticated searching algorithm, it is followed by open source and commercial products. Firewall rules usually are dominated by TCP protocol rules. For example, a typical distribution with regards to the protocols is:

75% TCP, 14% UDP, 4% ICMP, 6%, 1% other [13]. Taking into consideration that firewall rules are examined sequentially and UDP rules are usually positioned at the bottom of the hierarchical list, the performance of firewall degrades sharply. Towards this direction research efforts propose several optimization approaches such as rule reordering, multilevel filtering, statistical analysis and data mining techniques to predict the rules best suit to every packet, etc. Since firewalls usually work in synergy with IP routers, GPU is a promising alternative for firewall as well and firewall implementations can exploit the GPU features that are also exploited for routing schemes to speed up their performance.

Hardware-based firewall schemes are also either TCAM-based or SRAM-based solutions. TCAM solutions can perform fast parallel searches over all entries in one clock cycle but are not scalable to bigger rulesets. SRAM-based solutions are more scalable but cannot perform parallel searches.

However, when combined with pipelining and bit vector (BV) splitting algorithms [11] they can perform parallel searches on individual fields of a packet header to increase performance. Finally, when firewall schemes combine BV splitting algorithms, deep pipelining and multiport RAMs in modern FPGAs, these hardware implementations can achieve high performance by processing up to two packets per clock cycle.

III. EXPERIMENTAL RESULTS

In this section, we examine the three considered NFs (routing, firewall, DPI) that are included in the NFV middlebox. We evaluate the achieved performance both in CPU, GPU and FPGA implementations of the above described algorithms for these NFs. We have utilized the implementations of [7] for routing and firewall CPU and GPU implementations, enhanced by essential modification to address the challenges that are discussed in Section 3. Our purpose is to evaluate the throughput of IP lookup and firewall rule traversal algorithms independently, without examining additional overheads from NIC packet buffering. Considered implementations are composed of three consecutive phases: i) pre-shading, ii) shading and iii) post-shading. Pre- and post-shading phases run on CPU worker threads and perform the actual packet batching, host-to-device and device-to-host batch transfers (in case of GPU implementation) and other miscellaneous tasks. Shading process, which realizes the actual NFs functionality is executed either on a single core CPU implementation, or is offloaded to GPU and performed by GPU master threads. Our FPGA routing implementation is based on the architecture that is proposed in [9]. The routing FPGA architecture implements a full binary search trie (BST) for the IP look up process by exploiting FPGA's embedded memories. Pipelining is used to increase the throughput. Our firewall FPGA implementation is based on the architecture that is proposed in [11]. A memory optimized Field Split Bit Vector (FSBV) was implemented that utilize TCAM/CAM for rule fields with a very small number of unique values compared with the ruleset size. Moreover, multiple bits (k bit stride) inspection was exploited to reduce pipeline length and increase the achieved performance [12].

In order to achieve realistic case study conditions, we have exploited real network traffic measurements so as to highlight the benefits and peculiarities of each of the three NFs and their provided solutions, either software or hardware based. Regarding the IP routing NF, our purpose was to examine the effectiveness of FIB storage and FIB traversal. For these reasons, we have exploited CAIDA FIB records so as to construct FIB tries with varying size. In case of software and GPU solutions, multi-bit tries guarantee balanced tries with minimum depth extension, and FIB entries storage in coalescenced memory positions. Regarding the firewall NF, our purpose was to construct firewall rules that conform to typical protocol distribution [13] and examine realistic firewall rules cardinality. Moreover, DefCOM provide us with various traffic patterns (TCP/UDP intensive, TCP/UDP balanced), so as to examine firewall performance under normal and malicious traffic conditions (DoS). In Fig. 3 and Fig. 4 respective results are presented.

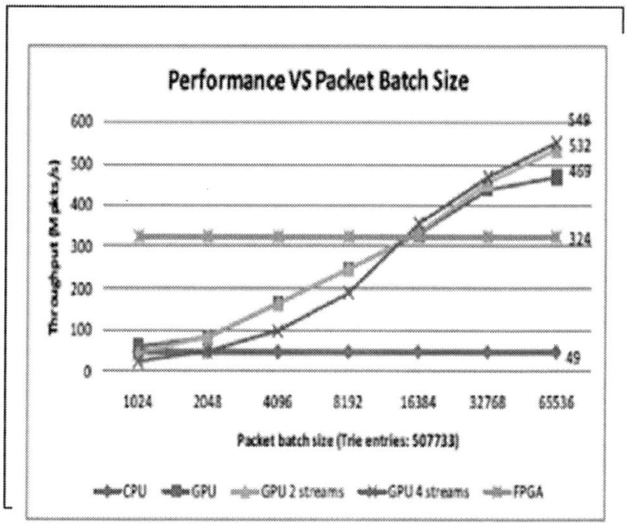

Figure 3. Routing scheme performance analysis: scaling packet batch size.

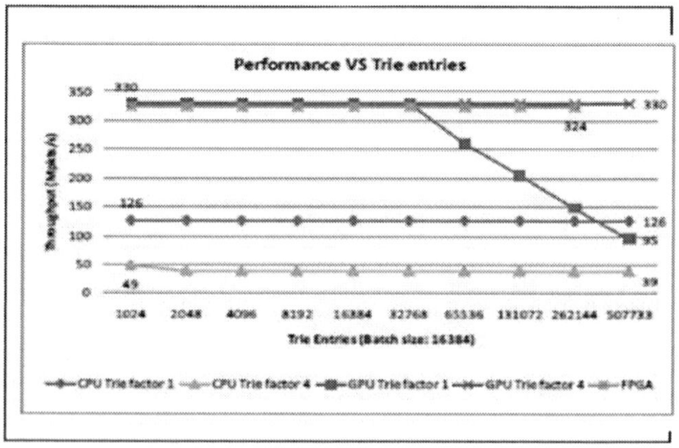

Figure 4. Routing scheme performance analysis: scaling trie entries

In case of routing NF, Figure 3 shows that scaling in batch size boosts up GPU configurations and FPGA and CPU present stable performance. GPU routing implementations achieve a peak performance of more than 500Mpkts/s and FPGA routing implementations can achieve a peak performance of 330 Mpkts/s while CPU-only implementations can achieve a performance of 49Mpkts/s. Moreover, GPU implementation that utilizes 2 streams has better performance compared to the single stream GPU implementation especially in case of heavy traffic (~12% improvement). GPU implementations outperform CPU ones in all cases, presenting up to ~10x acceleration in heavy workloads (65K packets per batch). The use of 4 GPU streams is not efficient in low workload conditions and achieve slightly better throughput (compared to GPU with 2 streams) in traffic congestion. Finally, FPGA implementations have significantly higher throughput in most traffic conditions but are outperformed from GPU implementations in extremely heavy traffic conditions (65K packets per batch). In Figure 4, we also examine the achieved performance in correlation with the FIB entries. There is a 3x performance acceleration in GPU implementation when compared with the CPU implementation when large FIBs are utilized regardless of the trie factor (either 1-stride or 4-stride multi-bit tries in both use cases). Additionally, GPU implementation that exploits 4-stride trie has better performance compared to GPU implementation that utilizes 1-stride due to memory coalescence. In case of CPU implementation, the performance degrades for more complex trie structures. Finally, for FPGA implementation, the performance is stable even when large FIBs are utilized.

We have evaluated the memory utilization for both GPU and FPGA implementation. The GPU implementation utilizes up to 50% of the available memory in our GPU card even for the larger FIB set that we have examined. In contrary, the FPGA routing implementation dominates our chip in large FIB sets since the 256K FIB set needs about 95% of the chip embedded RAM.

Experimental results for the firewall NF when scaling both the packet batch size and the firewall ruleset size are shown in Fig. 5 and Fig. 6, respectively. GPU firewall implementations achieve a peak performance of more than 35Mpkts/s and FPGA firewall implementations can achieve a peak performance of 32 Mpkts/s while CPU-only implementations can achieve a performance of only 2.48 Mpkts/s. The experimental results show a significant performance boost in GPU implementation when large packet batches are utilized. Moreover, the utilization of multiple GPU streams further improves the achieved performance. FPGA firewall implementation has stable performance that is not correlated with packet batch size scaling and is significantly higher than the CPU and GPU implementations in small batch sizes .In large batch sizes, the GPU implementation outperforms the FPGA implementation. When the firewall ruleset increases, the achieved performance is seriously affected in both CPU and GPU implementations as depicted in Fig. 6. Finally, since the FPGA implementation builds a parallel hardware structure for every rule, its performance is not affected by the number of the firewall rules. Finally, in case of heavy traffic load (65K packets per batch) and large input batches GPU outperforms FPGA implementation for real traffic.

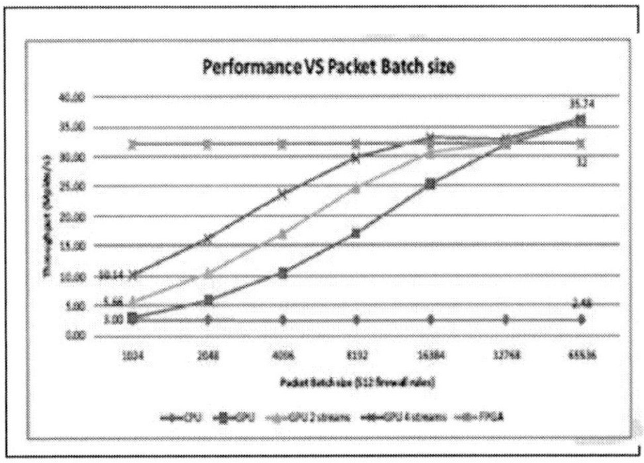

Figure 5. Firewall scheme performance analysis: scaling packet batch size.

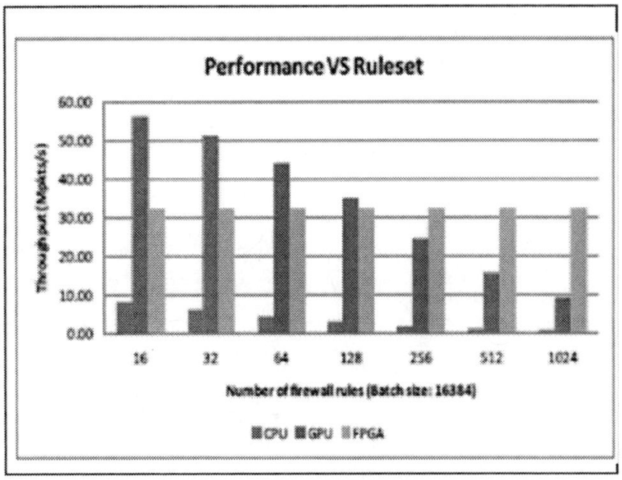

Figure 6. Firewall scheme performance analysis: scaling firewall ruleset size.

Concerning the resource utilization of these implementations, we have evaluated the memory utilization for both GPU and FPGA implementation. The GPU implementation utilizes almost 2% of the available memory in our GPU card even for the larger input batches that we have examined. The FPGA FSBV firewall implementation needs about 18% of the chip embedded RAM even for the larger implemented ruleset (1024 rules) since the chosen architecture is optimized for memory utilization.

The acquired results confirm the feasibility to consider the virtualization of such NFs in the 5G domain, both in the terms of operational performance, scalability but also in terms of their reconfigurability and dynamicity such implementations entail, enabling transparent integration and service continuity between 5G 3GPP and BBF network segments.

IV. CONCLUSIONS

We have presented an analysis of two commonplace network functions: a) Routing, b) Firewall in the context of NFV and function "softwarization". Experimental results for CPU, GPU and FPGA solutions for these functions have been evaluated for their performance to verify the abovementioned functions suitability for incorporation in hardware-accelerated NFV platforms. The results have shown that there are several benefits in scaling, reconfiguration and operational efficiency without compromising performance for the virtualization of NFs studied in the presented work, especially considering the requirements for 5G. As the studied NFs are very important n view also of the needs for Broadband Forum (BBF) and 5G 3GPP interworking for the seamless application provision and QoS requirements between the involved network segments, the results confirm the applicability of such solutions in the 5G domain.

ACKNOWLEDGMENT

The author gratefully acknowledges the NKUA and HUAWEI collaboration project in SDN and the fruitful inputs and comments from the relevant colleagues related to the presented results.

REFERENCES

[1] ETSI GS NFV 001,"Network Functions Virtualisation (NFV):Use Cases". [Online]. Available from: http://www.etsi.org/technologiesclusters/technologies/nfv [retrieved 11,2012].

[2] V. Sekar, N. Egi, S. Ratnasamy, M.K. Reiter, and G. Shi, "Design and implementation of a consolidated middlebox architecture", Proc. 9th USENIX conference on Networked Systems Design and Implementation (NSDI), 2012, p.24-38.

[3] "*5G: A Technology Vision*", Position paper, Huawei, [Online]. Available from: www.huawei.com/ilink/en/download/HW_314849 [retrieved: 9,2017].

[4] M. A. Ruiz-Sanchez, E. W. Biersack, and W. Dabbous, "Survey and Taxonomy of IP Address Lookup Algorithms", IEEE Network: The Magazine of Global Internetworking archive, vol. 15, no. 2, pp 8-23, March 2001.

[5] S. Haoyu, M. Kodialam, H. Fang, and T. V.Lakshman, "Efficient Trie Braiding in Scalable Virtual Routers," IEEE/ACM Transactions on Networking, vol. 20, no. 5, pp. 1489-1500, Oct. 2012.

[6] M. Dobrescu, N. Egi, K. Argyraki, B. G. Chun, K. Fall, G. Iannaccone, A. Knies, M. Manesh, S. Ratnasamy, "RouteBricks: exploiting parallelism to scale software routers", ACM Symposium on Operating Systems Principles (SOSP), 2009, p. 15-28, ISBN: 978-1-60558-752-3.

[7] S. Han, K. Jang, K. Park, and S. Moon, "PacketShader: a GPU-accelerated software router", ACM SIGCOMM Computer Communication conference (SIGCOMM), pp. 195-206, 2010.

[8] W. Sun and R. Ricci, "Fast and flexible: parallel packet processing with GPUs and click", 9th ACM/IEEE symposium on Architectures for networking and communications systems (ANCS), pp. 25-36, 2013.

[9] H. Le and V. K. Prasanna, "Scalable High Throughput and Power Efficient IP-Lookup on FPGA", 17th IEEE Symposium on Field Programmable Custom Computing Machines (FCCM), April 2009, p. 167- 174 , ISBN: 978-0-7695-3716-0.

[10] U. Mustafa, M. M. Masud, Z. Trabelsi, T. Wood, and Z.Al.Harthi, "Firewall performance optimization using data mining techniques," 9th International Wireless Communications and Mobile Computing Conference (IWCMC), pp. 934-940, 2013.

[11] T. Ganegedara and V. K. Prasanna, "Stridebv 400g+ single chip packet classification", IEEE Conference on High Performance Switching and Routing (HPSR), pp. 1-6, 2012.

[12] H. J. Jung, Z. K. Baker, and V. K. Prasanna, "Performance of FPGA implementation of bit-split architecture for intrusion detection systems", 20th International Parallel and Distributed Processing Symposium (IPDPS), 2006, p. 124-124, DOI: 10.1109/IPDPS.2006.1639434.

[13] D. Rovniagin and A. Wool, "The geometric efficient matching algorithm for firewalls", IEEE Transactions on Dependable and Secure Computing, vol. 8, no. 1, pp. 147–159, 2011.

[14] Broadband Forum TR-203 "*Interworking between Next Generation Fixed and 3GPP Wireless Networks*" Issue: 1 Issue Date: August 2012, [Online]. Available from: https://www.broadband-forum.org/technical/download/TR-203.pdf .

On V2X Network Slicing: Using Context Information to Improve Mobility Management

Panagiotis Spapis, Chan Zhou
Huawei German Research Center
Munich, Germany
email: panagiotis.spapis@huawei.com
chan.zhou@huawei.com

Alexandros Kaloxylos
Department of Informatics and Telecommunications
University of Peloponnese
Tripoli, Greece
email: kaloxyl@uop.gr

Abstract— **Network slicing in for 5th Generation (5G) networks enables the support of multiple logical networks, tailor-cut to the requirements of specific services. Initial specifications have already been produced by the 3rd Generation Partnership Project (3GPP) that describe the operation of slicing. However, the existing specifications lack specific details on how the network functions can be fine-tuned to fully optimize the network performance for specific use cases. This paper provides a comprehensive overview related to the latest status of the 3GPP standardization process related to slicing. Also, it proposes a new mobility management scheme, called Context Enhanced MOBility management (CEMOB), that is tailor-cut for communicating vehicles. The point we make is that by taking advantage of contextual information, in this case for vehicle-to-everything (V2X) communications, the performance of network control functions such as mobility management can be significantly improved. Slicing and the overall 5G architecture, support a simple introduction of contextual information into the network functions of a slice.**

Keywords-network slicing, mobility management, V2X communications.

I. INTRODUCTION

5G networks target, apart from the support of the telecommunications sector, also the "vertical industries" like autonomous driving, smart factories, new health services, etc. An extensive list of 5G use cases can be found in [1] [2]. A thorough examination of the verticals has identified that these sectors have diverse requirements. These requirements are mapped to different network Key Performance Indicators (KPIs). These KPIs indicatively include throughput, transmission reliability, latency, energy consumption, blocking probability, etc. Since every vertical has a different operation environment in terms of the density and mobility of the users, the arrival rate and the duration of different application and services, it is evident that no single network can support efficiently all these different use cases.

Thus, it appears that the deployment of parallel logical networks over the same network infrastructure is a necessity. These logical networks may have network functions (NFs) configured differently or even introduce new network functions both in the Radio Access Network (RAN) [3] as well as the Core Network (CN) [4].

The 3rd Generation Partnership Project (3GPP) has defined a network slice to be " A logical network that provides specific network capabilities and network characteristics" [5]. A "Network Slice" is implemented by a "slice instance" that in its turn is created by a "network slice template". The latter is a template that defines a complete logical network including the NFs, their interfaces and their corresponding resources.

Network slicing has been intensively investigated during the past years both by industry and academia. There are several research proposals that target full flexibility in terms of selecting, organizing and deploying NFs [6]. At the same time, 3GPP is currently working on the phase one specifications for 5G networks that include also the support for slicing. The standardization activities follow a more cautious path and attempt to re-use existing NFs or share NFs across different slices as much as possible. Note that although the use cases to be supported, as well as their requirements, have been thoroughly studied [7], current specifications do not provide fully tailor-cut solutions for them. In order to do this, it is needed to work really close with the representatives of the so called "vertical industries" (e.g., transportation, health, factories, energy). This is needed to understand not only the requirements and the operational environment, but also the contextual information produced and how these can be used to optimize network functions. For example, the newly founded 5G Automotive Association 5GAA [8] is working towards such a direction. Still, the activities towards the proposal of mechanisms driven by these organizations in the standardization are in primitive steps.

In the current paper, we present the latest status of the standardization activities related to network slicing. We also provide a new mobility management mechanism for autonomous driven vehicles that takes advantage of contextual information and we demonstrate how this information can be used by the standardized 5G NFs to bring significant benefits in a control operation such mobility management. This is an exemplary scheme to highlight that different requirements need very different solutions and the network shall support these solutions.

The rest of the section is organized as follows. In Section II we provide the latest status of 3GPP in relation to slicing. Section III discusses how mobility management is planned to be supported in the technical specifications and why we consider this not to be applicable for moving vehicles. In Section IV, we provide the details of our scheme design to use the 5G network functions. In Section V we present quantitative results that illustrate the benefits of our scheme. Finally, Section VI concludes the paper and describes future directions.

II. Slice Support in 3GPP

3GPP has decided to treat 5G specifications in two phases. The first one is to be completed by September 2018 (Release 15). This phase addresses a more urgent subset of the commercial needs. Phase 2 is to be completed by March 2020 (Release 16) for the IMT 2020 submission, having addressed all identified use cases & requirements. In relation to slicing, several working groups are currently progressing on the key elements and procedures that have to be specified.

In [5] and [9], the 5G network architecture is presented. There, a list of technical key issues, as well as potential solutions for slicing is presented. For example, in these documents the issues of slice selection, slice isolation, sharing of NFs, multi-slice connectivity, management of slices, etc. are being addressed.

Although several issues remain open, it seems that there is convergence in several principles. The first principle is that NFs, previously incorporated in monolithic network components, are now decomposed to smaller modules. The target is to allow a synthesis and configuration of the NFs on a per slice type basis. A second principle is the further splitting of user and control plane functions to facilitate a more flexible evolution of NFs. A third key principle is the exposure of NFs to service through appropriate APIs. This is expected to allow a better collaboration among network operators and service providers.

Figure 1 presents a summary of the supported NFs. The CP function in the CN are considered to be the following:

- **Unified Data Management (UDM):** supports the Authentication Credential Repository and Processing Function (ARPF).
- **Authentication Server Function (AUSF):** supports the Authentication Server Function (AUSF)
- **Policy Control function (PCF):** supports unified policy framework to govern network behaviour, provides policy rules to control plane functions
- **Core Access and Mobility Management Function (AMF):** supports mobility management, access authentication and authorization, security anchor functions and context management
- **Session Management Function (SMF).** supports session management, selection and control of UP functions, downlink data notification and roaming
- **User Plane Function (UPF):** is the anchor point for inter/intra RAT mobility and the external PDU session point of interconnection, supports packet routing and forwarding, QoS handling for user plane, packet inspection and policy rule enforcement
- **Network Exposure Function (NEF):** provides a means to securely exchange information between services and 3GPP NFs.
- **NF Repository Function (NRF):** maintains the deployed NF Instance information when deploying/updating/removing NF instances
- **Network Slice Selection Function (NSSF):** supports the functionality to bind a UE with a specific slice

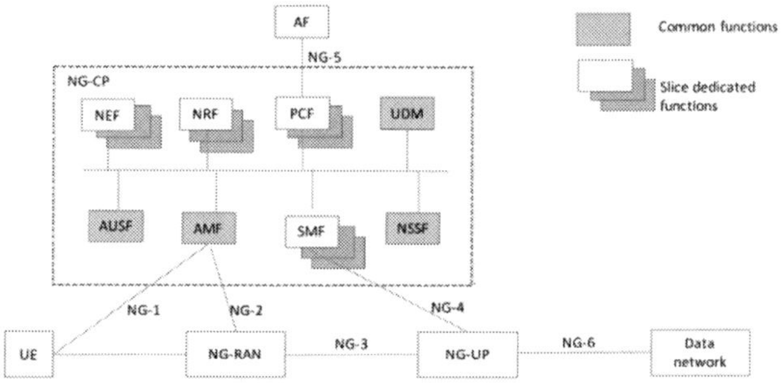

Figure 1: 5G service based architecture (adapted from [5])

Note that some of these functions are common for all slices while others can be dedicated for different slices. A UE may access multiple slices concurrently via a single RAN. For such cases, it is assumed that the involved slices should share some control plane functions, like the AMF. The abovementioned logical network allows the support of Application Functions (AF) and provides connectivity to typical external data networks.

Interestingly enough the question whether RAN is sliced or not still remains open. However, it has been agreed that RAN will be slice-aware so as to treat slice traffic according to the customer needs. Also, RAN shall support resource isolation among slices so as to avoid shortage of shared resources in one slice to break the service level agreement on another [6].

However, detailed alternative solutions have been proposed on how RAN is involved in slice selection by passing an appropriate identifier to the core network elements. Currently slicing for RAN essentially focuses on different scheduling schemes for different slices and also by providing different L1/L2 configurations. Moreover, it is considered that even if a User Equipment (UE) is connected to multiple slices a single Radio Resource and Control (RRC) entity will be used were as different protocols (i.e., Packet Data Convergence Protocol – PDCP and Radio Link Control - RLC) can be used.

Every slice is identified by a Single Network Slice Selection Assistance information (S-NSSAI) identifier. This identifier consists of a Slice/Service type (SST) and a slice Differentiator (SD) which optional information used to differentiate among different slices of the same type. Currently only 3 SST values have been agreed to be supported. These are a) enhanced Mobile Broadband (eMBB), b) Massive Internet of Things (MIoT), and c) Ultra Reliable Low Latency Communications (URLLC) [5]. This information is exchanged as part of Non-access stratum signalling through the RAN.

In [11], the lifecycle of a network slice is described by the following phases: a) Preparation phase, b) Instantiation,

Configuration and Activation phase, c) Run-time phase and d) Decommissioning phase.

III. CURRENT STATUS FOR MOBILITY MANAGEMENT IN 5G NETWORKS

Mobility management for legacy systems was performed as follows. The network was divided into non-overlapping regions called Tracking Areas (TAs). Idle UEs would have to inform the network each time they cross the border of such areas or when a timer, typically set at 54 minutes) expires. However, this design was initially static and the cost for re-arranging the coverage areas of TAs was quite high. Moreover, a problem appeared from excessive Tracking Area Update (TAU) messages due to the movement of the users near the Tracking Area boarders. That's why the notion of Tracking Area Lists (TAL) was introduced. TALs were assigned per UE and allowed the overlapping of TAs. The algorithm to define the TAL is proprietary and the operator according to his strategy decides whether to allocate large or short TALs. Whenever a UE has to be discovered for delivering data to it or in case of an incoming call, paging is executed in a subset or all the cells in the TAL according to the operator strategy [12]. If a subset of the cells of the TAL is paged there is a risk of increased delay due to page misses or but if all the cells are pages there is increased signalling cost. Also the size of the TAL relates to a signalling tradeoff since small TALs have reduced paging signalling cost but require frequent TAU and large TALs vice versa.

Even with these improvements, it has been noticed that for idle UEs that had to switch to connected mode, signalling had again to be exchanged up to the core network and more specifically the Mobility Management Entity (MME) where contextual information (such as security credentials) were kept. Considering that smartphones have a number of applications (e.g., facebook, skype, instant messaging) that have to wake up asynchronously and exchange small amount of information, this created in practise significant signalling load.

This is why for the 5G systems, mobility for idle terminals had to be redefined [10]. In the latest specifications, the RAN-based Notification Area (RNA) has been defined. This can be considered as a smaller subset of a TAL where a UE can move within without informing the network about its exact location. Also, a new state called RRC_INACTIVE is introduced where the context information of a UE is kept locally so as to avoid contacting the CN entities (i.e., AMF) when the UE switches again to the connected mode. This addresses the problem of frequent waking-up of devices (e.g., smartphones) and minimizes that signalling load towards the CN. In terms of mobility management, the UE context is kept in the last serving base station, called gNB in 5G systems. If the UE wakes up and becomes connected under a new gNB inside the same RNA then it uses the *RRCConnectionResume* messages to force the new gNB retrieve its context from the last serving gNB. The new gNB may also trigger a path switch by communicating with the AMF. Paging a UE takes place from the last serving gNB to all gNBs that are member of the RNA. These procedures are illustrated in Figure 2. On top of these messages, note that whenever a UE crosses the border between RNAs it needs to receive the gNBs identifiers that are members of the new RNA.

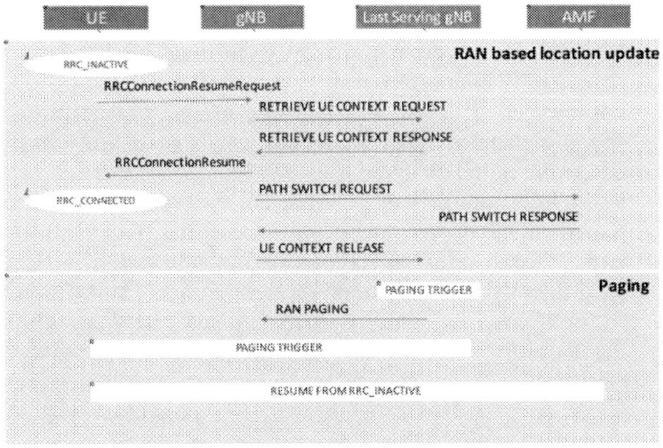

Figure 2: RAN based mobility management (adapted from [10])

This mechanism treats indeed several of the inefficiencies present in existing cellular systems. However, as explained in [13], the RAN based mobility management scheme suffers from excessive load for high moving UEs. This is why Hailu and Säily suggest a hybrid scheme where a typical CN mobility management takes places for high moving UEs, while RAN based mobility management is executed for UEs of lower mobility. To do this the UEs have to report the mobility to the CN at some intervals (e.g., during location update). Moreover, the authors also indicate potential delay issues that may arise if there is no direct interface between the last serving gNB and the new one. In such a case signalling has to travel essentially through the CN. The lack of a direct link between base stations is not uncommon in deployed and operating mobile networks. Note that in the current standard specification both the typical CN mobility management as well as the RAN based are supported.

The adoption of RAN based mobility management scheme will be beneficial for some of the 5G use cases but totally inefficient for others. A not applicable use case is the one of the autonomously driving vehicles because of the high mobility. To optimize a control procedure like mobility management, one has to take advantage of contextual information that will be available to operator as we discuss in the next section.

IV. CEMOB: CONTEXT ENHANCED MOBILITY MANAGEMENT

Autonomous driving is one of the key targets of the industry for the next decade. 3GPP has already specified an architecture and mechanisms to support inter-vehicle communication and access to service specific servers (i.e., V2X application server - [14]). The support of such services introduces additional contextual information that if used can greatly improve even control operations for a mobile network. More specifically, it is expected that in order to form a route, a vehicle will communicate with a server to receive the path to be followed. These servers can also estimate the time a vehicle will need to be at a certain position in the path. Such functionality exists even today with well-established applications like Google maps or any other GPS navigators. Obviously, these applications do not and they should not know any information about the deployed base stations of an operator. However, by passing the information of a route to an operator, it is an easy task to perform a translation of path coordinates to predicted serving gNBs. Furthermore, the specific geography of the roads can significantly assist in determining the exact cells a vehicle is going to pass through. Such information can be used to really optimize mobility management operation by optimizing the TALs allocation, and at the same time optimizing the paging strategy. Additionally, the functions modularization in 5G facilitates the optimum functionality placement in the network which for the mobility management functionality in certain use cases (like the V2X ones) would make sense to be split between the RAN and the Core. Moreover, 5G networks will allow, through secure APIs, for services to communicate with network components and exchange information.

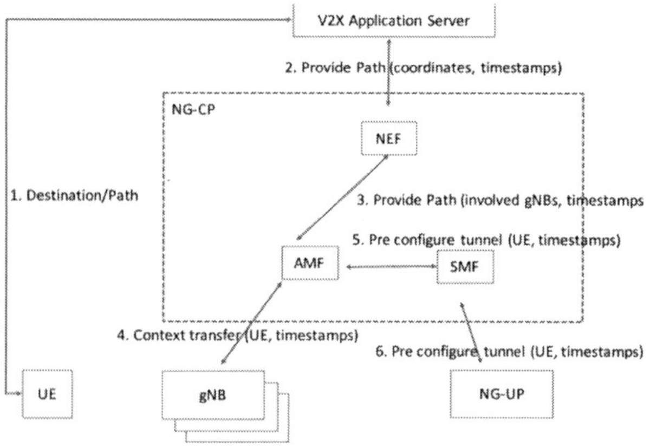

Figure 3: Mobility management for vehicles in 5G networks

In Figure 3, we present how a new mobility management scheme for vehicles operating in 5G networks can be implemented. Whenever a UE/vehicle wants to reach a specific destination, it will communicate with a V2X application server and it will receive the path so as the computer inside the car to start the autonomous driving functions. Upon calculation of such a path by the server the information in terms of coordinates and timestamps (time when the vehicle will be at a specific point) can be communicated to the mobile operator. This will take place through message exchange with the NEF. The NEF can also translate the coordinates into specific gNBs and forward further this information to the involved AMFs. These entities on their turn can transfer the UE context to the involved gNBs. Moreover, they will communicate with the corresponding SMFs so as to pre-configure the data path for the vehicles. Note that this pre-configuration does not imply that resources will be allocated for large period of times but rather only for a short time for which a vehicle is expected to be in a certain area. Obviously, a vehicle (or the respective server) may need to re-calculate a path, but this again will take place through the same communication with the V2X application server, so the same process will be repeated. The communication of a UE with an application server, especially if located inside the domain of the mobile operator can be in terms of a few tenths of millisecond [15], thus any updating of network components is not expected to affect the location management process, since even high moving vehicles will not have change their position more than a few meters.

When a UE wants to communicate with a neighbouring one, the request will stop in the gNB and the gNB mobility management function will perform the paging to this cell and the neighbouring ones, since there is no need to communicate with the core for transferring the UE context in the RAN because it already resides there and the actual location of the UE is well known with quite good accuracy.

The benefits of such scheme are manifold. Firstly, the mechanism is fully optimized for moving UEs no matter their speed. Thus, it is not necessary to revert to the typical CN mobility management scheme if their speed is high and reach high paging load. Secondly, there is no need to exchange control messages for UE location updates over the wireless interface which is the bottleneck for any wireless system. Furthermore, delay for transferring the context information of a UE from a serving to a new gNB is zero, since this information is in place before hand. This delay in the RAN based scheme can be significant as we have already explained in the cases where the gNBs have no direct interface and their communication takes place through the CN. Finally, the paging cost is significantly lower than the CN based scheme and as well better than the RAN based one since the known geography of the streets can minimize the number of involved cells only to very few ones. All these benefits are possible because the proposed scheme takes advantage of contextual information that can be available to the NFs of the mobile operator through the modularized architecture that allows different NFs to be used for different logical networks (i.e., slices).

In the next section, we quantify the aforementioned gains of the proposed scheme.

V. PERFORMANCE ANALYSIS

To evaluate the performance of CEMOB we compare it with the CN and RAN based mobility management schemes. Firstly, in order to calculate the signalling cost during paging we follow the analysis in [13]. Let M be the number of cells and N the number of gNBs. As an exemplary analysis we also consider 3 cells are supported by a single gNB. The RAN based scheme requires M messages over the radio plus N-1 messages (from the last serving gNB to the neighbouring gNBs inside the RNA). As for the CN based mobility management scheme, M messages over the radio plus N messages from the CN to the gNBs of an area (considered in this analysis of having the same size like the RAN based scheme), plus 6 additional messages that are needed to inform the CN NFs that the UE is in RRC_INACTIVE state. Concerning CEMOB, the knowledge of the position of a UE with a high accuracy even under some time coarse time period require to page only the gNB where the vehicle is camped under. Also knowing the topology of the streets and the direction of the vehicle, it is easy to make sure that there will be no page miss by also paging the previous and the following gNBs. Considering an inter site distance (ISD) of even 500m, the vehicle is paged in an area of 1,5 Km that makes the probability of success rather high. As shown in Figure 4, as long as the number of gNBs increases the benefits of the RAN-based scheme, compared to CN based is rather low. On the other hand, CEMOB outperforms these two schemes considerably since we take advantage of the accurate information about the location of the UE/vehicle.

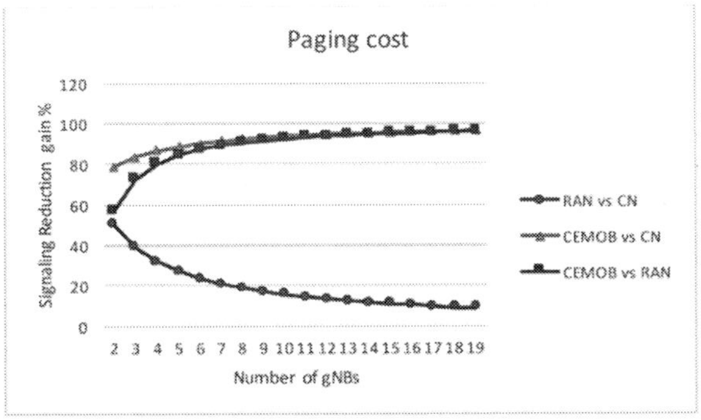

Figure 4: Paging cost CEMOB vs. RAN baseb vs CN based

To estimate the number of messages to be exchanged during a location update we perform the following analysis. As shown in Figure 2, for the RAN based scheme 7 messages need to be exchanged every time a UE crosses the border of an RNA or when it resumes an RRC connection in a gNB different from the last serving gNB. A similar number of messages is needed for the CN based scheme, but this time the communication takes places between a gNB and AMF instead of the last serving gNB. For the CEMOB case, context needs to be transferred to all gNBs of an area before the UE enters into it. Also, in case a UE selects with a probability p, a different path for any reason, then it will communicate again with the V2X application server and the context will have to be updated to all the gNBs of an area.

To perform an evaluation of CEMOB for the signalling load we consider an area of 15 gNBs divided into 3 RNAs. We also consider that a street has two lanes. According to [16], vehicle traffic flow with measurement at a point is "the number of vehicles that pass a point on a highway or a given lane or direction of a highway during a specific time interval". Traffic flow q is expressed in vehicles/hour is given by:

$$q = \frac{n_t}{t} \qquad (1)$$

Related to the flow of vehicles the space headway parameter can also be used. It is defined as the distance measured between the front ends of two successive vehicles (as the sum of the vehicles' in-between space and a vehicle's length). Based on this parameter the traffic flow can be calculated as:

$$q = \frac{\bar{v}}{\bar{hs}} \qquad (2)$$

where the flow q is calculated as the average speed of the vehicles divided by their average space headway. Based on this we are able to calculate the traffic flow of vehicles passing through the 3 RNAs border areas per hour. Our assumption is also that for the baseline, a UE will resume its connection once every 5 cells. Having also a fixed road topology and assuming a uniform distribution of vehicles with fixed space headway distance among them, it is easy to calculate the number of vehicles in this area. Using this number, we can select a probability that some of the vehicles will change their path, so CEMOB will have to update all the gNBs of an RNA. Figure 5 presents the results for different vehicle speeds (from 20 to 60km/h) and different space headways (from 4.5 to 22.5 meters). For this experiment , we consider that every 30 sec the 20% of the vehicles will request a path update.

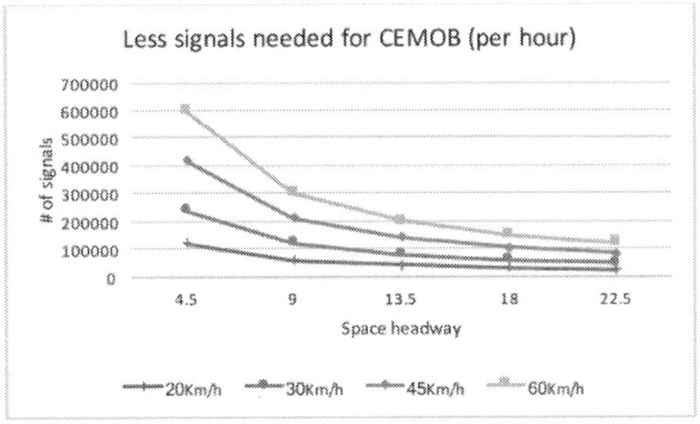

Figure 5: Signaling comparison between CEMOB and baseline scheme

As seen from the figure, CEMOB significantly outperforms the baseline scheme. The reason is that the on demand context transfer requires a lot of signalling even if this requested from one gNB to another. In this case the CN has to be notified so that path switching is performed. On the other hand, CEMOB has to notify the gNBs once and pre-configure the RAN-CN path at the same time. For a small number of cells like this discussed example topology, this means a considerable reduction. Also note that although CEMOB needs to update the gNBs every time a UE changes its path this is cost is at the end related only to the number of gNBs. In the case of the baseline, the cost is heavily affected by a complex process that may take place every time a UE is paged or resumes a connection to transmit data.

Obviously the penalty for CEMOB is the transfer of context information much more gNBs (all the gNBs inside an RNA) compared to the baseline where this is transferred only from one gNB to another. According to [17], the security information that needs to be transferred consists of a) K-ASME key (256 bits), b) K-eNB key (256 bits) and c) NONCE (32 bits). Also the Globally Unique Temporary UE Identity GUTI (80 bits) needs to be transferred to be associated with the abovementioned values.

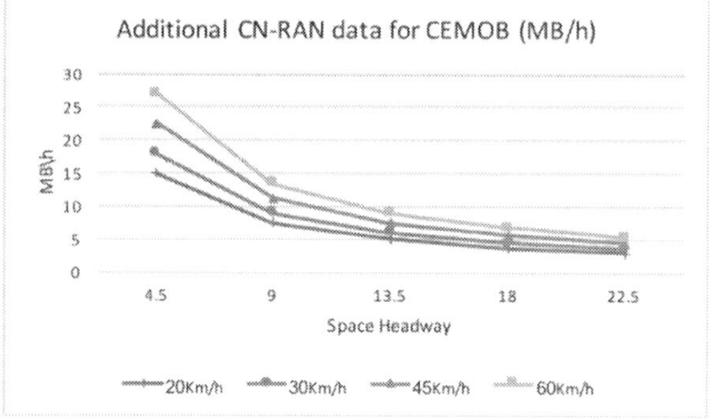

Figure 6: Additional data transfer needed for CEMOB

In Figure 6, we present the additional information needed to be transferred for CEMOB when compared to the baseline in terms of MB/h. The settings of this experiment were the same with the previous one (e.g., number of gNBs, size of an RNA, probability of changing path, etc.). As expected CEMOB always underperforms compared to the baseline, although the amount of information over wireline CN-RAN link seems to be rather manageable from today's networks. This would be the case additional context information is needed. For example, for the worse case of our experiment where vehicles are moving with 60Km/h and the 5000 bits need to be transfered per context transfer, then the overall traffic between CN-RAN would be 225MB/h.

VI. CONCLUSIONS

This paper makes the case that although the specification of 5G networks is well underway and slicing is gradually reaching a mature status several inefficiencies still exist. Standardization activities have sensibly focused on introducing new principles like NF modularization and the support of different numerologies in RAN and ported existing functionalities into the new principles.

What is still missing though are further optimizations, that can be realized if use case specific context information is taken into account. In this paper we have presented a new mobility management scheme that outperforms the baseline for the case of high moving UEs, like the autonomous driven vehicles. By taking advantage of the knowledge of the path that a vehicle will follow and by tailoring cut the involved network functions (e.g., AMF, NEF) appropriately, then significant benefits can be achieved in terms of signalling load with a manageable penalty of additional information being moved inside the network. As a next step of the current work, we will evaluate the proposed scheme using event driven simulations.

REFERENCES

[1] NGMN Alliance, 5G white paper, v 1.0, 2016 available from: https://www.ngmn.org/uploads/media/NGMN_5G_White_Paper_V1_0.pdf, access date 12-09-2017.

[2] SE Elayoubi, M. Fallgren, P. Spapis et al., "5G service requirements and operational use cases", European Conference on Networks and Communications - EuCNC 2016, DOI: 10.1109/EuCNC.2016.7561024.

[3] P. Marsch et. al., "5G Radio Access Network Architecture: Design Guidelines and Key Considerations", IEEE Communications Magazine, vol. 54, issue 11, pp 24-32, November 2016.

[4] X. An, et. al., "Architecture Modularisation for Next Generation Mobile Networks", European Conference on Networks and Communications - EuCNC 2017, DOI: 10.1109/EuCNC.2017.7980664.

[5] 3GPP, TS 23.501 "System Architecture for the 5G System; Stage 2 (Release 15)", Version 1.2.0, July 2017.

[6] 5G-PPP Architecture Working Group, "View on 5G Architecture (Version 2.0), July 2017, available at: https://5g-ppp.eu/5g-ppp-revised-architecture-paper-for-public-consultation/, access date 12-09-2017.

[7] 3GPP, TS 22.261, "Service Requirements for the 5G System", V16.0.0, June 2017.

[8] 5G Automotive Association -5GAA, "The case for Cellular V2X for Safety and Cooperative Driving", available at: http://5gaa.org/pdfs/5GAA-whitepaper-23-Nov-2016.pdf, access date 12-09-2017.

[9] 3GPP, TS 23.502, "Procedures for the 5G System", Stage 2 (Release 15), Version 0.6.0, August 2017.

[10] 3GPP, TS 38.300, "NR and NG-RAN Overall Description", Stage 2 (Release 15), September 2017.

[11] 3GPP TR 28.801, "Study on management and orchestration of network slicing for next generation networks", Release 15, Version 1.2.0, May 2017.

[12] K. Chatzikokolakis, A. Kaloxylos, P. Spapis, N. Alonistioti, and C. Zhou, "A survey of location management mechanisms and an evaluation of their applicability for 5G cellular networks", Recent advances in Communications and Networking Technologies, vol. 3, no. 2, 2014.

[13] S. Hailu and M. Säily, "Hybrid paging and location tracking scheme for inactive 5G UEs", European Conference on Networks and Communications - EuCNC 2017, DOI: 10.1109/EuCNC.2017.7980730.

[14] 3GPP TS 23.285, "Architecture enhancements for V2X services", Release 14, March 2017.

[15] R. Trivisonno, R. Guerzoni, I. Vaishnavi, and D. Soldani, "Towards zero latency software defined 5G networks," in IEEE International Conference on Communication Workshop (ICCW), June 2015, pp. 2566–2571.

[16] T. V. Mathew and K. V. Krishna Rao, "Introduction to Tranportation Engineering", Chapter 30, Fundemental parameters of traffic flow, May 2007, available at: http://nptel.ac.in/courses/105101087/downloads/Lec-30.pdf, access date 12-09-2017.

[17] 3GPP, TS 33.401, "Security Architecture", Release 15, Version 15.0.0 June 2017.